Collins

Cambridge IGCSE™

English

TEACHER'S GUIDE

Also for Cambridge IGCSE™ (9–1)

Series Editor: Julia Burchell
Claire Austin-Macrae, Julia Burchell, Nigel Carlisle,
Steve Eddy, Joanna Fliski, Mike Gould, Ian Kirby and Robin Wilson

William Collins's dream of knowledge for all began with the publication of his first book in 1819.

A self-educated mill worker, he not only enriched millions of lives, but also founded a flourishing publishing house. Today, staying true to this spirit, Collins books are packed with inspiration, innovation and practical expertise. They place you at the centre of a world of possibility and give you exactly what you need to explore it.

Collins. Freedom to teach.

Published by Collins
An imprint of HarperCollins*Publishers*
The News Building
1 London Bridge Street
London
SE1 9GF

Browse the complete Collins catalogue at
www.collins.co.uk

© HarperCollins*Publishers* Limited 2018

10 9 8 7 6 5

ISBN 978-0-00-826201-3

All rights reserved. No part of this publication may be reproduced, stored in a retrieval system, or transmitted in any form by any means, electronic, mechanical, photocopying, recording or otherwise, without the prior written permission of the Publisher or a licence permitting restricted copying in the United Kingdom issued by the Copyright Licensing Agency Ltd., Barnard's Inn, 86 Fetter Lane, London, EC4A 1EN.

British Library Cataloguing-in-Publication Data

A catalogue record for this publication is available from the British Library.

Series Editor: Julia Burchell
Authors: Claire Austin-Macrae, Julia Burchell, Nigel Carlisle, Steve Eddy, Joanna Fliski, Mike Gould, Ian Kirby, Robin Wilson
Project manager: Sonya Newland
Development editor: Sonya Newland
Commissioning editor: Catherine Martin
In-house editors: Hannah Dove, Helena Becci, Natasha Paul
Copyeditor: Catherine Dakin
Proofreader: Kim Vernon
Text permissions researcher: Rachel Thorne
Cover designer: Gordon MacGilp
Cover illustrator: Maria Herbert-Liew
Typesetter: Hugh Hillyard-Parker
Production controller: Tina Paul
Printed and bound by CPI Group (UK) Ltd, Croydon, CR0 4YY

All exam-style questions and sample answers in this title were written by the authors. In examinations, the way marks are awarded may be different.

MIX
Paper from responsible sources
FSC C007454

This book is produced from independently certified FSC paper to ensure responsible forest management.

For more information visit: **www.harpercollins.co.uk/green**

The publishers gratefully acknowledge the permission granted to reproduce the copyright material in this book. Every effort has been made to trace copyright holders and to obtain their permission for the use of copyright material. The publishers will gladly receive any information enabling them to rectify any error or omission at the first opportunity.

We are grateful to the following for permission to reproduce copyright material:

Extracts on p.9 from *The No.1 Ladies Detective Agency* by Alexander McCall Smith, Abacus, copyright © 1998, 2005 by Alexander McCall Smith. Reproduced by permission of David Higham Associates Ltd and Anchor Books, an imprint of the Knopf Doubleday Publishing Group, a division of Penguin Random House LLC. All rights reserved. Any third party use of this material, outside of this publication, is prohibited. Interested parties must apply directly to Penguin Random House LLC for permission; Extracts on pp.10-11, 173 from *Q & A* by Vikas Swarup published by Doubleday, copyright © 2005 by Vikas Swarup. Reproduced by permission of The Random House Group Ltd and Scribner, a division of Simon & Schuster, Inc. All rights reserved; Extracts on pp.16-17 from *The Salt Road* by Jane Johnson, Viking 2010, Penguin Books 2011, pp.1-2, copyright © 2010 by Jane Johnson. Reproduced by permission of Penguin Books Ltd; Baror International, Inc.; and Anchor Canada/Doubleday Canada, a division of Penguin Random House Canada Limited; Extracts on p.21 from *Set in Stone* by Linda Newbery, published by David Fickling Books, copyright © 2006 by Linda Newbery. Reproduced by permission of The Random House Group Limited and David Fickling Books, an imprint of Random House Children's Gooks, a division of Penguin Random House LLC. All rights reserved. Any third party use of this material, outside of this publication, is prohibited. Interested parties must apply directly to Penguin Random House LLC for permission; Extracts on p.27 about Dubai from https://www.visitdubai.com/en/articles/best-beaches, copyright © 2018; Extracts on pp.28, 29 from "Social media is harming the mental health of teenagers. The state has to act" by June Eric Udorie, *The Guardian*, 16/09/2015, and "Social media gets a bad press, but it was a lifeline for me" by Grace Holliday, *The Guardian*, 24/04/2017, copyright © Guardian News & Media Ltd, 2018; Extracts on p.33 from "J Hus - 'Common Sense' Review" by Joe Madden, *NME*, 15/05/2017, http://www.nme.com/reviews/album/j-hus-common-sense-review, copyright © Time Inc. (UK) Ltd. All rights reserved; Extracts on p.33 from "Restoration of a king's art is long overdue" by Ben Macintyre, *The Times*, 27/05/2017, copyright © The Times / News Licensing; A speech on pp.54-55 by Angelina Jolie from World Refugee Day, 18th June 2009 Washington DC; Extracts on pp.58-59 from *Tales from Kulafumbi: Diary of a Nature Lover's blog* by Tanya Trevor Saunders, www.wildernessdiary.com. Reprinted with kind permission; Extracts on pp.63, 202 from "Mountain Goat kills Hiker" by Alex Robinson, *Outdoor Life*, 19/10/2010, copyright © 2018. Reproduced with permission of Outdoor Life. All rights reserved; Extracts on pp.63, 202 from "First, catch your feral kitten. Then call in the experts" by Patrick Barkham, *The Guardian*, 07/11/2016, copyright © Guardian News & Media Ltd, 2018; Extracts on p.77 from "Fracking: the pros and cons", *Country Life*, 23/05/2013, copyright © Country Life Picture Library. Reproduced with permission; Extracts on p.86, 215, 217 from "Undiscovered south-east Asia: remote towns and secret beaches" by Ling Low, *The Guardian*, 10/05/2017, copyright © Guardian News & Media Ltd, 2018; Extracts on pp.89-90 from *A Game of Polo with a Headless Goat* by Emma Levine, p.71. Reproduced with permission of MBA Literary Agents on behalf of Emma Levine; Extracts on p.91 from *The Rough Guide to The Italian Lakes*, p.4, copyright © Rough Guides. Reproduced with permission from APA Publications (UK) Ltd; Extracts on p.92 from *Welcome to Crete, 6th edition*, p.4, copyright © 2016, Lonely Planet. Reproduced with permission; Extracts on pp.93-94 from "Review: In Documentary 'Maidentrip,' Laura Dekker Looks for Paradise in a Sea that Never Ends" by Beth Hanna, www.indiewire.com/2014/01/review-in-documentary-maidentrip-laura-dekker-looks-for-paradise-in-a-sea-that-never-ends-194139/; Extracts on pp.98-99, 224, 227 from *The Beach* by Alex Garland, Penguin, 1997, first published by Viking 1996, Penguin Books 1997, copyright © 1996 by Alex Garland. Reproduced by permission of Penguin Books Ltd and Andrew Nurnberg Associates Ltd; Extracts on pp.111-112 from "Should pandas be left to face extinction?" by Chris Packham, *The Guardian*, 23/09/2009, copyright © Guardian News & Media Ltd, 2018; and Extract on p. 222 from "Lynx could return to Britain this year after absence of 1,300 years" by Damian Carrington, *The Guardian*, 07/07/2017, copyright © Guardian News & Media Ltd.

Contents

	Introduction	4		
	Two-year scheme of work	6		
SECTION 1	**BUILDING KEY SKILLS**			
Chapter 1	Key reading skills	8	Worksheets	173
Chapter 2	Key technical skills	34	Worksheets	188
Chapter 3	Key writing forms	54	Worksheets	198
Chapter 4	Writing for purpose	66	Worksheets	205
SECTION 2	**APPLYING KEY SKILLS**			
Chapter 5	Comprehension	84	Worksheets	215
Chapter 6	Summary writing	89	Worksheets	220
Chapter 7	Analysing language	96	Worksheets	223
Chapter 8	Extended response to reading and directed writing	103	Worksheets	231
Chapter 9	Composition	119	Worksheets	239
SECTION 3	**APPLYING KEY SKILLS IN COURSEWORK**			
Chapter 10	Approaching written coursework	132	Worksheets	248
SECTION 4	**SPEAKING AND LISTENING**			
Chapter 11	Approaching speaking and listening	151	Worksheets	266
SECTION 5	**EXAM PRACTICE**			
Chapter 12	Practice papers and guidance	169	Worksheets	271

© HarperCollins *Publishers* Ltd 2018

Introduction

Welcome to the Collins *Cambridge IGCSE™ English Teacher's Guide (Third Edition)*. This guide has been fully updated to support teaching of the syllabus for first examination in 2020. We hope it will provide invaluable support to teachers worldwide as they prepare students for the freedom, challenge and enrichment offered by the Cambridge IGCSE and IGCSE (9–1) in First Language English (syllabuses 0500 and 0990).

Using the Student's Book

The Student's Book is structured to build the fundamental skills that underpin the course before giving students the opportunity to apply and develop these skills in combination to tackle a range of different tasks.

The book opens with four chapters in Section 1 Building key skills that systematically cover the reading and writing skills required by all IGCSE English students. These are divided as follows:

- Chapter 1: Key reading skills
- Chapter 2: Key technical skills
- Chapter 3: Key writing forms
- Chapter 4: Writing for purpose.

The book then focuses in Section 2 on applying these skills in combination to tackle the following types of IGCSE task:

- Chapter 5: Comprehension
- Chapter 6: Summary writing
- Chapter 7: Analysing language
- Chapter 8: Extended response to reading and directed writing
- Chapter 9: Composition.

The book moves on in Sections 3 and 4 to cover each written coursework assignment and the requirements of the Speaking and Listening tasks:

- Chapter 10: Approaching written coursework
- Chapter 11: Approaching speaking and listening.

The book closes, in Section 5 / Chapter 12, with resources for exam practice. These could be set together as a practice exam-style paper to provide a formative assessment opportunity or used at relevant points throughout your teaching.

In our opinion, the best way to approach the course would be to work through Chapters 1, 2, 3 and 4 early in the course, to secure students' understanding of the skills and the writing conventions that they will need to apply throughout the IGCSE.

Alternatively, it would be possible to work through Chapter 1 and then tackle the comprehension, summary and writer's effects chapters (5, 6 and 7). However, it is not advisable to use the extended response and directed writing, composition or coursework chapters (8–10) until students are familiar with the skills introduced in Chapters 2, 3 and 4. The tasks in Chapters 8–10 require a blend of skills and students need to be confident with these individual skills before they can begin to apply them successfully in combination. Please see the suggested **Two-year scheme of work** on pp. 6–7 of this Guide.

Features of the Student's Book

The book offers lively approaches to exciting texts and ensures that students have access to a wide range of fiction and non-fiction.

Successful writing and analysis is exemplified throughout, in particular by longer sample responses at different levels in the exam-style **Practice questions and responses** sections that end each chapter in Section 2 and 3. The sample tasks, responses and commentaries have been written by our authors, not by Cambridge Assessment International Education.

The **Check your progress** summaries will help to consolidate students' learning and give them the opportunity to self- or peer-assess their work.

Using the Teacher's Guide

Each two-page or four-page Topic in the Student's Book is intended to provide work for one lesson, or occasionally two lessons, and is supported in the Teacher's Guide by a lesson plan, plus worksheet(s) and PowerPoint slides (PPT).

The Teacher's Guide is designed to help you with the following:

Planning

- Key references to the syllabus are listed at the start of each lesson plan, with the **Assessment objectives** identified so that the wider application of learning is clear.
- Detailed, ready-to-use **lesson plans** offer all you need to teach: these are divided into sections that match the Student's Book – *Explore the skills*, *Build the skills*, *Develop the skills* and *Apply the skills* – ensuring progression and pace as well as opportunities for consolidation. Often, the *Develop the skills* section focuses on a deeper understanding or more sophisticated approach to the skill or concept in focus.
- **Worksheets** and **PowerPoint slides** (PPTs) supplement, support and extend activities in the Student's Book and are itemised in each lesson plan, meaning that time-consuming preparation is kept to a minimum.

Differentiation

- Differentiation opportunities are provided in the **Extra support** and **Extra challenge** boxes, ensuring that all students are able to access and be challenged by the Student's Book tasks, while **Taking it further** boxes suggest ways of extending learning beyond the lesson.
- **Worksheets** allow students to fill in grids or annotate texts from the Student's Book and **PPTs** offer readymade resources for front-of-class teaching.

Assessment

- A complete suite of exam-style practice papers is provided in Chapter 12, with supporting sample responses at different levels.
- Peer- and self-assessment is encouraged throughout, particularly in the end-of chapter **Practice questions and responses** sections, to help students understand how to progress and improve their work.

As above, the sample tasks, responses and commentaries have been written by our authors, not by Cambridge International.

Our resources are designed to build confidence so that learners can build all the skills they need for success in their IGCSE course. We hope you enjoy using them.

Julia Burchell
Series Editor

Two-year scheme of work: Year 1

These tables suggest a structure for using the materials in the Student's Book and Teacher's Guide over a two-year course. Each year is divided into six 'units', with each unit equating to approximately 18 to 24 hours of teaching time.

Year 1

Unit 1	Unit 2	Unit 3
Skills focus: An introduction to reading skills: • form and purpose *Student's Book Chapter 1, Lesson 12* • skimming • scanning • selecting • synthesis • recognising explicit meaning • recognising implicit meaning *Student's Book Chapter 1, Lessons 1–7* **Exam focus:** Comprehension and short answer questions *Student's Book Chapter 5* *Student's Book Chapter 7, Lessons 1–2* **Speaking and listening:** Individual presentation: opportunity 1 Choosing and researching an individual presentation *Student's Book Chapter 11, Lessons 2 and 3* Using the right language and engaging your audience *Student's Book Chapter 11, Lessons 1 and 4*	**Skills focus:** An introduction to reading skills: • skimming • scanning • selecting • recognising explicit meaning • recognising implicit meaning • synthesis. *Student's Book Chapter 1, Lessons 1–7* **Exam focus:** Summary questions *Student's Book Chapter 6* **Speaking and listening:** Individual presentation: opportunity 2 (Individual presentation in role) *Student's Book Chapter 11, Lesson 5*	**Skills focus:** An introduction to writing skills: The conventions of forms *Student's Book Chapter 3, Lessons 1–6* Key technical skills *Student's Book Chapter 2* **Exam focus:** Extended response to reading *Student's Book Chapter 8, Lessons 1–4* **Speaking and listening:** Individual Presentation: opportunity 3 *Student's Book Chapter 11, Lessons 1–4*
Unit 4	**Unit 5**	**Unit 6**
Skills focus: Writing for a purpose *Student's Book Chapter 4: Lessons 1–6* **Exam focus:** Extended response to reading *Student's Book Chapter 8* **Speaking and listening:** Paired activity: opportunity 1 *Student's Book Chapter 11, Lessons 6 and 9*	**Skills focus:** Recap on recognising implicit meaning Recognising words that stimulate the senses Recognising words that stimulate the emotions *Student's Book Chapter 1, Lessons 5–9* **Exam focus:** Language questions *Student's Book Chapter 7, Lessons 3–5* **Speaking and listening:** Paired activity: opportunity 2 Focus on listening and responding *Student's Book Chapter 11: Lessons 7–8*	**Skills focus:** Descriptive writing *Student's Book Chapter 9, Lessons 1, 4–7;* *Chapter 10, Lessons 4, 5 and 8* **Exam focus:** Descriptive writing *Student's Book Chapter 9, Lessons 1, 4–7;* Coursework Assignment 2 *Chapter 10, Lessons 4, 5 and 8* **Speaking and listening:** Paired activity: opportunity 3 *Student's Book Chapter 11: Lessons 6–9*

Two-year scheme of work: Year 2

Year 2

Unit 1	Unit 2	Unit 3
Skills focus: Narrative writing *Student's Book Chapter 9, Lessons 5–7; Chapter 10, Lessons 6–9* **Exam focus:** Narrative writing *Student's Book Chapter 9, Lessons 5–7* Coursework Assignment 3 *Chapter 10: Lessons 6–9* **Speaking and listening:** Individual presentation: opportunity 4 (Individual presentation in role) *Student's Book Chapter 11, Lesson 5*	**Skills focus:** Directed writing *Student's Book Chapter 1, Lesson 8* *Student's Book Chapter 1, Lessons 10 and 11* **Exam focus:** Directed writing *Student's Book Chapter 8, Lessons 5–7 and 9* Coursework Assignment 1: *Student's Book Chapter 1, Lessons 10 and 11* *Chapter 10, Lessons 1–3* **Speaking and listening:** Individual presentation: opportunity 5 *Student's Book Chapter 11, Lessons 1–4*	**Exam focus:** Re-cap comprehension and language questions *Student's Book Chapter 1, Lessons 5–9* *Student's Book Chapter 5* *Student's Book Chapter 7, Lessons 1–5* **Speaking and listening:** Paired activity: opportunity 4 *Student's Book Chapter 11: Lessons 6–9*
Unit 4	**Unit 5**	**Unit 6**
Examination practice *Chapter 12*	Examination practice *Chapter 12*	Examination practice *Chapter 12*

Chapter 1: Key reading skills

1.1 Locating information: skimming

Resources:
- Student's Book: 1.1, pp. 8–9
- Workbook: 1.1, pp. 7–8 can be set as homework
- PowerPoint slides 1.1a–d

Assessment objectives:

R5 Select and use information for specific purposes

EXPLORE THE SKILLS

As a class, read through the beginning of this section of the Student's Book and ensure that everyone understands the term 'skimming'. Read the extract from *The No. 1 Ladies Detective Agency* and then put students in pairs to answer **Q1**. Take feedback as a class. Responses will include:

a) a novel
b) Africa (Kgale Hill, Botswana) – strong sense of setting
c) Mma Ramotswe is introduced with some larger-than-life features.
d) There is no action.
e) sets the scene and introduces Mma Ramotswe and her agency; purpose is to entertain
f) One message is that she is a strong character.
g) Yes – we get a clear, itemised picture of the office and its view.
h) We might expect a client/problem to be introduced; we might get a sense that the agency is in trouble (from the mention of assets and inventories).

As an extension, use **PPT 1.1a–b** to develop the skill of skimming with some pair challenges. After each activity, discuss how easy it is to gain a quick understanding and why some information seems more important than other details.

In **PPT 1.1a**, students should note the aunt's age and old-fashioned ways. In **PPT 1.1b**, they should pick up on the writer's attitude towards London, the range of things to do, sighting David Beckham, and the pros and cons of city travel.

BUILD THE SKILLS

Read through this section with the class. Put students in groups of four to work on **Q2**. Test the effectiveness of their skimming by reading out questions a), b) and c) one by one, with students pointing to the relevant area of text as quickly as they can.

If students are finding the tasks difficult, repeat them using the opening paragraphs of any novel and get them to answer the same questions that appear in **Q1**. Then ask them three text-specific questions about where information is located. This could be done as a small group, with one group member challenging the others to find certain information from the text.

DEVELOP THE SKILLS

Read this section of the Student's Book and complete **Q3**. Ideas might include:

➢ **Paragraph 1:** describing the agency; introducing Mma Ramotswe; who and what
➢ **Paragraph 2:** the surroundings (vegetation); the view from the door

Students complete **Q4** in pairs, deciding what information is held in the different sentences of each paragraph. You can display the text of the passage from page 8 of the Student's Book using **PPT 1.1c–d**. To aid this discussion, **PPT 1.1d** is already annotated to show where information on 'vegetation' can be found in the second paragraph.

Chapter 1: Key reading skills

APPLY THE SKILLS

For **Q5**, ask students to write up answers to questions a), b) and c) from **Q2**. Remind them of the importance of putting the ideas into their own words, and of using appropriate quotations as evidence.

> **Extra support:** Help students to find relevant sections or appropriate quotations. Help could also be given with sentence starters, such as:
>
> ➢ *Some of the vegetation looks quite big and harmful...*
>
> ➢ *The phrase 'great white thorns' makes the vegetation sound...*
>
> **Extra challenge:** Encourage students to be detailed yet concise. Remind them that it is good practice to refer to any relevant techniques, such as the effect of using adjectives or metaphor.

Class feedback might include:

➢ Vegetation: big, harmful-looking acacia trees ('great white thorns'); the trees look unusual because, in contrast, their leaves seem pretty ('so delicate'); it seems dry rather than lush ('scrub bush').

➢ Staff: one member of staff ('her secretary').

➢ Mma Ramotswe: unique ('only lady detective', or 'no inventory...'); polite, generous or down to earth (she brews tea for her own secretary); clever or skilful ('human intuition and intelligence' or 'in abundance').

After feeding back as a class, invite students to share their work in pairs and use the 'Checklist for success' on page 9 to assess how well they have done and what they need to do to improve.

TAKING IT FURTHER	Students need to skim texts for quick understanding. They should quickly find the most appropriate information for the question being asked. They also need to do this in order to quickly select the 'best' quotations that will allow them to analyse the effects of a writer's language choices. Encourage students to practise the skill of skimming on a regular basis in order to sharpen their abilities. Students could, for example, skim newspaper articles from which the headlines have been removed and then devise their own headlines to sum up the news story. Or they could read different stories in groups and then sum up the story for the group in a few sentences.

Chapter 1: Key reading skills

1.2 Locating information: scanning

Resources:
- Student's Book: 1.2, pp. 10–13
- Workbook: 1.2, pp. 9–11 can be set as homework
- Worksheet 1.2

Assessment objectives:

R5 Select and use information for specific purposes

EXPLORE THE SKILLS

As a class, read through the opening sections on page 10 of the Student's Book and ensure that everyone understands the term 'scanning'. Students should complete **Q1** in pairs. Take feedback, eliciting the following answers: 1G, 2D, 3F, 4A, 5B, 6C, 7E. In each case, discuss the features that match the text type and what made them easy to scan for.

Ask students whether they can think of any other real-life situations where they have used scanning skills (they may make suggestions, such as reading a bus timetable, finding out what time a television programme starts, searching for something on the internet, checking food labels for an allergy-causing ingredient).

BUILD THE SKILLS

Read through the information on page 11 of the Student's Book, up to the extract, as a class. Explore how to unpick a question and scan for appropriate information. For **Q2**, hand out **Worksheet 1.2** and ask students to discuss the extract from Q & A in pairs, before completing the table. Please note that reference is made to a non-metric measurement in the extract. 100 square feet is approximately equal to 9 square metres.

Extra support: Ask students questions that will help them to explore the different phrases in the table. For example:
- Why isn't artificial light as nice as *natural light*?
- Why would you want *ventilation*?
- What do you think of when you imagine *corrugated metal*?
- What does the adverb *violently* add to the roof image?
- What would a train *passing overhead* be like?
- What do you need running water for?
- What does it mean by *no sanitation* and how would this affect the house?

Extra challenge: Encourage students to consider the connotations (implied meanings) of specific words. This is getting them to consider *how* and *why*, not just *what*.

DEVELOP THE SKILLS

As a class, read this section in the Student's Book and complete **Q3**, discussing with students what they can tell about migrants from the whole sentence given. Explain the importance of using context to gain full understanding of certain meanings. Responses might include:

➢ *destitute* shows they are poor and suggests homelessness

➢ *from all over the country* suggests that migrants move away from their home towns, presumably for economic reasons

➢ *jostle* suggests that there are lots of migrants

➢ *their own handful* suggests they are grateful for what they can get

➢ *slum* suggests that they are in extreme poverty and have to put up with a lot of hardship.

Chapter 1: Key reading skills

As an extension, ask students to scan the extract to select the 'best' word or phrase to describe the following things. Encourage them to explain their choices by thinking about how the language suggests or enhances meaning. For example:

- not having much room (*cramped, million... packed, squabbles over inches*)
- the surrounding landscape (*swampy urban wasteland*)
- suggestions of aggression (*jostle, squabbles, turn deadly*)
- lack of self-esteem (*live like animals, die like insects*).

APPLY THE SKILLS

Ask students to use the extract from *Q & A* to complete **Q4**: 'How does the writer suggest that life is not easy for the narrator?'

> **Extra support:** Remind students to use the information they have already gathered. Help them with sentence starters, such as:
> - *The writer suggests that life is not easy for the narrator by describing a lack of hygiene...*
> - *The phrase 'no sanitation' implies that life would not be easy because...*
>
> **Extra challenge:** Encourage students to be detailed yet concise, grouping their ideas and considering the connotations of the words that they select and their context. Advise them to refer to specific techniques, such as use of adjectives or simile.

Feed back as a class, taking examples of the points that they identified, the phrases that students selected, and how the choice of language within their phrases conveys that life is not easy. Responses might include:

- the state of the house (as already explored in **Q2**)
- the narrator's lack of money (emphasised by the short sentence) and people's desperation (*inches of space... bucket of water*)
- the local area (*packed... swampy urban wasteland*)
- his feeling of being unvalued (the simile *live like animals*)
- the sense of danger (the simile *die like insects*, and the reference to *daily squabbles... which at times turn deadly*).

After feedback, ask pairs to share their work and use the 'Checklist for success' on page 13 of the Student's Book to assess how well they have done.

TAKING IT FURTHER	To respond effectively, students need to scan texts and quickly find the most appropriate information for the question being asked. They also need to do this in order to select quickly the 'best' quotations that will allow them to analyse the effects of a writer's language choices. Encourage students to practise this skill with a variety of forms of writing that they encounter, such as newspapers, leaflets, or their favourite magazine. Students could scan a poem, picking out words which suggest emotion or words which describe a place. They could scan Tennyson's 'The Charge of the Light Brigade' and pick out words that suggest bravery, loss or error.

Chapter 1: Key reading skills

1.3 Selecting information

Resources:
- Student's Book: 1.3, pp. 14–15
- Workbook: 1.3, pp. 12–14 can be set as homework
- PowerPoint slides 1.3a–i

Assessment objectives:
R5 Select and use information for specific purposes

EXPLORE THE SKILLS

As a class, read through the opening section of this topic on page 14 of the Student's Book. Ensure that students understand how skimming and scanning lead to selecting the most relevant information for their answers.

For **Q1**, use **PPT 1.3a** to show the two alternative answers. Either through teacher-led discussion, or through individuals coming up to the board, highlight the less relevant information that could be removed. Make sure that students understand why, for this question, they only really need two points from this list:
Petchey wanted people to experience walking on the beach, swimming in the sea or the view.

BUILD THE SKILLS

For **Q2**, read through the two sample answers. Ask students to discuss which is more effective and, using the bullet points, why.

During feedback, use **PPT 1.3b–f** to highlight the different pieces of unnecessary information in the first sample answer, and how this extra detail has been summarised to make a clearer response in the second sample answer.

As an extension, ask students to complete the activity on **PPT 1.3g**, explaining what Uncle Howard is like. They should extract that he is in his sixties, is bald, likes music, is nostalgic, is sociable and has difficulty walking. During the activity, ask students to explain how they know what is and is not important to select; encourage them to highlight the specific examples, descriptive detail and unnecessary additional information that they decide to remove. Encourage them to summarise points where appropriate.

DEVELOP THE SKILLS

Introduce the purpose of the anecdote on page 15 of the Student's Book, and discuss **Q3**. Students should pick out that the writer is conveying why he hates cats. The anecdote starts with the phrase, 'It all started...' and ends, '...even louder than it had'.

Students should then complete the rewriting task in **Q4** in pairs.

Extra support: Help students to select alternative words. For example: *looked* (*seemed, appeared*), *harmless* (*innocent, docile*), *cuddly* (*sweet, furry*), *kind* (*friendly, considerate*).

Chapter 1: Key reading skills

APPLY THE SKILLS

Ask students to use the text on cats to answer **Q5**: 'How does the writer feel about cats and why?'

> **Extra support:** Help students by providing sentence starters, such as:
> - The writer finds cats...
> - The phrase, 'I hate our furry friends', shows...
>
> **Extra challenge:** Encourage students to consider the effectiveness of the language – for example, the use of irony in the phrase *our furry friends*.

Take feedback as a class, discussing the different feelings that students came up with and how these are made clear by the writer's language choices. Ideas should include:

- He/she hates cats.
- He/she is scared of cats.
- He/she finds cats mysterious.
- He/she was clawed across the face by a cat when he/she was a child.

After feedback, get students to share their work in pairs and assess how confident they now feel about a) selecting the correct information to answer a question, and b) using synonyms and their own words to achieve a concise answer.

As an extension, ask students to answer one of the following questions about the cat extract:

- What features of a cat doesn't the writer like and why?
- What animal does the writer like and why?

This can be supported using **PPT 1.3h–i**. Share and mark students' responses, using the criteria on Student's Book p. 15. For the question, responses should include:

- the way they look and move (*slinky, panther-like frames*)
- they aren't friendly (*mysterious, aloof creatures*)
- their claws (*swiped me across the cheek*, *they scare me*).

TAKING IT FURTHER	Students need to filter out any irrelevance and select the most appropriate information for the question type. Encourage students to practise this skill of summarising key ideas and selecting only the most relevant information in the different forms of writing that they encounter. They could reread the passage under 'Develop the skills' and select information that reveals that the author regards cats as a threat.

Chapter 1: Key reading skills

1.4 Synthesis

Resources:
- Student's Book: 1.4, pp. 16–19
- Workbook: 1.4, pp. 15–17 can be set as homework
- Worksheet 1.4
- PowerPoint slides 1.4a–d

Assessment objectives:

R5 Select and use information for specific purposes

EXPLORE THE SKILLS

As a class, read through this section on page 16 of the Student's Book, checking that students understand the term 'synthesis' and asking them to come up with other examples from everyday life. Read the Top tip and get pairs to complete the sorting task in **Q1**, checking their understanding via class feedback.

BUILD THE SKILLS

Read through this section of the Student's Book, then hand out **Worksheet 1.4** for **Q2**. As a class, read through the extract and ask students to underline and number all the different statements about the problems caused by extreme weather conditions. Tell them to be as thorough as possible, highlighting each idea when they come to it and not worrying about any repetition of information. Explain that they should be able to underline and number about 20 phrases from the main extract.

Take feedback and, as you go through the answers, ask students to underline and number any that they missed. (It doesn't matter if their numbers are in a different order to the ones here.) Students should have found:

1) can overturn caravans
2) tear off roofs
3) topple trees
4) causing extreme distress to many people
5) and financial hardship to whole communities
6) some of the strongest tornadoes can demolish houses completely
7) leaving people homeless
8) and vulnerable to disease
9) and criminal harm
10) people may be knocked down or struck by debris
11) and many places may lose electricity
12) flooding and storm surges can destroy buildings
13) and [destroy] roads
14) contaminate water supplies
15) halt other essential services
16) and drown people
17) large hail stones can damage cars and roofs
18) and destroy crops
19) but rarely kill people
20) heat waves can lead to drought
21) which causes crop loss
22) as well as health issues
23) and death from dehydration.

DEVELOP THE SKILLS

Explain that, by grouping ideas together when making notes from a text, you can save valuable time. Discuss how this can be done after all the ideas have been selected, but that it is much more efficient to do it while students are selecting their ideas.

For **Q3**, ask students to reread the text on **Worksheet 1.4** in pairs. As they read, they should put the phrases that they have numbered under different headings in the boxes provided. They need to decide whether each of their numbered phrases needs a new heading or goes under a heading that they have already created. Come up with between five to nine headings.

Chapter 1: Key reading skills

Feed back and discuss the different headings that the students have come up with. Groupings might include:

- destruction of property (1, 2, 6, 12)
- damage to nature (3, 18)
- other dangers to people (10, 16, 17, 19)
- problems with health and hygiene (8, 14, 22)
- short-term effects on communities (4, 7, 11, 13, 15)
- social problems (9)
- wider effects on communities (5, 20, 21, 23).

These can be shown to students, to compare with their own ideas, using **PPT 1.4a**.

Extra challenge: Ask students to order their points within their headings and consider whether any points overlap (for example, dehydration could be a health problem as well as a wider effect after possible heat waves).

APPLY THE SKILLS

As a class, read through the sample directed writing task in **Q4** and ask students to complete the note-making task. Students' notes might include:

Problems arising:

- injury or loss of life
- damage to, or destruction of, homes
- financial hardship
- flooding, but also drought
- loss of infrastructure
- spread of disease
- crop damage
- crime.

What can be done in advance:

- have stockpiles of supplies, fresh water, medicines, tents, pipes
- individuals to take out private insurance
- have trained and equipped rapid response teams.

What needs to be done after the disaster:

- rapid response teams search for survivors, treat injured and remove debris
- set up temporary homes
- distribute emergency supplies
- fix broken water pipes and ensure clean water
- deploy extra police to deal with looting
- warn locals of how to deal with heat waves, including support for the vulnerable.

Feed back as a class; the points above can be shown using **PPT 1.4b–d**. Ask students to share their work and use the **Sound progress** and **Excellent progress** criteria on page 50 of the Student's Book (bullet 3) to assess how well they have done.

TAKING IT FURTHER	Students need to select and sort a full range of information from multiple sources. They need to be able to arrange their information in a cohesive and highly convincing manner. To practise this, they could: ➢ read news stories on the same topic from different papers and synthesise the key information. ➢ synthesise descriptions of a place in two different travel guides ➢ write short biographies of a celebrity synthesising information from two different online sources.

Chapter 1: Key reading skills

1.5 Explicit meaning

Resources:
- Student's Book: 1.5, pp. 20–23
- Workbook: 1.5, pp. 18–21 can be set as homework
- Worksheets 1.5a–b
- Dictionaries

Assessment objectives:

R1 Demonstrate understanding of explicit meanings

EXPLORE THE SKILLS

As a class, read through page 20 of the Student's Book, making sure that students understand what 'explicit information' means.

Read the extract from *The Salt Road* (going through any difficult words in the Glossary) and set students the five comprehension questions in **Q1**, which ask for explicit information.

During class feedback, ensure that students do not include any comments that are either irrelevant or inferred (rather than explicit). Responses should include:

a) 'draped over' (paragraph 1, line 2)

b) 'found it preferable to' (paragraph 2, line 1)

c) 'suffocating' (paragraph 2, line 5)

d) 'lost civilisations' (paragraph 2, line 10)

e) 'complement' (paragraph 2, penultimate line).

Extra support: Guide students towards where to look for specific information.

As an extension, you could ask students to work in pairs on selecting explicit information to show how Izzy is different from her parents. Responses might include:

➢ She is imaginative while they are scientific and studious (paragraph 2).

➢ She is energetic while they are sedate (paragraphs 2 and 3).

➢ She is loud while they are quiet (paragraph 2).

BUILD THE SKILLS

As a class, run through this section in the Student's Book and reread the extract together. Students could tackle **Q2** in pairs or groups of four, then feed back to the class. Take feedback, drawing out the following possible answers:

Word	Precise meaning	Synonym	What the writer wanted to convey
stuffed	every available space filled	jammed	a lack of free space
yellowed	changed from pure white with age	faded	age; a depressing neglect
dusty	covered with dust particles	dirty	parents' lack of interest in material world

Chapter 1: Key reading skills

DEVELOP THE SKILLS

Read the sentence starters leading into **Q3**. Ask students to use them to write up their findings about three of the words from **Worksheet 1.5a or 1.5b**. For each chosen word, students should use either starter 1 and 2, or starter 3.

> **Extra support:** Help students to begin with starter 1 (referring to the first two columns of their table), and then use starter 2 (referring to the word again, followed by the last two columns of the table).

APPLY THE SKILLS

As a class, read the sample question types in this section. Ask students to complete **Q4** independently.

> **Extra support:** Give targeted students some sentence starters, such as:
> - *The girl likes to go outside because...*
> - *The phrase, 'felt small and suffocating' shows that the girl likes to go outside in order to...*
>
> **Extra challenge:** Encourage students to select information carefully, use their own words, and support their point with a quotation. As an extension, they could also complete the fifth (summary) question.

Feed back as a class, making sure that students' ideas are supported by quotations. Responses should include this information:

1. to escape parents' arguing; because the house felt oppressive; as a place to let her imagination free
2. beheaded or scalped them; buried them
3. going to the cinema; imagining things; being loud and messy; playing outdoors games; mutilating her toys
4. parents are unsociable; out of step with the rest of the world; self-absorbed; pay little attention to their daughter; trapped.

It may be useful to discuss with students why the second type of question is more difficult than the first: explanation involves the skill of 'translating' explicit meaning into their own words.

After feedback, ask students to assess their work in pairs using the **Sound progress** and **Excellent progress** criteria on Student's Book p. 50 (bullet 1) to see how well they have done.

TAKING IT FURTHER	Students need to select a range of the most relevant explicit information. It is important that they can recognise when they are being asked for this explicit information, so that they restrict themselves to it and consider its purpose. Students will need to pick out the 'best' quotations and analyse their effects on the reader.
	As an extension of **Q2**, students could use **Worksheet 1.5a** and **Worksheet 1.5b** in groups of four. Give one worksheet to one pair, and the other to the other pair (the examples are the same on both worksheets, but the words that each pair need to explore are different). Using the glossary entries and dictionaries, ask students to complete the exploration of the words in their chart, then feed back to the other pair in their group. (This offers possible differentiation, as the vocabulary on the second worksheet is a little more difficult.)

Chapter 1: Key reading skills

1.6 Implicit meaning: character

Resources:
- Student's Book: 1.6, pp. 24–27
- Workbook: 1.5, pp. 18–21 can be set as homework
- Worksheet 1.6a-b

Assessment objectives:
R2 Demonstrate understanding of implicit meanings and attitudes
R4 Demonstrate understanding of how writers achieve effects and influence readers

EXPLORE THE SKILLS

As a class, read through the opening section of the Student's Book. Make sure that students understand the five bullet points about character. Check understanding of the term 'implicit meaning' and explain that 'inferring' is a skill we use every day. Then ask pairs to complete the spider diagram task in **Q1**.

Afterwards, ask students what other things they have inferred today, for example:

➢ how their family and friends are feeling

➢ what the weather might be like later

➢ what a passer-by might be like from how they dress, move and so on.

BUILD THE SKILLS

Revisit the five bullet points about character. Check that students understand the technique demonstrated in the table, then ask them to complete **Q2** and **Q3** on implicit meaning in pairs.

Extra support: Select a certain phrase (for example, *the photographs of elaborate cakes*) and ask students what it might suggest about Sasha or her mother.

Invite class feedback. Responses may include:

➢ It appears that Sasha's mother has been trying to convince her.

➢ Sasha clearly doesn't like Tracey.

➢ Mother wants to be nice to her daughter but is disturbed by her behaviour.

➢ Mother is going to invite Tracey anyway.

➢ Sasha appears to have a short attention span; she also seems greedy.

➢ Mother has been planning her party for a long time.

➢ Sasha is spoiled and used to getting her own way.

Encourage students to explain which particular words or phrases suggested the implicit meanings that they have written down.

DEVELOP THE SKILLS

As a class, read through the extract from *Great Expectations*. Then hand out **Worksheet 1.6a** and ask students to complete the character table for Pip and Magwitch in **Q4**. During class feedback, responses on each character might include the following:

Chapter 1: Key reading skills

Pip	Magwitch
• 'you little devil' suggests Pip is young • 'sir' implies Pip is quite respectful • 'terror' shows how scared he is • 'nothing in them but a piece of bread' might suggest poverty • 'not strong' suggests that he doesn't exercise or is badly fed • 'expressed my hope that he wouldn't' conveys that he doesn't understand the man is not speaking literally	• 'you little devil' suggests he doesn't like children • 'cut your throat' shows he is violent and immoral • 'coarse grey... great iron' indicates that he is an escaped convict • 'soaked in water' and so on, implies that he has been sleeping rough and travelling across country • 'limped and shivered' suggests that he is ill and injured • 'glared and growled' makes him sound mentally ill • 'Show us where you live' and other orders convey his dominance • 'turned me upside down' demonstrates strength • 'ravenously' suggests that he hasn't eaten for a long time • 'Darn me if I couldn't eat em' suggests that the man is not well-educated or of a high class

Ask students to complete **Q5** independently using their notes from **Worksheet 1.6a** to write a paragraph about each character.

Students could tackle **Q6** independently or in pairs. Take feedback, drawing out the following answers:

a) Maria either dislikes Tom, and so is emotionally cold towards him, or she disapproves of him at this moment.

b) He was known to be an eloquently persuasive speaker, even to the point of misleading his listeners.

c) The speaker feels that the person addressed is trying to withhold information from them.

d) Smith spoke or behaved in a forceful but unsubtle way.

e) The speaker feels that the person referred to was keeping an emotional distance from him, not engaging with him in a friendly way.

APPLY THE SKILLS

As a class, read through this section of the Student's Book. Ask students to complete **Q7**, answering the two questions. Remind them to make use of their notes from **Worksheet 1.6a** and to comment on the effects of the language being used in the text.

> **Extra support:** Give students sentence starters, for example:
>
> ➢ *It is clear that Pip is scared when Dickens writes...*
>
> ➢ *When Dickens describes Magwitch as a man who 'limped and shivered, and glared and growled', this makes the character seem...*
>
> **Extra challenge:** Encourage students to explore implied meanings, not just select literal ones. Students should try to group their ideas, link phrases from the text together, and comment on the effect of specific features of language, such as the use of verbs and adverbs.

TAKING IT FURTHER	Students need to select a range of the most relevant implicit meanings. They need to link information together and analyse how language is being used to create different effects that convey information about character. For further challenge, students could undertake **Worksheet 1.6b**. Answers: 1 He runs a few steps, thinking Pip's mother is alive and in the graveyard. 2 He is deciding what to do – probably whether to trust the boy. 3 He is thinking that a blacksmith's tools could remove his leg iron. 4 'so as to give me a greater sense of helplessness and danger': a child would not understand this – only an adult looking back with hindsight. 5 He has been brought up to be polite.

© HarperCollins *Publishers* Ltd 2018

Chapter 1: Key reading skills

1.7 Implicit meaning: setting

Resources:
- Student's Book: 1.7, pp. 28–31
- Workbook: 1.5, pp. 18–21 can be set as homework
- Worksheets 1.7a–b
- PowerPoint slides 1.7a–b

Assessment objectives:

R2 Demonstrate understanding of implicit meanings and attitudes

R4 Demonstrate understanding of how writers achieve effects and influence readers

EXPLORE THE SKILLS

As a class, read through this section in the Student's Book, making sure that students understand the term 'inferring'. Then ask students to complete the spider diagram in **Q1** before sharing their ideas in pairs. Ideas might include:

- reference to other senses (such as smell)
- how many people are around (and what they are like)
- what time of day it is
- the temperature
- the age/history of the place
- its upkeep, and so on.

BUILD THE SKILLS

Introduce the first extract and ask students to talk generally about the atmosphere created. Class inferences will include that the text is describing some kind of party, that people are enjoying themselves, and that the atmosphere is happy and upbeat.

> **Extra support:** Select a particular phrase (for example, *The room buzzed with energy*), or just a single word (such as *balloons*) and ask students what it suggests to them about what is going on and what the mood is.

In **Q2**, students are asked to choose three words to sum up the atmosphere in the room. During feedback, ensure that students give evidence to support their ideas. Words chosen may include:

- excited: *buzzed with energy*; *everything appeared to be moving*; *couples danced or chatted animatedly*; *dresses swept by*
- relaxed: *cheerful voices*; *gently swayed*
- happy: *cheerful voices*; *balloons*; *bunting*; *couples*; *brightly patterned table cloths*.

Ask students to suggest the effect of these descriptions on the reader and consider why the writer may have done this (for example, to make us feel positive about the setting; to make us like any characters involved; to make us anticipate an exciting event; or even to surprise us by then making something bad happen).

Next, introduce the concept of pathetic fallacy using the glossary, and discuss how phrases such as *the room buzzed*, *balloons swayed gently* and *bunting swished* are examples of pathetic fallacy in the extract. For **Q3**, encourage students to create their own examples of the technique to extend the extract. Share examples as a class.

Chapter 1: Key reading skills

After discussion, use **PPT 1.7a** to develop students' understanding of pathetic fallacy by discussing the different emotions reflected in each setting. Ask students to consider use of place, lighting, colour, background and so on.

As an extension, discuss with students the different verbs, nouns and adjectives used in the extract. Ask them to think of other verbs, nouns and adjectives for a party that could suggest excitement, relaxation or happiness. Develop this with **Worksheet 1.7a**, on which students alter the atmosphere of a piece of writing.

Before students tackle **Q4**, check that they understand what connotations are. You could define this as 'ideas that you connect in your mind with a particular place or thing'. Draw the 'jungle' spider diagram on the board and ask students to suggest ideas, or get them to work on this in small groups. Possible connotations are: trees, forest, heat, dense growth that is hard to penetrate, danger, 'the law of the jungle'. The most obvious type of story to have a jungle setting is the adventure story, or a war story (as in Vietnam).

Students could discuss **Q5** in groups, or you could ask the class the questions. Draw out the difference between **a)**, which is an exaggerated description of an overgrown garden, and **b)**, which is a metaphor implying a harsh city upbringing where people have to be on the defensive, and where the rule is survival of the fittest.

DEVELOP THE SKILLS

As a class, read through the second extract from *Set in Stone* and ask students to complete the setting chart for **Q6** using **Worksheet 1.7b**. Other phrases that students might add include: *the mist clung, vaporous swamp, my heart pound and my nerves stretch taut, wailing shriek, the shadow of the wall, a sound of terrible distress, I felt the hairs prickle, some creature yowling*. During feedback, take ideas in the order of the chart: time of year, time of day, weather, landscape, objects, actions, sounds.

Use the final column of the setting chart from **Worksheet 1.7b** to complete the vocabulary task in **Q7**, considering how the piece could be made exciting and optimistic.

APPLY THE SKILLS

As a class, read through this section in the Student's Book. Ask students to complete **Q8**, using the notes from their table.

Use **PPT 1.7b** to provide a sample answer for part of the first question. Explain how the answer attempts to fulfil its requirements, using both the question and the **Sound progress** and **Excellent progress** criteria on page 50 of the Student's Book (bullet 2).

> **Extra support:** Help students with a sentence starter (for example, *One phrase that suggests he is afraid is...*) or a phrase to be working with (such as, *'The metal bit into my hands as I clung onto the gate'*).
>
> **Extra challenge:** Encourage students to select a variety of phrases and to use technical language (such as *verb, adjective, personification, metaphor*) as part of their explanation of effects. Advise students to link phrases together in order to show how mood is built up by a writer.

Feed back as a class, then ask students to assess their work in pairs using bullet 2 of the **Sound progress** and **Excellent progress** criteria to see how well they have done.

TAKING IT FURTHER	To respond effectively, students need to show they can select a range of the most relevant implicit meanings. A particularly good novel for further work on implied meaning in setting is Susan Hill's *The Woman in Black*. Students could analyse how menace is conveyed in a suitable passage, such as the chapter entitled 'Across the Causeway' ('As I neared the ruins...') or 'The Sound of a Pony and Trap' (paragraphs 3–6).

Chapter 1: Key reading skills

1.8 Emotive language

Resources:
- Student's Book: 1.8, pp. 32–35
- Workbook: 1.6, pp. 22–24 can be set as homework
- Worksheets 1.8a–b
- PowerPoint slides 1.8a–e

Assessment objectives:

R2 Demonstrate understanding of implicit meanings and attitudes

R4 Demonstrate understanding of how writers achieve effects and influence readers

EXPLORE THE SKILLS

As a class, read this section of the Student's Book, ensuring that students understand the terms 'emotive language' and 'connotation'.

Ask students to complete **Q1** in pairs. Feed back as a class, discussing the emotional effects of each word. Encourage students to identify where a word is relying on connotation to create a reaction. Display **PPT 1.8a–d**, which contain some suggested answers. Responses should include:

➢ *sullen* suggests sulky, uncommunicative dissatisfaction and might be annoying to others

➢ *sunset* might be linked to calmness, peace, romance, or even tiredness

➢ *red rose* suggests love again, especially Valentine's Day, but this might be interpreted differently by someone who sees this as clichéd

➢ *irritable* suggests someone who is bad-tempered, gaining little sympathy.

BUILD THE SKILLS

For **Q2**, ask students to discuss the words in pairs, then share ideas with the class. Show **PPT 1.8e** and ask students to place the words on the line, depending on how positive or negative they are. Move on to **Q3**; either invite students to place the feeling words on the scale of intensity in pairs, or recreate it at the front of the class (four students represent the emotions and the rest of the class arrange them). To make the latter more interesting, add the following words (and extra students): *appreciate, be fond of, admire, cherish*. You could also present this activity using a piece of string as a washing line, with students pegging the words on paper to the line in the order they choose.

Repeat the activity with the 'dislike' words in **Q4**. Again, this could be written in pairs, or done physically in small groups or as the whole class. Words might include: *abhor, be averse to, detest, disgust, dislike, displease, hate, loathe, put off by, scorn*.

DEVELOP THE SKILLS

To introduce how we choose words to express our feelings or provoke a reaction, ask students how they might use the like/dislike words they explored. For example, ask them how they honestly feel about a food they don't enjoy (such as Brussels sprouts or pineapple) and then how they would say they felt about that food if their parents tried to make them eat it.

To develop understanding of how we choose words to provoke a reaction, write these two headlines on the board:

➢ Football Player Has Car Accident

➢ Football Hero in Car Smash Horror.

In pairs, students decide which is the better headline and why. During feedback, encourage them to consider the effects of *hero*, *smash* and *horror*. Emphasise that writers choose particular words to achieve effects and influence the reader.

Chapter 1: Key reading skills

Q5 and **Q6** will reinforce students' understanding of the purpose of a piece of writing. They could discuss the sentences in **Q5** in groups or pairs. As an extension, ask them to write a second sentence to follow on from each of these sentences, which uses emotive language to maintain or increase the effect of the first. Take feedback. Possible responses are:

a) The language aims to create horror at the savagery of the wolves, and sympathy for the children. *Ravening* suggests crazed with hunger. *Snarling* suggests fierceness. (You could ask how 'razor fangs bared' differs from 'sharp teeth showing'.)

b) This suggests hope and emotional uplift – partly because of the traditional (originally biblical) association of the rainbow with hope. The sun shining *bravely* is an encouraging personification. *Glorious* suggests praise and positivity.

c) The language describing the creatures makes them sound very non-human, and threatening. Pus is associated with infection. People usually find slime disgusting. The alliteration accentuates the effect.

Read the story extract as a class. Point out that H(erbert) G(eorge) Wells often wrote what we now call science fiction. Check to see whether any words need explanation (possibly *excrescence* – an unattractive, abnormal or diseased obtruding lump on a body). Get initial feedback on the overall effect of the passage.

Ask students to copy and complete the table in **Q6**, or use either **Worksheet 1.8a** or **1.8b** (which gives more support by identifying emotive words).

During feedback, draw out the effects of the words and how Wells uses them. Basic responses on their effects might include:

- 'coiled copiously': the tentacles must be very long – therefore able to reach further
- 'glistening texture': unnatural
- 'tentacle-surrounded mouth': alien – not like a human mouth
- 'curious excrescence': strange and disgusting
- 'evil interest': ill-intentioned intelligence
- 'preying upon human flesh': they are predatory; humans are vulnerable
- 'slowly uncoiling': as if their power means they need not hurry
- 'creeping': approaching in a stealthy way
- 'soft purring': weird, because like a cat (perhaps they are pleased to have new human prey)
- 'pouring': unstoppable

APPLY THE SKILLS

Ask students to answer **Q7** independently, using the bullet-point prompts and their notes from **Worksheet 1.8a** or **1.8b** to help them. Remind them to keep focusing on the purpose of the writing (to entertain by exciting the reader with a sense of horrific threat).

The responses should incorporate some of the ideas in the list above, but they should be in continuous prose, and with an awareness of the 'context' of an entertaining science-fiction horror story.

> **Extra support:** Give students a sentence starter. For example, *The writer uses the phrase 'coiled copiously' to convey a sense of ...*
>
> **Extra challenge:** Ask students to think of words or phrases that would have similar effects to those used by Wells. Students could also use technical terms, such as 'alliteration' for *coiled copiously*, or *The use of the adjective 'curious'...*

TAKING IT FURTHER	Students need to select a range of emotive words and phrases, analysing how language is used to create specific effects. To develop their awareness of emotive language further, ask them to write their own sci-fi description of some threatening creatures, copying Wells' techniques but using their own language.

Chapter 1: Key reading skills

1.9 Sensory language

Resources:
- Student's Book: 1.9, pp. 36–37
- Workbook: 1.6, pp. 22–24 can be set as homework
- Worksheets 1.9a–c

Assessment objectives:

R4 Demonstrate understanding of how writers achieve effects and influence readers

EXPLORE THE SKILLS

As a class, read through the opening section of the Student's Book, checking that students understand the importance of appealing to the senses in writing. Remind them what 'connotations' are.

For **Q1**, hand out **Worksheet 1.9a** and instruct students to complete the sensory connotations flowchart.

Extra support: Help students to think about which of the five senses the phrase links to, how the narrator would react, and what mood or atmosphere it creates.

Feed back as a class, drawing out the different sensory connotations and effects on the reader of each phrase.

Read through the extract about a summer's day. Ask students to work in pairs on **Q2**, again using **Worksheet 1.9a** to make their list of words or phrases that use the senses. Feed back as a class, collecting ideas for each of the five senses.

BUILD THE SKILLS

Set students the **Q3** writing task and give them ten minutes to try to use each of the senses in an effective way.

Extra support: Help students to select sense words, or give them sense pairs to include – for example:
- *sun, hot*
- *girls, laughing.*

Extra challenge: Encourage students to use the full range of senses. Use the last sentence of the extract to show students how the senses can be used in quite unusual ways.

Either get pairs to swap their work and try to spot each other's use of senses, or feed back as a class. If working as a class, consider dividing students into groups of five and allocating each person in a group one of the senses; each time they spot that sense being used in someone's writing, they have to stand up. This could lead to discussion of why some senses are used more than others.

DEVELOP THE SKILLS

Read through this section of the Student's Book with the class. Discuss the use of the adjective *slush-grey* and encourage students to consider the connotations of 'slush' (suggesting a dirty grey, perhaps – thinking about snow – a sense of something being spoiled or horrible). Check that students understand what the words *noun*, *adjective*, *verb* and *adverb* mean before they undertake **Q4**.

Ask students to work in pairs to complete the table, exploring the impact of using different word types in **Q4**, using **Worksheet 1.9b**. Take feedback as a class, asking students to explain and explore the effects of the words they have selected.

Chapter 1: Key reading skills

As an extension, introduce students to the idea of 'nuances': subtle differences in meaning. Ask students to revisit the beach extract in pairs, exploring how the language and senses used in the first paragraph create a more positive mood than those in the second paragraph. Share ideas and discuss students' findings as a class, trying to draw out the different effects of language and senses. Responses might include:

- see – 'toddlers wrestle over plastic spades' suggests play and togetherness, while 'stray flip flops' suggests desertion
- hear – 'giggling carelessly' suggests happiness and freedom, whereas 'there is no laughter in my mouth' uses a lack of sound to suggest unhappiness
- touch – 'the warm wind' sounds nice and comforting, but 'water sucks at my feet pulling me inwards' seems threatening
- smell and taste – 'sweet smell of candyfloss' sounds innocent and pleasurable, while 'salt spray lingers' sounds harsh and difficult to get rid of.

APPLY THE SKILLS

Ask students to answer **Q5**, making use of their notes from **Worksheets 1.9a** and **1.9b**.

> **Extra support:** Help students with a sentence starter. For example:
> - *The writer makes the beach seem...*
> - *The phrase 'sticky toddlers wrestle' suggests that the beach is...*
>
> **Extra challenge:** Encourage students to select a variety of phrases that cover all the senses, and to use technical language (*verb, adjective, personification, simile,* and so on) as part of their explanation of effects. Advise students to link phrases together in order to show how mood is built up by a writer.

TAKING IT FURTHER	Give students **Worksheet 1.9c**, which asks them to read a passage from *Wuthering Heights*, find examples of sensory language, and comment on their effects. The passage includes words and phrases relating to sight, hearing and touch. The overall effect is to contrast Cathy's ideal day (full of life, movement and energy) with Linton's (lazy, comfortable, sedate).

Chapter 1: Key reading skills

1.10 Recognising fact, opinion and bias

Resources:
- Student's Book: 1.10, pp. 38–39
- Workbook: 1.7, pp. 25–27 can be set as homework
- PowerPoint slides 1.10a–d

Assessment objectives:

R3 Analyse, evaluate and develop facts, ideas and opinions, using appropriate support from the text

EXPLORE THE SKILLS

Check on the class's initial understanding of the terms *fact*, *opinion* and *bias*. Read the lesson introduction with them. Ask students to think of other sentences beginning *The Tower of London is…* that are either statements of fact or opinions.

Students could consider **Q1** in pairs, then feed back to the class. Statements **a)** and **d)** are opinions. Note that some students might think that statement **e)** is an opinion because it could involve people having opinions.

To emphasise the distinction, ask students for further examples of facts, then further examples of opinions.

BUILD THE SKILLS

Show students the image of Dubai in the Student's Book. Point out that the extract comes from a well-known series of travel guides, and ask students how far they would expect travel guides to feature facts or opinions.

Read the extract on Dubai with the class, then ask students to work in pairs to tackle **Q2**, copying the table and completing it with facts and opinions from the text. They should then use their tables to complete **Q3**.

Extra support: For **Q2** and **Q3**, display **PPT 1.10a**, which contains some tips for the facts and opinions students should try to find for their tables, and some ideas for words that present a judgement.

Use **PPT 1.10a–c** to present suggested answers and discuss any points arising.

DEVELOP THE SKILLS

Refer to the 'Key terms' box on page 38 of the Student's Book and ask for examples of bias. Students might think of particular newspapers or news channels, or of a football referee, or sports reporting being biased.

To emphasise the point that even facts can be used in a biased way, challenge students to think of three facts that could show your school in a positive light, and three that could show it in a negative light. Develop this by giving an example of how a single fact could be presented positively or negatively. A house could be described as 'overlooking a busy motorway' or, by an estate agent as 'excellently situated for the motorway'.

Students could consider **Q4** in pairs, then feed back to the class. Statement a) could be biased in favour of Nettlefield United, using facts selectively, if the team has only achieved draws at home and has always been beaten when playing away. Statement b) uses the statistic of the Antarctic's 24-hour sunlight – in summer, without mentioning the 24-hour night in winter, and the low temperatures all year round.

Read the second Dubai text with the class and invite comments on how it could be biased. For **Q5**, students could work in small groups for discussion first, then copy three sentences from the extract giving explanations of how they could be biased.

Chapter 1: Key reading skills

> **Extra support:** Tell students to test whether a statement is biased by asking themselves how the same basic fact could be presented in a negative way instead.
>
> **Extra challenge:** Ask students to select especially positive words or phrases and analyse their effect in depth. You could refer them to Topic 1.8 on Emotive language (pages 32–35), relating to 'connotations'.

Review possible answers with the class:

- 'crystal clear waters' suggests pollution-free; 'crystal' has connotations of precious stones and cut glass
- 'soaring' suggests flight and freedom; compare with 'overbearing'
- 'selfie' suggests a focus on the reader, and the informal language implies fun
- 'pampered' implies luxury and comfort
- Negative details that might have been included, if they were applicable, could include beach tar, high prices, uncomfortably high temperatures, city centre traffic.

APPLY THE SKILLS

Students could begin by discussing in groups what they could write about. The 'place where you live' could be interpreted as a locality, town, city or country. If your student intake is widespread, it would be helpful for pairs or groups of students living in the same place to discuss options.

> **Extra support:** Help students to address the types of attraction they might write about – for example:
> - historic buildings
> - scenery
> - parks (or even theme parks)
> - the weather
> - the people
> - museums and art galleries.

TAKING IT FURTHER	Students could study newspapers and magazines and look for examples of facts, opinions and bias. Newspaper editorial sections will provide examples of opinion. Reviews of theatre, concerts, books and so on, will also provide examples.

© HarperCollins *Publishers* Ltd 2018

Chapter 1: Key reading skills

1.11 Analysing and evaluating

Resources:
- Student's Book: 1.11, pp. 40–41
- Workbook: 1.8, pp. 28–30 can be set as homework
- PowerPoint slide 1.11

Assessment objectives:

R3 Analyse, evaluate and develop facts, ideas and opinions, using appropriate support from the text

EXPLORE THE SKILLS

Read the introductory sentence with students. Explain the difference between analysis and evaluation: analysis involves *how* a text or argument works; evaluation is about *how well* it works.

Work through **Q1** with the whole class. Read the text together, then look more closely at the annotations. Ask students how well they think the title works as a summary of the text, and how well the topic sentence works.

There is no clear correct ranking for **Q1**. You could point out that some titles do sum up a text, while others simply attract attention to it – especially, for example, in a tabloid newspaper. Factual evidence tends to be more reliable than anecdotal evidence, but the latter may make more of an impression on the reader. Students will be able to judge its effect when reading the text.

Ask students to complete **Q2**. A possible answer is that Udorie makes the point that the wide range of social media apps available puts damaging pressure on young people to keep in touch with all of their social group all of the time. Point out that this is summed up in the topic sentence.

For **Q3**, Udorie names several apps as evidence for the range available. She also gives an extended personal anecdote about the way that apps put social pressure on her younger sister. This is not hard factual evidence, but the fact that it is based on her own sister (rather than, say, a story she heard about someone else) gives it more weight.

Extra challenge: Show **PPT 1.11** and ask students how the underlined words and phrases add to the persuasive effect of Udorie's anecdote. (Overall, the word choices make the younger sister appear to be in the grip of a compulsion that makes her behave in a desperate and unreasonable way.)

BUILD THE SKILLS

Students could work on **Q4** and **Q5** in pairs, then feed back to the class. Draw out the following answers:

➢ The point Udorie makes is that social media damages teenagers' sleep, leading to anxiety and depression.

➢ The evidence is in the form of her citing (rather vaguely) 'a new study'.

DEVELOP THE SKILLS

Emphasise the point that evaluating the argument involves weighing it up. For example, you could ask whether Udorie's anecdotal evidence about her sister is persuasive because of being personal, or makes her a less reliable witness because of her emotional involvement.

Read the text with students and ask how its basic message differs from that of the first text. For **Q6**, the main point is that social media can increase young people's happiness by making them feel better about friendships and increasing their capacity for empathy.

For **Q7**, students could discuss in pairs and then write an answer evaluating the text.

Chapter 1: Key reading skills

Extra support: Tell students to consider what they would need to know in order to make a more confident evaluation. For example:
- How was the research carried out?
- What was the relative benefit for boys?
- What was the evidence that expressing empathy became 'habitual'? (That seems particularly difficult to quantify.)

Extra challenge: Ask students to write a comparison between the views and evidence in both texts. They should remember to analyse and evaluate both.

APPLY THE SKILLS

Discuss with the class what kinds of points they could make in their speech. You could either limit them to the evidence of the two texts, or you could allow them to use their own experience as well.

Extra support: Get students started by getting them to make lists of positive and negative effects of social media, based on the texts and their own experience. These could be in the form of spider diagrams, mind-maps or conventional lists in two columns. They should then attempt to weigh up the two sides and reach a conclusion towards which they would then aim in their speech.

Extra challenge: Students could write and even deliver the whole speech.

TAKING IT FURTHER	Students could devise their own research into young people's use of social media, collecting data from other class members on: <ul><li>what apps they use</li><li>how often they use them</li><li>how many times a day they check for messages</li><li>whether they ever log in in the middle of the night</li><li>how this affects their lives.</li></ul> They could write up their results, and then analyse and evaluate each other's arguments.

© HarperCollins *Publishers* Ltd 2018

Chapter 1: Key reading skills

1.12 Understanding the form and purpose of different texts

Resources:
- Student's Book: 1.12, pp. 42–45
- Workbook: 1.9, pp. 31–33 can be set as homework
- Worksheet 1.12

Assessment objectives:

R3 Analyse, evaluate and develop facts, ideas and opinions, using appropriate support from the text

EXPLORE THE SKILLS

Read the opening paragraph with the class and ask for feedback on other forms. These could include workshop manuals, recipes, travel magazine articles or magazine problem page replies. This lesson focuses on non-fiction, but at this point students could also consider fictional forms, such as novels, poetry and drama.

Ask students to use **Worksheet 1.12** to answer **Q1** and **Q2**, then share their answers as a class. Alternatively, approach these as whole-class activities using the whiteboard.

For **Q1**, draw out answers such as:

a) Air passengers will generally want relatively light, entertaining articles that they can easily complete in the duration of a flight. Subjects may relate to holiday activities, sight-seeing in the destination country, or more widely to international interest. They may be calculated to encourage customers to take future flights.

b) This would be in full-length book form. Readers would probably expect a chronological account starting with the celebrity's childhood. The book would probably contain an account of how the celebrity became successful, including challenges, obstacles and influences.

c) People might read this for several reasons: to decide whether to go to the play themselves; to compare the reviewer's views with their own if they have seen it; or it they took a general interest in the theatre. It would therefore give information on when and where to see the play, the actors, the director's approach and so on.

For **Q2**, suggested answers are:

a) news report: inform (and to some extent entertain)

b) holiday brochure: inform, persuade (a travel guide would advise)

c) accident prevention leaflet: inform, advise

Discuss any alternative views with the class.

BUILD THE SKILLS

The text here and in the 'Develop the skills' section can be used alongside the activities to help students practise for the coursework assignments, and to encourage them to come up with ideas and creative topics of their own.

To begin, explain to students that, as a way of generating ideas and practising key writing skills needed for their assignments, they are going to work with two non-fiction texts that both relate to physical danger. However, remind them that it is only in **Assignment 1** that they will need to respond directly to texts.

After students have read 'Alone in the balloon', put them into groups of four to work through **Q3** and **Q4**. They should be aware that the form and purpose of this text (as a personal prose account) is perhaps less important than it might be in a media text or poem.

Chapter 1: Key reading skills

Extra challenge: Ask students to consider creative writing opportunities based on what they have read. Do they know of anyone who has faced danger in a similar way? Could they find out more about the incident, or about other balloon adventures, and write about them in a similar way to Branson? A web search for 'Branson Balloon Crash 1987' will lead to more detailed accounts.

DEVELOP THE SKILLS

Read the introductory paragraph of this section to the class and make sure that students understand that form and purpose are related. As a further example, you could add that an in-flight magazine distributed on a short-haul flight would not have a long, complex article that would take longer than the flight time to read.

Read 'Confessions of a high-rise window cleaner'. Get the class to work on **Q5** and **Q6** in pairs, and then feed back to the class. Draw out from **Q5** that the feature cannot be breaking news as it covers something that the subject has been doing for two and a half years. The description of his hair suggests that at least one purpose of the feature is to entertain. For **Q6** the use of present tense and the phrase *He tells me…* reveal that the basic format is an extended interview, with the interviewer sometimes quoting the window cleaner and at other times presenting his findings in the third person.

APPLY THE SKILLS

Students should discuss **Q7** in pairs, then feed back in class discussion. Draw out that the ballooning text aims to create a gripping, exciting narrative, using suspense and details that make the reader imagine what it was like to be in Branson's situation. The second text conveys what the job is like, and why Maple enjoys it, entertaining and informing the reader, but there is no narrative, suspense or any attempt to convey a real sense of danger.

Extra support: For the *Metro Toronto* report, tell students to begin by making up a number of short quotations that Richard Branson might say to explain why he goes ballooning and what challenges there are in it. For the window-cleaner's account, you could give students an opening, such as: 'It started off as just another day of high-rise window-cleaning. As I looked up at the clear blue sky …'

Extra challenge: Tell students to work in groups, then individually, to devise at least two very different ways to present the window-cleaning story. For example, there could be a narrative element, recreating, or inventing, a dangerous episode, or snapshots of one day's work.

TAKING IT FURTHER	Make sure that students have a clear command of the main conventions of different types of texts, but then challenge them to try out different ways of mixing those conventions – for example: ➢ a story with a clear moral message persuading the reader not to do what the writer has done ➢ a travelogue with personal emotions alongside a descriptive account and factual information about a place or event.

Chapter 1: Key reading skills

1.13 Deducing audience

Resources:
- Student's Book: 1.13, pp. 46–49
- Workbook: 1.10, pp. 34–35 can be set as homework
- Worksheet 1.13
- PowerPoint slides 1.13a–c

Assessment objectives:

R3 Analyse, evaluate and develop facts, ideas and opinions, using appropriate support from the text

R4 Demonstrate understanding of how writers achieve effects and influence readers

EXPLORE THE SKILLS

Read out the introduction and explain that this lesson focuses on how audience influences content and style.

Q1 introduces 'target audience' by encouraging students to identify themselves as one. Discuss the listed factors with the whole class, or use **Worksheet 1.13**. Students should fill this out, commenting on the *relative importance* of factors in determining which target audience they fit.

After the discussion or filling in the worksheet, discuss the order as a class. Encourage them to think of how the factors listed would relate to particular texts. For example, do they ever read any specialist interest magazines or books?

BUILD THE SKILLS

For **Q2**, students should read the three sentences in small groups and discuss the profiles of their target audiences. They could refer to the factors listed under 'Explore the skills' or in **Worksheet 1.13**. They could write target audience profiles for each extract individually, then feed back to the class.

Suggested answers:

a) This appeals to people who care about the natural world and the effects of global warming. They might be young, but not necessarily. The text could be part of a campaign appeal, so it would be aimed at people who could donate some money or time.

b) This is aimed at parents of teenagers and younger children (though Mum and Dad could also be the grandparents) who want their children to enjoy themselves, and have a chance to relax themselves.

c) This is an introduction to the manual for a sophisticated camera. Buyers will need money to spare, and the enthusiasm for photography. It is aimed at users who will understand it. (Lens aperture affects how much of the field of vision comes into focus; shutter speed determines how much light enters the camera; ISO relates to the camera's sensitivity to light.)

Extra support: For a), ask whether there are particular types of people who care about global warming (for example, the young, because they will be more affected by it?), and draw attention to the phrase 'people like you and me'. For b), ask who will be paying. For c), ask what the technical language suggests.

Extra challenge: Ask students to write similar texts aimed at similar or other specific audiences, such as retired people or the fashion-conscious. **PPT 1.13a–c** provides examples.

Read the text for **Q3** with the class and check that they understand it all. Make it clear that they do not need to have heard any 'Ghanian hiplife' or 'Atlanta rap'. However, the reviewer assumes that at least some of the audience will know what these are.

Students could complete **Q4** and **Q5** in small groups, and then write individual answers. Afterwards, they could compare as a class.

Chapter 1: Key reading skills

> **Extra support:** Play students part of a J Hus track to give insight into what the review describes, but listen to it first, to make sure that there is nothing potentially offensive. ('Spirit' might be a good track to choose.) Otherwise, point out that many readers would have no previous knowledge of the artist, so the review has to convey what the music is like.

Suggested answers to **Q4**:

a) *NME* is a music enthusiasts' magazine, and it assumes that readers will have at least some knowledge of the genres mentioned.

b) The reviewer provides brief descriptions of each type of music. These are enjoyable in themselves, but they also inform anyone unfamiliar with them. For example, Ghanian hiplife is bouncy, and Atlanta rap is hypnotic ('zoned-out'). Ask whether any students are familiar with any of these types of music.

c) The phrase might appeal to a younger audience. However, it also assumes an audience who like to be surprised or challenged by music rather than just wanting familiarity.

For **Q5**, 'Aggy' and 'zoned-out' are 'street' language. The others are likely to be used by well-educated or well-read readers, especially 'louche' and 'prodigious'. This suggests that the review is aimed at literate readers who are also aware of popular culture.

DEVELOP THE SKILLS

Students could consider **Q6–8** in pairs or small groups and write answers, or feed back ideas to the class.

Suggested answers:

Q6 It assumes that readers will know that Stormzy, Skepta and Drake are all rappers, and that they will want the UK to become more prominent in the rap world.

Q7 It assumes that they live in the UK.

Q8 Generally, a music review reader will want to know what the music is like, and whether the artist is someone they might enjoy. If they already know the artist, they will be interested in the artist's development. If they already know the album, they will enjoy reading the reviewer's views.

APPLY THE SKILLS

Read the text with the class and check that they understand the moral question: Should works of art 'confiscated' by a government and sold abroad eventually be returned to the nation they came from?

Students could discuss, then write answers.

Q9 Suggested answers:

➢ The content appeals to readers interested in art, British history and moral issues.

➢ 'Cabal', 'restitution' and 'mores' (say it is pronounced 'more-ayz') imply any educated audience.

➢ The jokily casual description of the English Civil War ('flogs it') implies an audience familiar with its history.

➢ Readers might want to go to the exhibition.

Q10 Students should discuss details for the brief before they write individually. The exercise should bring together all they have learned in the lesson so far. The key points are all in the answers above.

TAKING IT FURTHER	Students could write a piece to appeal to the audience of one of the texts in the lesson. They could write a review of music they know well, for *NME* or a similar publication in their own country.

© HarperCollins *Publishers* Ltd 2018

Chapter 2: Key technical skills

2.1 Vocabulary and word classes

Resources:
- Student's Book: 2.1, pp. 52–55
- Workbook: 2.1, 2.2, pp. 36–41 can be set as homework
- Worksheet 2.1
- PowerPoint slides 2.1a–d

Assessment objectives:

W3 Use a range of vocabulary and sentence structures appropriate to context

W5 Make accurate use of spelling, punctuation and grammar

EXPLORE THE SKILLS

As a class, look at the noun table on page 52 of the Student's Book and recap on the differences between common and proper nouns. Read through the text and complete **Q1** by asking whether the students notice anything in particular about proper nouns. Expect comments about real names and ask what makes the words different in the two columns. Students should be identifying the capital letter.

Explain that pronouns do not have a capital letter when they replace proper nouns, referring back to the example *Shaheed was in the middle of explaining when suddenly he raced out of the room*.

Read through the text about verbs, checking that students are clear about the different types of verb: main, auxiliary and modal. Use the 'Top tip' if necessary.

Move on to adjectives and adverbs and their role in modifying nouns and verbs. Using the examples about the mouse, discuss how the text changes when adjectives such as *timid* or *dangerous* are used or omitted. Also look at adverbs and the effect of *really* or *incredibly*. You could take suggested examples of their use in other sentences and evaluate their importance together. For example:

➢ *The ice on the playground is dangerous and really needs extra grit to stop it being incredibly slippery.*

Students could improve or extend this in pairs before completing **Q2** when a bank of adjectives and adverbs might be useful to start them off. Have some ready to help.

Extra support: Provide students with a few adjectives and adverbs to start them off in **Q2**. For example:

➢ The **impatient** woman.
➢ The film was **petrifying**.
➢ I am **justifiably** tired.

BUILD THE SKILLS

Recap on the role of pronouns. You could refer back to the sentence: *Shaheed was in the middle of explaining when suddenly he raced out of the room*. Point out how *he* makes the sentence flow better than repeating *Shaheed*.

Read through the text about pronouns, prepositions, conjunctions and determiners as a class, then set **Q3**, which asks students to identify the prepositions (at), determiners (the) and pronouns (I'll). You could encourage students to write alternatives to the four sentences given in this section.

Extra support: Make sure that targeted students are secure in their understanding of word classes with **Worksheet 2.1**. You could cut the strips out so that it is easier to match the terms with their descriptions.

Chapter 2: Key technical skills

Extra challenge: Ask students to use the example sentences in this section to come up with their own sentences using prepositions, determiners and pronouns.
- *I gave the chocolate cake to Mr Green.*
- *I want that guitar.*
- *The red bike belongs to me.*
- *All morning I paced about the room, waiting for the exam results letter to arrive.*
- *I'll meet him at the entrance to the railway station at 6 o'clock with them.*

DEVELOP THE SKILLS

Go through the information about vocabulary on page 54, and make sure that all students understand what is meant by 'emotive words' and 'technical terms or phrases'. Display **PPT 2.1a**, which contains the short text from the Student's Book with some vocabulary highlighted to help with **Q4**.

Allocate groups to describe the effects of specific words. You will probably find a range of reactions to the experience of playing in a band. The narrator feels exhilarated by the nerve-wracking event but they might feel petrified of letting other band members down. Discuss these different emotions and how vocabulary conveys these feelings.

Ask students to stay in their groups to complete **Q5**. They need to evaluate the word choice *serious* and compare it with *grave, important, worrying* and *drastic*. Encourage students to give each word a score out of 5 in terms of the strength of their shock, panic and concern. Display **PPT 2.1b**, which contains the words and some example rankings of strength. Ask students whether they agree with these scores. Can they suggest words that might score 1, or go above the highest ranking and score 6?

See whether students agree with the scores above and ask whether they can suggest words that would score 6 or 1.

For **Q6**, display **PPT 2.1c** for students to use as reference for copying and replacing the highlighted words. If they need help getting started, you could suggest *atrocious* instead of *very bad* and/or *splattered* instead of *thrown*.

Students should complete **Q7** on their own. For an alternative that offers more support, you could display **PPT 2.1d**, which provides a completed version of the paragraph that students can evaluate and change.

Extra challenge: Ask students to use adjectives and adverbs to change the tone of a piece of writing. For example: *A storm kept me awake last night* becomes *A malevolent storm vindictively kept me awake last night*. Alternatively, they could use the same sentences for different purposes by adding or changing words.
- Sentence: *A storm kept me awake last night.*
- Diary entry: *A malevolent storm vindictively kept me awake last* night.
- Travel guide: A spectacular storm excitedly kept me awake last night.

APPLY THE SKILLS

Remind students of the skills that they have been using: precise choice of vocabulary, effective use of adjectives and adverbs to suit different purposes. When students complete their first paragraph in response to **Q8**, invite trial of their initial ideas with peers to check that the tone is correct for the intended purpose. Share adjectives to modify the noun *cave* and try different adverbs to describe the mountain *precariously balanced on the side of a cliff*. Students should give feedback to each other about the effects of their vocabulary choices. Ask what detail could they add to *as night falls*. Suggest how frightening it could be and how the fear could be shown rather than told. So *hands are shaking* rather than *I was really scared.*

| TAKING IT FURTHER | Sophisticated and pertinent choice of vocabulary can be quite minimal. It can be appropriate to use one well-chosen word where 20 had been used in an early draft. Encourage students to find words they have never heard before such as *copious, arcane, subterfuge, obtuse, plethora, verbose* and practise using them to describe a dark setting where a spy is plotting to break in to a high security official building. |

Chapter 2: Key technical skills

2.2 Accurate sentences

Resources:
- Student's Book: 2.2, pp. 56–57
- Workbook: 2.3, 2.4, pp. 42–47 can be set as homework
- PowerPoint slides 2.2a–d

Assessment objectives:
W3 Use a range of vocabulary and sentence structures appropriate to context
W5 Make accurate use of spelling, punctuation and grammar

EXPLORE THE SKILLS

As a class, read through the information at the top of page 56 in the Student's Book, reminding students about the different ways of punctuating the end of a sentence. Review the different types of sentence indicated by each of these punctuation marks: declarative, interrogative, exclamatory and imperative. Ask students to work in pairs to answer **Q1**, writing down sentences for each function in a copy of the table. Take feedback as a class and discuss any examples that are incorrect, and why.

To consolidate understanding of sentence functions, display **PPT 2.2a**, which contains some more sentences, and ask students to classify them. The answers are on **PPT 2.2b**. Use this to clear up any remaining confusion that students might have about sentence functions.

BUILD THE SKILLS

Introduce the three different sentence types, which students may have come across before: simple, compound and complex. Read through the explanations of each of these types carefully and ensure that everyone understands the difference between them, especially between compound (two clauses *of equal weight*) and complex (a main clause and a subordinate clause).

Ask students whether they have received feedback on their writing (either verbally or through marking) that is similar to the following:

➢ 'Your piece of writing would have been stronger if you had used more complex sentences.'
➢ 'Please try to add more detail to your sentences.'
➢ 'Sometimes less is more when writing narrative. A complex sentence can provide detail and subject concisely whereas a compound sentence can extend the word count rather than expand the imagination of the reader.'
➢ 'Try to use fewer "ands" and more "because", "although" and "since".'

Ask students to identify a comment that feels relevant to their own writing, or copy out similar comments from their own books to focus their minds on what they need to improve.

Read the text about the Nile as a class, and then ask students to answer **Q2**:

➢ Sentence 1 = compound and declarative
➢ Sentence 2 = simple and exclamatory
➢ Sentences 3 and 4 = complex and declarative
➢ Sentence 5 = simple and declarative

Extra challenge: After students have identified the different sentence types and functions in **Q2**, challenge more able students to rewrite the compound sentence (*The River Nile was incredibly wide, and we saw crocodiles basking in the midday sun.*) into a complex sentence.

An example answer might be:

➢ The River Nile, where we saw crocodiles basking in the midday sun, was incredibly wide.

Chapter 2: Key technical skills

DEVELOP THE SKILLS

As a class, recap on the structure of compound sentences and how generally they offer detail rather than tension or layers of meaning. Explain that compound sentences can present two balanced or contrasting points or ideas. Then read the information about subordinate clauses at the start of the 'Develop the skills' section in the Student's Book. Display **PPT 2.2c** and discuss the advantages of using subordinate clauses rather than linking two or more clauses with commas and 'and' or 'but'. Draw out the benefit of making clauses dependent rather than adding extra information. The red complex sentence shows two linked clauses. The blue compound sentence shows two clauses that could be made into individual sentences. Concise writing, using subordinate clauses, conveys information quickly and removes ambiguity. If the red sentence was compound, replacing *although* with *and,* the reader might question why it was important to look after your valuables when the police have stated there was no danger.

Before students tackle **Q3**, evaluate the complex-complex-simple paragraph structure on **PPT 2.2d**. Elicit from students what can be inferred about what the old man does next. Draw out what effect the long sentence has at the start of the paragraph. Does it suggest that things were happening quickly or slowly? Ask students to consider the effects of the second and third sentences.

Answers for **Q3** will vary but might include responses such as:

a) *As the jeep approached a crocodile*, we insisted the driver stopped.

b) We placed Clark under the shade of the only tree, *in order that he could sit out of the glare of the midday sun.*

c) Finally, his fever began to subside, *although he still remained very weak.*

> **Extra challenge:** Ask targeted students to rewrite the paragraph on **PPT 2.2d** so that it conveys sympathy for the old man rather than frustration towards him. What type of sentences would best convey detail about the old man and perhaps recollection about his past?

APPLY THE SKILLS

Consider **Q4** as a whole class and decide together on the success criteria for the writing task. These may include:

- effective selection of sentence types to have an effect on the reader
- sentence choices match the tone and create appropriate pace
- an appropriate blend of simple, compound and complex sentences
- creating effects with punctuation.

Once students are confident about the success criteria, they should write their narrative account individually. They could swap their writing afterwards and peer-assess against the criteria listed above.

TAKING IT FURTHER	Students could collect sentences used in different texts for different audiences and purposes, and compare. For example: - from a website explaining the help available for older people with filling out forms - a flyer for a sports club in the school holidays for under-10s - an advertisement for a playgroup for mums and toddlers - the description of a character from a Dickens novel. Ask students to write a comparison of how different authors use sentences for different purposes.

Chapter 2: Key technical skills

2.3 Tenses and verb agreement

Resources:
- Student's Book: 2.3, pp. 58–59
- Workbook: 2.5, pp. 48–50 can be set as homework
- Worksheet 2.3
- PowerPoint slides 2.3a–f

Assessment objectives:

W5 Make accurate use of spelling, punctuation and grammar

EXPLORE THE SKILLS

Use the information at the start of this section in the Student's Book to explore the meaning of 'tenses' and 'verb agreement'. Build on the example here by creating further sentences, such as:

➤ *The students write.*

➤ *The student writes.*

Point out the rule in these examples, when a verb ends in '–s', the noun should not have an 's' and that if the verb does not have an 's', the noun should have one (i.e. be plural):

➤ *The child laughs.*

➤ *The children laugh.*

Ask students how many further examples of regular verbs following this rule they can find.

As a class, look at the table on page 58 of the Student's Book, which clarifies how the verb 'jump' is conjugated. Then ask students to complete **Q1**. When they have done so, display **PPT 2.3a**, which shows the original paragraph and the corrected version, and discuss the mistakes in the original version.

BUILD THE SKILLS

Discuss with the class the statement:

➤ *Exceptions to the rule often stick in your mind quicker than the rule.*

Display **PPT 2.3b**, which contains the following paragraph, and ask students to copy and complete it.

➤ 'Before you b_____ writing, check you have ink in your pen. After you have b_____ writing, be careful not to smudge your work. Tell your partner how you b_____ your story.'

When everyone has completed the paragraph, display **PPT 2.3c** to provide the answers. Discuss any they got wrong and why. Invite students to come up with a further three examples of irregular verbs and how they conjugate. Ask which verb they find most difficult to conjugate in past, present and future tenses and create a PPT slide listing the challenges of these verbs – for example:

➤ ride/rode/ridden

➤ wake/woke/woken

Ask students to apply what they have just learned to **Q2**. The correct paragraph should be:

I had run home when Sadiq texted me and asked what we had to do for homework. I told him the teacher had taken our books in so we didn't have any.

DEVELOP THE SKILLS

Review the information on modal verbs in the Student's Book, and make sure that all students understand that these are 'helping' verbs, indicating degrees of possibility or probability. Discuss how modal verbs convey meaning in a variety of ways.

Chapter 2: Key technical skills

Explain that it is important to be careful not to use modal verbs excessively, and model this using the paragraph on **PPT 2.3d**:

> 'Would you mind if I closed the window? Will it rain do you think? Could we work together and tidy up the trays on my desk by any chance? Can we all take our bags off the carpet because I've been told that a special vacuum cleaner is coming that we must use if there are any particularly bad patches on our carpet.'

Point out how using too many modal verbs makes speech or writing seem uncertain and a bit irritating! Like many language devices, modal verbs should be used in moderation.

Ask students to complete **Q3** in pairs. If necessary, clarify that the speaker is saying that they will not be going, but is doing so in a polite way. The answers are:

a) Unlikely: that the speaker is going to go

b) Definite: that the speaker will be watching Rav in his tennis final

As an extension to this activity, display **PPT 2.3e**, and ask students to:

➢ try using *could* in place of both *would* and *will*

➢ change *would* for *will*, then use *could* in place of *will*.

For these changes, *was* needs to change to *am*. It tells the reader that there is a possibility that she might be free and that Rav might not be in the final.

Extra support: Give students **Worksheet 2.3**, which provides some additional activities for consolidating understanding of modal verbs.

Extra challenge: For further practise on how modal verbs help to convey 'definite' or 'unlikely', display the table on **PPT 2.3f** and ask students to copy and complete it with sentences that represent a vague hypothesis or a high level of certainty.

APPLY THE SKILLS

Read the task in **Q4** and ask students to use their experience of changing tense carefully. They will need to blend past and future. Advise students to create word banks using the future and past tense to describe events that have happened (certain) and might happen (vague hypothesis).

You could assess how effectively students are using this advice by checking the work in progress after 20 minutes. Offer reminders about using their word banks as they write, and draw attention to the 'Checklist for success' on page 59 of the Student's Book.

TAKING IT FURTHER	Ask students to collect examples of when modal verbs are and are not appropriate to use and then explain their choices. For example: ➢ Yes: When serving food to guests. 'Would you like to order dessert?' ➢ No: When giving instructions. 'You might want to add an egg to the cake mix here.'

Chapter 2: Key technical skills

2.4 Sentence punctuation

Resources:
- Student's Book: 2.4, pp. 60–63
- Workbook: 2.6, pp. 51–55 can be set as homework
- Worksheets 2.4a–c
- PowerPoint slides 2.4a–i

Assessment objectives:

W5 Make accurate use of spelling, punctuation and grammar

EXPLORE THE SKILLS

Recap on the use of commas and apostrophes by asking students to read through the information on pages 60–61 of the Student's Book in pairs and discuss any rules they were unsure of. Come back together as a class and list any misunderstandings and confusions on the board. For example:

➢ *a comma indicates a pause in a long sentence or all words ending in 's' need an apostrophe.*

Extra support: Give students **Worksheets 2.4a** and **2.4b**, which contain further activities on the correct use of commas and apostrophes. Direct them to the rule they are having particular trouble with – for example, commas in lists, separating parts of a sentence, adding more information, apostrophes of omission or possession, and ask them to complete the appropriate activities.

Display **PPT 2.4a** and ask students to use it to complete **Q1**. When everyone has finished the task, display **PPT 2.4b** and go through the answers, identifying where students might have missed the incorrect uses of punctuation.

BUILD THE SKILLS

Work through the rules of brackets and dashes as a class, then ask students to complete **Q2** in pairs. Ask the pairs to present a case for brackets with part **a)** and dashes for part **b)**. Select groups to present their cases and draw out how the feature's use is not set in stone – there is some negotiation when it comes to which one is used, and the effects are more subtle. The first thing to establish is the main clause and the subordinate part. How the parts are separated and linked is up to the writer.

PPT 2.4c shows an answer for students to evaluate.

DEVELOP THE SKILLS

Use pages 62–63 of the Student's Book to clarify the use of colons and semi-colons, then ask students to complete **Q3** in pairs. The answers are:

a) My phone has lots of things wrong with it: broken screen; no audio; dead battery.

b) Grime is my favourite type of music; Sasha has always loved techno.

c) Javed carefully opened the box; it was completely empty.

If students still seem unsure about when to use colons, explain that a colon signals to the reader '…and I'm going to tell you why'. Demonstrate this by reading the two example statements in this section and replacing the colon with 'and I'm going to tell you why':

➢ *We can be proud of last year [and I'm going to tell you why] increased sales, more customers and higher profits.*

➢ *She was overjoyed [and I'm going to tell you why] the bag was exactly what she wanted.*

Chapter 2: Key technical skills

Ask students to complete **Q4** in pairs, correctly punctuating the paragraph about the school library. Display the answer on **PPT 2.4d** and discuss the positioning of the colons and semi-colons, reinforcing how:

➢ colons are used to introduce a list and separate two parts of a sentence where the second part explains the first

➢ semi-colons are used to separate items in a list and split two parts of a sentence where the second part is a contrast or comparison with the first.

Extra support: Show students the text on **PPT 2.4e** and ask them where colons and semi-colons could be used in the unpunctuated paragraph describing Shamira's picnic. The answer is on **PPT 2.4f**.

Extra challenge: Ask students to complete **Worksheet 2.4c**, which contains an extended writing activity involving the use of brackets, dashes, colons and semi-colons.

Extra support: Display **PPT 2.4g** and ask students to use semi-colons, colons, brackets and dashes to improve the sentences. If students are struggling, you could display **PPT 2.4h**, which gives some tips. Go through the answers on **PPT 2.4i**.

APPLY THE SKILLS

Ask all students to complete **Q5**, making use of the bullet points to structure their writing.

Help students to engage with the subject by sharing articles on the internet.

TAKING IT FURTHER	Students need to balance content and skills carefully. They should concentrate on careful use of writing techniques and not get too involved in supporting or disputing an argument. To practise this, ask students to compile a checklist before they start, which could help them to keep track of time spent constructing an argument against time spent using impressive writing techniques while they are writing.

Chapter 2: Key technical skills

2.5 Reported and direct speech

Resources:
- Student's Book: 2.5, pp. 64–65
- Workbook: 2.6, pp. 51–55 can be set as homework
- Worksheet 2.5
- PowerPoint slides 2.5a–c

Assessment objectives:

W5 Make accurate use of spelling, punctuation and grammar

EXPLORE THE SKILLS

Ask students to recall a conversation they had earlier in the day. It might have been at breakfast, on the school bus, in registration or with a tutor. Then ask them to write out part of the conversation and try to punctuate it accurately. Students should swap their work and identify errors in the speech punctuation.

Next, ask students to look at the annotated dialogue on page 64 of the Student's Book and see whether there are any other features missing from their own written conversation. Ask them to redraft their conversations.

Recap on all the features of direct speech, using the annotations, then ask students to complete **Q1** in pairs. When everyone has finished, display the answers on **PPT 2.5a** and discuss any punctuation that students got wrong.

Extra challenge: Give students **Worksheet 2.5** and ask them to complete the task, which involves rewriting a piece of text using the correct speech punctuation.

BUILD THE SKILLS

Read through the information about reported speech in the Student's Book. Look at the example, which shows the difference between direct and reported speech. Display the table on **PPT 2.5b**, which shows examples of when you might use direct and reported speech.

Explain to students that when changing from direct to reported speech, it is important to use pronouns carefully to indicate the ownership of the spoken word:

➤ *Jenna said, 'I can't believe that you could be so thoughtless!'*

➤ *Jenna said she couldn't believe that he could be so thoughtless.*

Ask students to suggest why *I* becomes *she* or when *you* becomes *he* in the above examples. Then return to **Q2** to practise more changing of direct speech to reported speech. Sample answers are:

a) The police officer told us that the fire was still burning.

b) The president said that she was delighted with the outcome of the meeting.

Extra support: Ensure that targeted students have the annotated examples from the Student's Book in front of them when answering **Q2**.

Extra challenge: Put students in pairs and either ask them to write a continuation of one of the conversations on **PPT 2.5b** (Natasha/Lola or Mrs Wise/Arnold) or show them the example below:

'I can mend Natasha's phone, Mrs Wise.' said Arnold.

'I doubt that, Arnold.' replied Natasha's mum.

'No, really I think I can,' Arnold carried on. 'It's what I've been studying at college. I have the tools at home that you need to open the case up properly. I changed the screen on my own phone when it got cracked.'

Chapter 2: Key technical skills

> *Mrs Wise looked at Arnold. 'Arnold,' she said, 'that is not the same as drying out a phone that has been in a swimming pool.'*
>
> When they have done so, ask them to convert the text to reported speech.

DEVELOP THE SKILLS

Explain to students that inverted commas are used for titles of poems and short stories, and for quotations, as well as for presenting direct speech. Use the sentences on **PPT 2.5c**, which includes examples of all types of use of inverted commas, to explore this as a whole class. Then ask students to complete **Q3** in pairs. The answers are:

a) 'Tidy your room first' was all she would say when I asked her if I could go round to Ben's.

b) When Wordsworth writes 'I wandered lonely as a cloud' we get a vivid picture of him strolling through the mountains.

> **Extra challenge:** Ask students to report on how their favourite poet has used rhyme to make their poems easy to remember. Remind students to use quotations in inverted commas to provide exemplification.

APPLY THE SKILLS

For **Q4**, students have to continue a dialogue. Remind them how they did this in the 'Build the skills' section and encourage them to look at examples of how dialogue is presented elsewhere in the classroom before they start. Caution students about lengthy 'ping-pong' conversations when dialogue does not move the story forward and does not give opportunity for creative use of punctuation.

Discuss the key words in the question – 'burst in' and 'hissed' – and what this indicates about the tone students should be aiming for in the dialogue. Talk about the type of sentences that might reflect this. Then suggest that students make a suitable word bank for each so that they have a collection to work with.

TAKING IT FURTHER	Students should be able to show that they can discriminate between opportunities for using a punctuation feature and a place where there is a real need for emphasis. They will also understand which kinds of punctuation are appropriate to the purpose, audience and form of the piece of writing they are undertaking. Encourage students to question their decisions on the use of punctuation. Share the use of speech in works by Dylan Thomas, such as the opening to *Under Milk Wood*, where no speech marks are used and even the narrative is made of voices: *Look. It is night, dumbly, royally winding through the Coronation cherry trees; going through the graveyard of Bethesda with winds gloved and folded, and dew doffed; tumbling by the Sailors' Arms.* *Time passes. Listen. Time passes.* *Come closer now.* *Only you can hear the houses sleeping in the streets in the slow deep salt and silent black, bandaged night.* Ask students to discuss how Dylan Thomas uses a narrative voice in this extract.

© HarperCollins *Publishers* Ltd 2018

Chapter 2: Key technical skills

2.6 Accurate use of paragraphs

Resources:
- Student's Book: 2.6, pp. 66–67
- Workbook: 2.7, pp. 56–59 can be set as homework
- PowerPoint slides 2.6a–e

Assessment objectives:

W2 Organise and structure ideas and opinions for deliberate effect

EXPLORE THE SKILLS

As a warm-up, ask students what they know about when to start new paragraphs. They may comment that paragraphs are used when a new person is introduced to a story or when they are going to start writing about a new place. Open the Student's Book and, using the information there, explain that there are four specific rules for paragraphing. Read the bullet points that outline these rules.

Explain how topic sentences are used to start a paragraph and use the annotated example in the Student's Book to discuss how a point of view can be introduced and then changed through the use of paragraphs.

Display **PPT 2.6a**, which contains all four paragraphs, and ask students to complete **Q1** in pairs. They should look at the different purposes of the last two paragraphs and how that change is signalled to the reader. Take feedback as a class. Responses for part **a)** should include:

➢ The third paragraph gives a personal example of a cruise.
➢ The fourth paragraph tells the reader about the relief the writer felt when the cruise ended.

For part **b)**, students should notice that

➢ The topic sentence in the third paragraph signals the introduction of evidence to support the viewpoint.
➢ The topic sentence in the fourth paragraph signals a change in time.

> **Extra challenge:** Ask students to identify the purpose of the first two paragraphs too:
>
> ➢ The first paragraph establishes that the writer does not like the idea of going on a cruise.
> ➢ The second paragraph switches to an alternative viewpoint.

BUILD THE SKILLS

Use the table on page 67 to explain the different types of paragraphs (introductory, body and concluding) and their uses.

> **Extra challenge:** Put students into groups of three and give each member a paragraph type to work with (introductory, main or concluding). Allocate each group one of the following desserts:
>
> ➢ cake
> ➢ pudding
> ➢ ice cream
> ➢ jelly
> ➢ fruit.
>
> Ask them to write a brief article in three paragraphs, detailing the good points of the dessert they have been allocated. For example:

Chapter 2: Key technical skills

Cake	
Introduction	*Who doesn't like cake? Cakes are famous as a pudding or a treat. There have been cakes in the centre of tables for thousands of years, causing an outbreak of smiles for young and old.*
Main	*You can make a cake as complicated as you like. Layers, icing, candles – it really is up to you. My favourite is a traditional fruit cake with marzipan and icing.*
Conclusion	*Cakes are the ultimate celebration. Next time you have guests, make them feel special by presenting a unique centrepiece. You won't regret it!*

As a practice task, display **PPT 2.6b**, which contains a new paragraph about cruise ships. Ask students where they would place the new paragraph in the text, then display the answer on **PPT 2.6c** and explain briefly why this is the best place for it.

Students could then work in pairs on **Q2**, identifying that the paragraph must come near the beginning of a story. They should stay in their pairs or join up into fours to discuss **Q3** – how the single-sentence paragraph has been used for effect (it suggests a dramatic new turn of events, taking the story on a new path).

DEVELOP THE SKILLS

A well-structured paragraph extends from the topic sentence by:

➢ adding a follow-up sentence that develops the subject or idea

➢ giving more detail with evidence and examples

➢ offering a comment or drawing conclusions.

For **Q4,** students need to extend two topic sentences. Ask them to work in small groups to create these extra sentences. **PPT 2.6d** shows two possible answers. Display these and ask students to identify which of the features of a well-constructed paragraph they represent: (a) is evidence and b) is comment).

Extra support: Display **PPT 2.6e** to show the features of a well-constructed paragraph while students are working through this section of the Student's Book.

APPLY THE SKILLS

Students should complete **Q5** individually. Display **PPT 2.6a** again as a reference if they choose to write an opinion piece.

TAKING IT FURTHER	Students who quickly adapt to shaping paragraphs for effect could experiment further with the structure recommended. Encourage them to do this using one-word paragraphs, interrupted conversations, disputes and unexpected evidence or comment when writing a paragraph about the difficulties being encountered by extreme weather. Support trial of *comment* then *evidence* then *consequence*, finishing with a *topic sentence* and *refinement*. For example: ➢ *I think I've bought six hats this winter! Hat sales are increasing in our village according to the assistant at the shop. This has led to the employment of Faaria in the outdoor clothing section. People are not hiding away indoors; they are getting properly equipped to deal with whatever weather is presented. 'There is no such thing as extreme weather, just a lack of clothing to deal with it,' says Faaria.*

© HarperCollins **Publishers** Ltd 2018

Chapter 2: Key technical skills

2.7 Paragraph cohesion

Resources:
- Student's Book: 2.7, pp. 68–69
- Workbook: 2.7, pp. 56–59 can be set as homework
- Worksheet 2.7
- PowerPoint slides 2.7a–d

Assessment objectives:

W2 Organise and structure ideas and opinions for deliberate effect

EXPLORE THE SKILLS

To introduce this topic, display **PPT 2.7a**, which shows a paragraph that lacks cohesion. Read it together and discuss how the way this paragraph has been written leaves the reader feeling confused. See whether students can suggest how the paragraph could be improved. Then display **PPT 2.7b**, which shows the improved version of the paragraph from page 68 of the Student's Book. Discuss how this works better and is clearer for the reader. Then work through the whole text in the Student's Book, considering the annotations.

Explain to students how there needs to be cohesion both *between* paragraphs and *within* paragraphs. Then ask them to work in pairs to complete **Q1**, commenting on how cohesion holds the well-structured paragraph together. Responses might include:

➢ The topic in paragraph 1 is how the writer has been looking forward to the holiday. In paragraph 2 the topic is the problems the writer had with the bus journey to the airport. The topic of paragraph 3 is the relief of arriving at the check-in desk. The topic in paragraph 4 is the mistake made with the dates.

➢ The sequence phrases used to help give cohesion to the text are: *looking forward… for weeks, eventually, next morning, Finally,*

➢ Content is organised chronologically and details are minimal, assuming that the reader will recognise that *check-in, airport, passport, ticket printout* and *flight* all refer to the same experience.

Extra support: Explain to students that to structure a paragraph effectively, it is important to make sure that a topic sentence sets up the subject at the start. They should then expand on the topic with a follow-up sentence. Next, the paragraph might need a connective linked to time. Finally, it needs a comment and a consequence, which draws it all together.

BUILD THE SKILLS

For **Q2**, students need to create a further paragraph for the text. Support choice of ideas to develop in this paragraph by numbering students 1, 2 and 3, then allocating all 1s 'the ride back in the bus', all 2s 'Mum and Dad arguing back at the house' and 3s 'the next morning'. Help students engage with the new scenario by asking them to create a brief role-play for each of the three new subjects.

The ride back on the bus	Mum and Dad arguing back at the house	The next morning
You have three things to deal with on the ride back to the airport: roadworks, a demonstration and a herd of cattle. Dad starts arguing with the bus driver, Mum starts arguing with the farmer. The children start arguing with each other. Can you create the scene?	Mum is upset because so much of the holiday went wrong. She feels guilty for getting the flight date mixed up but she blames Dad for using the cheap tour operator. Dad is upset too. He is cross about the amount of money they spent on transport for a low quality experience. Can you create their argument?	The sun is shining and your cousins have arrived keen to hear about your holiday. Mum and Dad have made breakfast for everyone. The whole family is on best behaviour, trying to forget about all the mishaps on holiday. Can you present this positive picture?

Chapter 2: Key technical skills

Draw out the dialogue that might be heard in each and the tableau that might be created if photographs were taken to promote the film version.

Extra challenge: Ask students to reduce the text to five sentences that are all linked together. Suggest that some sentences start with 'Because' or 'Since' or 'Although' to promote cohesion.

DEVELOP THE SKILLS

Give each student a sheet of lined paper on which to list cohesive devices. Recommend the words *Because*, *Since* and *Although* to start their lists off. Invite further contributions from the class, then add the connectives shown on page 69 of the Student's Book.

Put students into groups of four to complete the email in **Q3** using **Worksheet 2.7**. When all groups have finished, display **PPT 2.7c**, which contains the email skeleton, and work through the task as a class, inviting different groups to try out the connectives they have chosen for each gap. Evaluate the different choices or, if they all choose the same, ask for suggestions of what they could have chosen. **PPT 2.7d** contains a possible completed email.

Extra support: For **Q3**, make sure that students fully understand the *type* of connective required (in brackets). It might be useful to highlight the connectives in different colours on the cohesive devices page 68 (for example, connectives linked to time in green, cause/effect in yellow and contrast in pink).

APPLY THE SKILLS

Q4 requires students to use a provided plan. Clarify that everyone understands the points on the 'Checklist for success', then advise students to start by selecting the order they are going to use when arranging their paragraphs. You might discuss labelling the bullet points 1–4 in whatever order they prefer and express a preference for starting with the negative aspects then moving towards the more positive ones at the end.

TAKING IT FURTHER	Some students might feel confident enough to want to structure their work in a more unconventional way. Share examples of unusual travel writing with them, and ask for a brief summary of how paragraphs are structured in different ways. The example below shows how a writer might use comedy when describing restaurants visited in unfamiliar places: ➢ *I'm sure that somewhere in the world there are food outlets worse than this one. I am certain of that in the same way that I am certain that planets orbit other stars. I cannot imagine what they are like and I have no desire whatsoever to go there. However, I accept that they must exist.* Discuss how this style of paragraph does not use the conventions we might expect yet does present a compelling narrative. Ask students whether they can identify a topic sentence, refinement, evidence, comment or consequence then discuss why.

Chapter 2: Key technical skills

2.8 Proofreading

Resources:
- Student's Book: 2.8, pp. 70–71
- Workbook: 2.9, pp. 62–64 can be set as homework
- Worksheet 2.8
- PowerPoint slides 2.8a–e

Assessment objectives:

W5 Make accurate use of spelling, punctuation and grammar

EXPLORE THE SKILLS

Explain to students that they are going to be developing strategies to improve their work by checking what they have already done and making corrections, alterations and extensions. Read through the two stages of proofreading described on page 70 of the Student's Book, and ask students to think about errors that they commonly make, such as missing out words or confusing homophones. Discuss mistakes that you know are made frequently in class and in the wider world. For example:

- *potato's for sale*
- *steak and egg's*
- *We Bye Used Cars*
- *quite please*

Create a 'mistakes' display in the classroom, where students can post examples anonymously of errors they have made or have seen when they are out and about.

Students then complete **Q1** independently, by applying Stage 1 and Stage 2 of the proofreading process to a recent piece of work. Mistakes could be posted on the display.

BUILD THE SKILLS

Introduce the concept of making corrections by drawing attention to the date displayed on the whiteboard – which should read *Wensday 18th Febuary* – then to a notice you have put on a display board, which invites students to join *the hocky club*. Ask whether anyone had noticed the mistakes. Ask the question:

What is going to make us more vigilant in checking the text we have written?

Ask students to keep track of their mistakes using the display and reward students who can prove that their mistakes have been corrected.

Remind students of the three stages that their proofreading should take:

- checking for sense
- checking for detail
- making corrections.

Collect examples of 'before' and 'after' as students start to commit to taking responsibility for improving their own performance in writing. Check students' workbooks in other subjects. For example, in science, have they spelled *oxygen, temperature, experiment* correctly?

Display **PPT 2.8a** and ask students to complete **Q2**. Allow one minute, then see whether all mistakes have been corrected. Students could use mini whiteboards, holding up the finished text after one minute.

Share answers, checking apostrophes (2), missing words (1), homophones (3), spelling errors (2). The correct version is on **PPT 2.8b**.

Encourage students to check their own work regularly for errors like these.

Chapter 2: Key technical skills

Extra support: Use **PPT 2.8c–e** to model how the three stages can be applied. Encourage detail to be added to *holiday* (Where? When? Who?), *Mum* (What is she doing in the kitchen?) and *street* (What else can be seen?).

DEVELOP THE SKILLS

Put students into groups of four. Set up a newspaper office scenario, in which stories are coming in, the print deadline is at the end of the lesson and they need to draft the copy, check for errors and go to print on time. Hand out **Worksheet 2.8** and ask students to select stories to write. Give them a time limit of 15 minutes, after which proofread articles must be submitted to the editor. The number of errors in each article is:

➢ Fire in Portugal turns UK sky red. (24)
➢ US airport brought to a standstill. (17)
➢ Brazil nut shortage sparks granola crisis. (18)
➢ Is the Antarctic ice cap shrinking? (18)

Set up rewards for the quickest and most accurate copy.

APPLY THE SKILLS

Ask students to complete **Q4** independently, then reflect on their own improvements. They should do so in view of the 'Mistakes' display to remind them of what not to do.

Explain how work can be improved hugely by using proofreading skills carefully. Give examples of how students have done this in the past. You could give tips about where the corrections need to go, using the version of **Q4** below.

*My **fathers** watch was a delicate item but it had a torn strap**,** it had scratches on the face. I placed it on the desk and **tryed** to read **it's** maker's label. But unfortunately, **It** was **to** faint, so I couldn't make it out. I picked it up and let it rest for a moment in the palm of my hand: it was surprisingly heavy. Then, from an angle**,** I was able to read the maker's name: **wright** and sons, London 1888. Wow – it was old! Later that day, my phone **rung**. Caller unknown. I answered and **herd** a strange voice on the line. 'Is that Sunil?' it asked. 'Yes,' I replied carefully. **'You don't know me'** the voice continued, 'But I know you.'*

*I had a sudden omen. Something bad **is** going to happen all because of that watch.*

TAKING IT FURTHER	Students need to be adept at proofreading, so they should take opportunities to practise frequently in their school work and beyond. Can they help out with proofreading the school newsletter or reviewing updates about school trips on the website? Could they help their parents/grandparents to do final checks on anything that needs to be sent formally? Working with real documents can lead to further familiarity with likely mistakes.

Chapter 2: Key technical skills

2.9 Audience and levels of formality

Resources:
- Student's Book: 2.9, pp. 72–75
- Workbook: 2.10, pp. 65–66 can be set as homework
- Worksheet 2.9
- PowerPoint slides 2.9a–c

Assessment objectives:

W4 Use register appropriate to context

EXPLORE THE SKILLS

Ask students to work in pairs on **Q1** to look at how vocabulary is modified to suit different circumstances. Spend some time with different pairs, drawing out the specific language features used by the teacher when talking to a parent and to a child. Look at the modification of nouns (*production* becomes *play*). How might the same teacher modify the nouns *vehicle, beverage, narrative* and the verbs *vaulted, transcribed, concocted*? Discuss as a whole class.

To help students choose the correct level of formality, practise role-plays between an adult and a child – at lunchtime, when visiting a zoo or at the cinema. Pick out the nouns, verbs and adjectives that need to be changed. For example:

➢ At lunchtime, would mum use the words *indulgence or excessive*?

➢ At the zoo, would the attendant use *deprivation or foliage*?

➢ At the cinema, would the marketing assistant use *futuristic,* or *dystopia*?

Ask students to work through **Q2** in pairs, with one student becoming the expert in formal written communication and the other student becoming the expert in informal writing, collected from A and B.

➢ Formal elements: invitation, attend and delighted.

➢ Informal elements: there's me, our backyard, trots by.

Extra challenge: Ask students to continue thinking about formality and informality in different situations using **Worksheet 2.9**. Give them a selection of nouns and verbs to start them off. For example:

➢ **Dentist:** cavity, extract
➢ **Judge:** witness, arbitrate
➢ **Bus driver:** ticket, pay
➢ **Student:** folder, read and so on.

BUILD THE SKILLS

Read through the information on page 73 of the Student's Book together, to secure students' understanding of the eight annotations on the formal letter. Clarify how these features make the letter formal. Then ask students to write a similar response to Mrs De Witt using just the annotations.

Use **PPT 2.9a** to practise different levels of formality. For example, try changing the underlined phrases as follows:

➢ 'Mrs De Witt' becomes 'Lady Penelope'

➢ 'your letter of the 17 May' becomes 'secret note'

➢ 'speak to new students at the school' becomes 'chat with my buddies', and so on.

Discuss how it is possible to offend by being too informal or too formal, depending on the relationship between the characters.

Chapter 2: Key technical skills

Students then complete **Q3**, continuing the informal letter. When they have finished, choose a few examples and use **PPT 2.9b** to annotate them with:

- friendly opening
- grateful for previous communication
- reacts to request
- suggests follow up action
- informal close with personal name.

Extra challenge: Ask students to respond to a letter from Auntie Tanya that complains of informality in their recent letter.

DEVELOP THE SKILLS

Define the terms *objective* and *impersonal* as a class using **PPT 2.9c**, then ask students to work in pairs to find examples of both objective and impersonal language in the extract for **Q4**.

Check that everyone understands how to identify the active and passive forms by using the following examples:

- *He kept slamming the door.* (Active)
- *The door kept slamming.* (Passive)
- *The children left litter all over the floor.* (Active)
- *Litter was left all over the floor.* (Passive)

Read the advice on how to create passive form in the Student's Book together, before asking students to complete **Q5** and **Q6** independently. The paragraph in **Q6** should look like this:

- *The shipwreck was discovered yesterday by a local fisherman, as the fishing boat he worked on was returning last night. After he had seen the hull shining in the water, he dived in and was able to take photographs with his waterproof camera before he returned to the surface. A mobile phone was used by the captain to pass the photographs on to a local newspaper.*

APPLY THE SKILLS

Check that everyone understands the meaning of *idiom* (informal style when a saying means more than its different parts – *over the moon*, *turn up for the books*), *contraction* (when words are joined together – *didn't*, *It'll*) and *tag* (using questions in a dialogue). Then set **Q7** to be completed independently, using the example to start if they choose.

TAKING IT FURTHER	Students need to vary their formality with assurance. If a student meets a barrister in a courtroom, the conversation might start off very formally, led by the professional (*Good Morning young man, how can I help you?*). The student would respond formally, matching his formality to that of the professional (*Good morning. I'm here on a work experience placement, hoping to see some courtroom practice. I hope I will not be an inconvenience.*) Once the barrister relaxes his formality (*Hey, did you see the rugby match last night? Wasn't it fabulous?*), that gives the student a cue to match tone (*I did, yes, the scrum half was incredibly brave, even though that defence was a brick wall.*)
	Ask students to carry the conversation on then introduce a further barrister, which makes the setting very formal again as she brings information about the robbery case they will be prosecuting.

Chapter 2: Key technical skills

2.10 Voice and role

Resources:
- Student's Book: 2.10, pp. 76–79
- Workbook: 2.11, pp. 67–68 can be set as homework
- Worksheet 2.10
- PowerPoint slides 2.10a–e

Assessment objectives:

W4 Use register appropriate to context

EXPLORE THE SKILLS

Read through the opening section in the Student's Book with the whole class to introduce/recap on prior knowledge about voice and role. Draw out examples of a voice that is 'chatty' or 'anxious' to confirm students' understanding of *voice*. Ask them to work in role to exemplify what a child of 10, a schoolteacher or an angry neighbour might say.

It might be helpful to discuss the concept of stereotyping, which can be patronising, insulting or inappropriate. It is important that students attempt to write with a sense of audience, so stress that a clichéd or inappropriately humorous voice would make a bad impression. On the other hand, voice used accurately and with a sensitive awareness and understanding will score highly.

Ask students to work in pairs on **Q1** to match each speech to a role or character. Spend some time with the pairs, drawing out the specific language features being used by each character to give them their voice and relating this to:

➤ what is being said
➤ how it is being said
➤ the conventions being used.

Students should conclude that the first voice is that of a bride-to-be and the second is the voice of a police officer.

Extra support: Give students **Worksheet 2.10**, which contains a task that will allow them to practise and reflect on how to identify speech with a particular role.

BUILD THE SKILLS

As a class, read through the information at the start of the 'Build the skills' section of the Student's Book, which establishes a scenario for students to use to practise voice and role. Use **PPT 2.10a–c** to focus students on picking out the context, the character and background behind the voice they will need to capture.

Once you have read the diary extract, discuss as a class the context of the tournament. Point out that Poppy might be feeling a bit vulnerable in strange company and anxious with the test looming. Then briefly discuss Pop'py's expressions in her diary entry:

➤ '– at least I thought I had'
➤ 'This made me laugh'
➤ 'I couldn't eat anyway'
➤ 'Am I going mad?'

Ask students to consider what kind of feelings, thoughts and attitudes Poppy has, then put them in pairs to complete **Q2**.

Chapter 2: Key technical skills

Extra support: Using **PPT 2.10c**, go through the text in detail and record ideas in a table, like the one below, to help students develop their ideas further.

Thoughts	Feelings	Attitudes
Can I trust Sonya?	Worried about the competition	Self-doubt questioning the purpose of the competition

DEVELOP THE SKILLS

Read the introductory information about creating an effective voice. Display **PPT 2.10d**, which contains the bullet points describing Poppy from page 78 of the Student's Book, and ask students whether they agree with these points. Ask them what other descriptive words could be added to the list, and whether it is possible to draw anything negative about her from the diary entry they have already read.

Make sure that students are able to pinpoint the section of text that has inspired each comment and steer them to sensitivity rather than caricature. It might be that Poppy is a little bit arrogant in not believing in last-minute preparation or it might be bravado as she realises that her peers are taking this more seriously than she is. Talk about the layers of meaning they could infer (for example, *Poppy is quite vulnerable underneath her carefree image*) and the fact that most people are multi-dimensional.

Direct students to the 'Top tip' on page 78, but encourage them to be careful when inferring character traits, particularly when only a small amount of stimulus text is provided.

For **Q3**, support students to show Poppy's characteristics in her writing: nervous, witty, close to her mum and dad, friendly but competitive, observant. You could continue to model the diary in character using **PPT 2.10e**.

Once students have written Poppy's next diary entry, introduce the concept of a change of context. Ask pairs to consider how their language changes when they are in different situations (for example, in the classroom, in the park, in the theatre, at a wedding, at a funeral.) Ask:

➢ How do we change our language in different situations?

➢ How might different people infer different things about us from meeting us in different contexts?

For **Q4**, support students to make brief notes as below:

a) The purpose of the speech is to motivate other students to take part in competitions, whereas the diary entry is to carry personal thoughts.

b) The two forms are speech and diary writing. The style of the speech is formal and the diary is informal.

c) The speech will include details about what the competition is like and it will leave out her doubts about herself.

d) Poppy would continue to display her wit, her comical observations of other competitors and her friendly but competitive manner.

Students should work in pairs to make notes for **Q5**. They should recognise that the purpose of the speech is persuasive rather than informative or reflective; the speech is formal while the diary is informal; the conventions of a speech are different to those of a diary, and the style is objective rather than personal.

APPLY THE SKILLS

Ask students to work independently to write the two entries from Sonya's diary for **Q6**, which requires a lot of inference about the character. It will be helpful for students to return to Poppy's original diary first to extract information, then to look at the new information within **Q6**. Remind students to create three-dimensional characters through a sensitive portrayal rather than clichéd stereotypes.

TAKING IT FURTHER	Students should vary their style with assurance to suit audience and context. Using appropriate voice for role requires an understanding of how character can be inferred from very small amounts of information. There is a clear transfer of skills from reading to writing here that students will benefit from practising. For example, how does the following information help us to ascertain a voice for Leon? *Distracted, as ever, Leon wandered into the room without noticing the shock and disappointment oozing from his mother's face.*

Chapter 3: Key writing forms

3.1 Conventions of speeches and talks

Resources:
- Student's Book: 3.1, pp. 82–85
- Workbook: 3.1, pp. 69–71 can be set as homework
- Worksheets 3.1a–b
- PowerPoint slides 3.1a–d

Assessment objectives:

W2 Organise and structure ideas and opinions for deliberate effect

W4 Use register appropriate to context

EXPLORE THE SKILLS

Explain to the class that speeches are written to be spoken and to have an immediate impact on listeners. For example, speeches are likely to make greater use of shorter sentences, repetition and signposting than texts that are designed to be read. It is important that students are aware of the needs of an audience.

As a warm-up, ask students to give examples of powerful speeches they have heard or heard of, then ask them to discuss in pairs what made these speeches memorable. You could share an example of a speech given at a recent inauguration of a president or prime minister.

Students should stay in their pairs to work on **Q1**, taking it in turns to talk for two minutes about a subject they feel strongly about. Afterwards, have a class discussion to answer the questions raised in **Q1** – how easy or difficult did they find it? Were they able to keep their partner interested? Show **PPT 3.1a** and discuss the techniques they may have used. Use **PPT 3.1b** to move the discussion on to the *purpose* of their speeches. Take some feedback to ensure that the concepts of purpose, audience, direct address, informal language and personal references are securely understood.

Extra support: If students struggle to think of a topic for their two-minute speech, help them by making some suggestions – for example, whether school uniform is a good thing or a bad thing or if young people spend too much time on social media.

Read the extract from Angelina Jolie's speech together, then ask students to use the annotations to compare the techniques Jolie uses to the techniques their partner used in their two-minute speech. They should discuss this in their pairs and use **Worksheet 3.1a** to keep track of how each feature has been used by Jolie and their partner.

Come back together as a class to decide on the tone of Jolie's speech. Ask students if the tone is:

➢ friendly and informal

➢ mocking and rude

➢ hard-hitting and serious.

In fact, it is both friendly and informal (paragraph 1) and hard-hitting and serious (paragraph 3). Ask students to stay in their pairs to answer **Q2**, reading the speech aloud and identifying the changes in tone or focus and where they appear. They might identify the powerful effect of the list of recognisable occupations (*farmers, teachers, doctors, engineers*) and the tone in which she discusses meeting with a vulnerable pregnant woman, then the moment of friendship in the dirt hut ('we sat and we talked and they were just the loveliest women'). The part when Jolie recounts the parable of the *Widow's Mite* moves the speech into a serious lesson for her audience to learn from.

To develop this thinking, put students into groups of four. Using a large print version of **Worksheet 3.1b,** divide Angelina Jolie's speech into four and distribute one to each of the groups. Allocate the shorter paragraphs to students who find formal language difficult.

54 © HarperCollins *Publishers* Ltd 2018

Chapter 3: Key writing forms

Ask students to discuss in their groups what information is shared in their paragraph of the speech and what effect it might have on the intended listeners. Take feedback in the correct order so that all students get a gist of the whole speech.

➢ **Paragraph 1** is introducing the subject of the speech and making sure the audience know that the speaker is sympathising with refugees.

➢ **Paragraph 2** is making the audience aware that these are ordinary people living through extraordinary hardships.

➢ **Paragraph 3** gives a real example of meeting a pregnant woman and sharing a cup of tea with her in an act of unexpected generosity from the refugee host. Jolie is humbled by this.

➢ **Paragraph 4** ends on a note of warning that we should not underestimate the kindness of the world's most desperate.

BUILD THE SKILLS

Ask students to work in pairs to answer **Q3–6**. Responses will vary. Generally, students should identify the following:

Q3 a) Jolie is presenting herself as a campaigner for refugees.

   b) She wants her audience to recognise their plight and help.

   c) Some or all of the examples Jolie gives in the speech of what happened when she met the refugees.

Q4 a) 'desperate', 'survivors', 'impressive' and 'vulnerable'

   b) 'cut-off from civilisation' and 'great loss'

Q5 'Millions' makes the numbers seem countless.

Q6 'two', 'old' emphasises how little these two women have; 'few twigs' and 'single cup of water', show the lack of facilities they have.

DEVELOP THE SKILLS

Ask students to think about how Jolie's speech is structured to have an effect on her audience. Can they see a formula for using structure effectively? Use **PPT 3.1c** and **3.1d** to discuss how each paragraph serves a purpose. The first shocks (red). The second evokes sympathy (blue). The third gives a personal story (green). The fourth finishes with a powerful, lingering message (purple). Keep the slides on display while students complete **Q7**, copying and completing the table.

Read through the bullet points given to support **Q8** and then ask students to answer the question in a pair discussion. Circulate while they are talking and, where necessary, direct them with examples such as how *millions* in the first paragraph become recognisable workers in the second and then *one pregnant woman* in the third.

APPLY THE SKILLS

Ask students to read through the task in **Q9** and think about the skills they could use to maximise their impact on their audience. Encourage students to make full use of Angelina Jolie's speech, reminding them of some of its best features. When they have finished, they should assess their partner's speech using the 'Checklist for success' on page 85 of the Student's Book.

TAKING IT FURTHER	Set a more unfamiliar task for high-attaining students. For example: ➢ *Write a speech for your head teacher to give to a local electricity company, persuading them to do more to cut down on pollution, waste and general disregard for the local landscape.* Encourage students to find the voice, the tone and then create the content rather than dwell on the details of the electricity company.

© HarperCollins *Publishers* Ltd 2018

Chapter 3: Key writing forms

3.2 Conventions of interviews

Resources:
- Student's Book: 3.2, pp. 86–87
- Workbook: 3.2, pp. 72–73 can be set as homework
- Worksheet 3.2
- PowerPoint slides 3.2a–e

Assessment objectives:

W2 Organise and structure ideas and opinions for deliberate effect

W4 Use register appropriate to context

EXPLORE THE SKILLS

Start by reading the introduction to the topic on page 86, and taking some initial thoughts on the questions raised:

➢ How do interviews usually start and end?

➢ Who tends to say more – the interviewer or the guest?

For **Q1**, students read the information from the conservation website in pairs. Hand out **Worksheet 3.2**, which contains the transcript of the dialogue. Display **PPT 3.2a** and ask students to annotate the dialogue on the worksheet with the statements:

➢ Repeats the question assertively.

➢ Simplifies the issue with four words.

➢ Makes sure that the task is not reduced to simple facts.

➢ Uses statistics to challenge.

➢ Distracts from the conversation by introducing a new topic.

➢ Explains the impact of just one problem.

➢ Defensively states the unmanageable size of the task.

➢ Tries to get the discussion back on track.

BUILD THE SKILLS

Draw students' attention to the words 'reporter' and 'expert' in the transcript, and the terms 'synonyms' and 'paraphrase' in **Q2**. Check that everyone understands what these words mean and discuss examples of each that they may have come across:

➢ **reporter:** someone who discovers information and writes news stories

➢ **expert:** a person with a high level of knowledge or skill about a particular subject

➢ **synonyms:** words that mean the same thing

➢ **paraphrase:** a rewording of something that has been said or written.

When all students are clear on this, ask them to complete **Q2**. Answers are:

a) The roles are different because one asks questions and the other is expected to know the answers.

b) 'Eastern Himalayas' is a synonym for China, Mongolia and Korea. 'Monumental task' paraphrases the issues that conservation has to deal with.

c) It is clearly an interview because of the formal greeting and close ('I'm here to talk to Dr Sandra Capello' and 'Thank you Dr Capello') and because of the conversation format.

d) The final bullet point 'Body parts used in traditional medicine' is not used in the interview.

Chapter 3: Key writing forms

Extra challenge: Display **PPT 3.2b–c**, which contain another interview and a list of conventions. Ask students to identify how each convention is used in the interview with the doctor.

DEVELOP THE SKILLS

As a class, read the text from a website on page 87 of the Student's Book, which suggests ways in which the tiger could be saved from extinction. Then put students in pairs to create the role-play for **Q3**. It may help to recap on the conventions of interviews using **PPT 3.2c** before they begin. Explain that there are two characters in the role-play – a reporter and an expert. Start students off by asking them to think about who would say the statements below. They could include these statements in their role-play if they wish, continuing the train of thought and keeping to the same style. Pairs should explore how the two characters might behave.

➢ 'So you have four things to do – how long is this going to take?' (Is this similar to the previous reporter?)
➢ 'We have a team of enthusiastic and committed conservationists who can't wait to develop a project in the local town.' (Does this sound like a forceful charity manager? Can you make him or her more forceful?)

Extra support: Display **PPT 3.2d**, which shows how this interview might begin. Ask pairs to read the interview aloud with each other, then continue it using the bullet point facts from the charity's website (on **PPT 3.2e**). Explore how forceful the charity manager can be and still be realistic for television/radio.

APPLY THE SKILLS

Ask students to complete their own written version of the interview independently, using the conventions of interviews. You could offer a range of suggested quotations they might use:

➢ *Every time we find a solution to one problem, another one raises its head.*
➢ *We are up against traditions that are centuries old here and communities do not want to reject what their ancestors did.*
➢ *Attempts to reforest areas where the Siberian tigers might settle are thwarted by the logging industry.*

TAKING IT FURTHER	Students should describe and reflect on interview conventions – how they are used effectively and how they can be subverted to achieve unexpected outcomes. For example, an expert might turn out to know very few relevant details and give an opinionated personal response: ➢ *If we don't have enough people giving money to charity, we won't have any more tigers. Simple as that. No science.* Ask students to continue the interview below, considering how a skilful reporter might respond to an expert that ignored questions, then gave blunt opinions: *Reporter: Could you tell me about the reclamation of tigers' habitat please?* *Expert: We need to stop the poachers I say. We need cameras set up as soon as we know where the tigers are. Then we watch and wait.* *Reporter: Can we talk about the poachers in a minute please? How are we getting the habitat back from the corporate developers?* *Expert: We won't have any tigers if we don't arrest all of the poachers, believe me.* *Reporter: ...*

© HarperCollins *Publishers* Ltd 2018

Chapter 3: Key writing forms

3.3 Conventions of diaries and journals

Resources:
- Student's Book: 3.3, pp. 88–89
- Workbook: 3.3, pp. 74–76 can be set as homework
- Worksheet 3.3
- PowerPoint slides 3.3a–d

Assessment objectives:

W2 Organise and structure ideas and opinions for deliberate effect

W4 Use register appropriate to context

EXPLORE THE SKILLS

As a starter, ask students to work in groups of four to discuss what they know about diaries and journals. Who writes them? Why are books and films made about them? Why are people interested in them? Do students write one themselves or do they know anyone who does? Mention some famous diaries and diarists (real and fictional): Samuel Pepys, Anne Frank, Henry David Thoreau, Bridget Jones, Eugene Delacroix, Adrian Mole.

Read the diary extract on page 88 of the Student's Book. Go through the features in the annotations and draw out what makes it instantly recognisable as a diary. For **Q1**, elicit who is writing the diary (a school student).

BUILD THE SKILLS

Ask students to tackle **Q2** in pairs, with one student looking at content and the other looking at structure and style. Give students five minutes to answer the part of the question they have been allocated; they should then share their findings with another pair. Responses might include:

- **Content:** the student missed the science trip; emotions: embarrassment at missing the trip; boredom while sitting outside the head teacher's office; fear of what might happen if his parents find out.
- **Structure:** the chronological order of events shows an unfortunate set of incidents that finish with the student hiding from his parents.
- **Style:** 'overslept', 'fool', 'boring', 'mad' suggest that this is a teenager.

Extra support: Give targeted students **Worksheet 3.3**, which explains the three headings – Content, Structure and Style – in more detail and gives help in answering **Q2**.

DEVELOP THE SKILLS

Read **Q3** and the diary entry by Tanya Saunders as a class. Use **PPT 3.3a** and **3.3b** to review significant features of the text:

- Red highlights features of content (specific descriptive details that help create a sense of setting and atmosphere).
- Green highlights features of structure (chronological progress – 'yesterday', 'today', 'tonight').
- Blue highlights features of style (a very long, complex sentence).

Ask students to answer **Q3** in pairs, then display **PPT 3.3c** to review possible responses. Identify literary devices such as:

- 'Goliath Heron'
- 'flowers prepare to launch'

Chapter 3: Key writing forms

- 'tiny pretty blue commelina flowers'
- 'spiky aliens'.

Students should stay in their pairs to answer **Q4**. Review the questions first, using **PPT 3.3d**. Responses might include:

a) The difference in literary style between in the two diary entries. Saunders is creating a vivid picture of rural West Africa while the student is looking at a day in school and at home in familiar settings.

b) She makes specific reference to the day (yesterday/today) and time of day (tonight) to structure the piece.

c) Saunders switches between past and present in her work (ask students to count the number of '-ing' verbs (5), which shows an active setting.

d) There is a sense of the unique landscape with the crocodiles, the flowers, the heron and so on.

APPLY THE SKILLS

Ask students to work in pairs on **Q5** to discuss the writer from Kenya. Ask them to summarise their thoughts in three bullet points, which could be based on:

- how she feels about the different weather
- how she feels about the wildlife
- how she feels about the unpredictability of the setting.

Students should then complete **Q6** independently. They could use the bullet points they created for **Q5** to guide their writing in terms of reflecting Saunders' style and her use of time, weather and nature.

Extra challenge: Ask students to write a diary in the same style as the description of the garden in Kenya, describing their own garden or a nearby park. They should be able to describe how they used content, structure, style in their writing.

TAKING IT FURTHER	Diary writing can seem straightforward to some students and it may be difficult to ensure that they use the full repertoire of writing skills on these tasks. Encourage students to read models of high-quality diaries and to imitate or subvert their style. Remind them that diary entries should be full and extended, and that in an exam they should include a maximum of two or three entries. Ask students to choose one of the following openings to a diary entry and then continue it to extend their diary writing skills: <ul><li>*The greatest view welcomed me as I woke up and looked out of the window…*</li><li>*The most disappointing view depressed me as I drew back the curtains…*</li></ul>

Chapter 3: Key writing forms

3.4 Conventions of reports

Resources:
- Student's Book: 3.4, pp. 90–91
- Workbook: 3.4, pp. 77–78 can be set as homework
- PowerPoint slides 3.4a–d

Assessment objectives:

W2 Organise and structure ideas and opinions for deliberate effect

W4 Use register appropriate to context

EXPLORE THE SKILLS

As preparation for this lesson, ask students to bring in examples of reports from magazines or websites. Explain that reports are common in the media and other contexts.

Display **PPT 3.4a–d**, which show four types of reports:

➢ **a** a police crime report
➢ **b** a school report
➢ **c** a weather report
➢ **d** a news report.

Students should work in pairs to discuss the types of text on the slides, the reports they have brought to the lesson and the features they share. As a class, read the extract from a report on page 90 of the Student's Book, then ask students to work through **Q1**. Reponses might be:

a) the successful school fundraising day

b) school staff and students

c) the first paragraph is a message of thanks to all; the second describes some events of the day and gives particular thanks to individuals

d) news report

e) school magazine

f) yes, because it is personal and mentions particular incidents.

> **Extra support:** If students are unsure where the extract may have come from, direct them to the phrases 'school fundraising day' and 'thanks to you all'. Ask who is involved in school fundraising days and therefore who the writer might want to thank. Use an example of a similar report from your school newspaper or magazine if available.

BUILD THE SKILLS

Remind students of the 'content, style, structure' approach covered in the lessons on writing diaries and speeches. Ask students to consider how the same approach might be useful when writing reports. In particular, get them thinking about who their audience is.

Ask students to copy the table in **Q2** and then complete it in pairs.

➢ **Content:** It gives clear information, but also covers the events and outcomes of the day.
➢ **Structure:** It could be in time sequence but could also jump around to topics such as the weather, money raised and number of people there; current structure is one paragraph providing a summary and the other details of the day and particular member's contributions.
➢ **Style:** Informal, because the writer knows the people who worked on the charity day and is celebrating their efforts.

Chapter 3: Key writing forms

DEVELOP THE SKILLS

Invite four students to each read a paragraph of the longer report on page 91 of the Student's Book to the whole class. Have a brief class discussion to pick out the facts in the extract, the number of paragraphs, and examples of formal and informal language to focus their thinking. Then put students in groups of three to discuss and make notes on **Q3–5**. Circulate as groups are having their discussion and make sure that they are keeping on track with the ideas of content, structure and style. The discussions might cover the following features.

3   a) Its purpose is to update staff and students on *recent research* that has been carried out and actions planned to encourage students to donate more so that funds can go to meeting the needs of *those less fortunate than ourselves*.

  b) There is evidence of research, contributions and plans; there is a quote from the head teacher.

4   a) The report uses four paragraphs effectively. The first is a call to action (*it's time we and the readers of this magazine did something about it*). The second provides evidence (*one in five students have given to charity*). The third celebrates fundraising (*raised over $2000*). The last calls interested parties to the school hall for all to get involved and be hopeful (*watch this space!*).

  b) The report is effective because it hooks the reader from the beginning and gives an uplifting, hopeful ending.

5   a) The report is clearly to inspire staff and students.

  b) It is semi-formal.

  c) It contains details such as statistics, quotes and high expectations as well as detailed, engaging accounts of what the speaker would like to do.

  d) It uses a variety of sentences, such as long, complex sentences, short simples sentences, rhetorical questions and commands.

Take class feedback and note down the key ideas on the whiteboard.

> **Extra challenge:** Ask students what changes might need to be made if the report's target audience was different – perhaps the school governors or former students. You could also consider changing the purpose. What would need to be changed if the purpose was to make people feel guilty about not getting involved?

APPLY THE SKILLS

Recap on the skills that students need to demonstrate in **Q6** – an understanding of purpose, audience, form and how these are matched by choice of content, structure, style. Explain the importance of choosing the right language to set an appropriate tone, and of using the right structure to make the information clear for the audience. Highlight the importance of openings, paragraphing and closing text.

Ask students to work through **Q6** independently. Use the 'Top tip' on page 91 to remind students of the structure they could use.

TAKING IT FURTHER	Students should be able to adopt a mature stance quickly, establishing a clear viewpoint that is sustained throughout. They need to flex their knowledge and understanding of content regardless of where their own sympathies or allegiances lie. Encourage students to work in role as reporters using one of the skeleton plans below: ➢ Police crime report – Disturbance at market ➢ School report scandal – Bogus grades found ➢ Wild weather report – freak conditions predicted ➢ Royal visit – Prince honours town Guide students through the content, structure and style expected using the exemplar reports on **PPT 3.4a–d** and encourage students to cover new ground using their different titles.

Chapter 3: Key writing forms

3.5 Conventions of news reports and magazine articles

Resources:
- Student's Book: 3.5, pp. 92–95
- Workbook: 3.5, pp. 79–80 can be set as homework
- Worksheet 3.5
- PowerPoint slides 3.5a–e

Assessment objectives:

W2 Organise and structure ideas and opinions for deliberate effect

W4 Use register appropriate to context

EXPLORE THE SKILLS

Explain the difference between news reports and feature articles using the text on page 92 in the Student's Book. Then ask students to work in pairs to decide which is which from the headings in **Q1**. You could put these titles on the whiteboard and ask students if they are news report or feature articles. The answers are:

- Temperatures dip to –30° for coldest night on record = news report
- Why are our winters getting colder? = feature article
- Ice causes chaos on motorways = news report
- Snow go – 36 hours stuck on train = news report
- How to predict cold winters = feature article

Ask students which features led them to place the headings in each category. Try to elicit the fact that there is often a link between declarative sentences and news reports, and interrogative sentences and feature articles. Explain that news reports try to put across the facts and the details quickly and clearly, while features interrogate the stories behind headlines. Discuss how news reports draw on social impact stories to some extent, while features take a more scientific approach.

BUILD THE SKILLS

Ask five students to each read a paragraph of the news report on pages 92–93 of the Student's Book. Invite the class to discuss the annotated features of the text as evidence of whether it is a news report or feature article (they should identify that it is a news report). Then develop the discussion around the following questions:

- How many facts are presented?
- Is this a social impact story or does it take a scientific approach?
- How many questions are asked?

Extra challenge: Ask students to rewrite the text so that it is a feature article, changing the facts to a scientific interrogation: Why would a goat kill a man?

Return to the 'content, structure, style' approach that students learned earlier to analyse writing for different purposes and audiences. Put students in groups of three to discuss **Q2** and **Q3**, exploring the content, structure and style of the article. Display **PPT 3.5a** and **3.5b**, which contain the questions for ease of reference during the discussion. After the discussions, take class feedback, with one member of each group nominated as spokesperson. The text is shown on **PPT 3.5c** and **3.5d**, with sections highlighted to indicate content, structure and style, and can be used either as support during the discussion, or during the whole-class feedback. Draw attention to the use of third person, the combination of complex and simple sentences, the use of facts and the sense of drama created by using 'but', 'when', 'if' and 'apparently'. Responses should include:

Chapter 3: Key writing forms

2   a) Who: Robert Boardman, a 63-year-old man; what: killed by a mountain goat; where: while out hiking in Olympic National Park; when: on Monday.

   b) We find out from Barb Maynes that the goat had 'shown aggressive behaviour in the past'. It couldn't be the first paragraph because we would not know what she was referring to unless we had information about the incident first. It provides extra detail.

   c) The final paragraph focuses on the causes of the attack and how the goat might have had a disease that caused it to act aggressively.

3   a) Yes – the report is written without using the first person. Words such as 'apparently' are used to show that no opinion is being formed.

   b) The article uses the time connectives 'on Monday' and 'an hour after the attack'.

   c) The headline and the concluding paragraph contain verbs in the present tense (*Mountain goat kills hiker,* and *The goat is being examined),* which shows that the events are current.

DEVELOP THE SKILLS

Put students in groups of four. Read the bullet points at the top of page 94 in the Student's Book together, then allocate one to each member of a group. Explain that you are going to read the article aloud and that when students feel their convention is being demonstrated, they should raise their hand. For example, in the first paragraph, the writer uses four personal pronouns, which indicates the personal nature of the writing (bullet 1). Read the article and students raise their hands as instructed.

Staying in their groups, students should discuss the content, structure and style of the article and answer **Q4** and **Q5**. Take feedback. Responses should include:

4   a) It not about a news event that has just happened; it is about a situation that is on-going.

   b) This article contains five paragraphs telling the reader about feral cats and how the writer caught one. The mountain goat news report also had five paragraphs and also started with a summary of the main events. Both articles present a balance between sympathy and concern (the goat might have had a disease causing its aggressive behaviour; the feral cats have hard lives and only survive for a couple of years).

5   a) The headline tells us it is a feature article by offering advice about taking responsibility for feral kittens.

   b) You can infer that the writer is an animal lover. The adjectives, *humane* and *adorable* and his sympathy to cats' *hard lives* tell us that he wants to support the work of the RSPCA in giving the cats a second chance.

> **Extra support:** Break down the questions for students who are finding this section difficult.
> ➢ **Content:** ask students to look for the *who, what, where* and *why*.
> ➢ **Structure:** ask how the article tells us about the event. Are there any references to time? What connectives are used (for example, 'next' or 'later')?
> ➢ **Viewpoint:** ask why the writer has chosen to describe his subjects as *scraggy wild things that cadge food.*

APPLY THE SKILLS

Ask students to complete **Q6** individually. Distribute **Worksheet 3.5**, which contains the two articles. Encourage students to spend ten minutes planning their writing by using the worksheet to highlight and make notes on which aspects of these two articles they are going to use. Invite one or two suggestions on the opening using the model opening **PPT 3.5e**.

TAKING IT FURTHER	Students will benefit from opportunities to represent information in increasingly challenging ways. For example, they could take a flyer advertising painting and decorating services and recast it as a report warning about bogus workmen posing as tradesmen in order to steal from your house. They could write a report with the title *Handyman proves to be charlatan'* demonstrating their skills in using past tense, simple sentences for clarity and appropriate material.

Chapter 3: Key writing forms

3.6 Conventions of letters

Resources:
- Student's Book: 3.6, pp. 96–97
- Workbook: 3.6, pp. 81–82 can be set as homework
- Worksheets 3.6a–b
- PowerPoint slides 3.6a–c

Assessment objectives:

W2 Organise and structure ideas and opinions for deliberate effect

W4 Use register appropriate to context

EXPLORE THE SKILLS

As a starter, ask pairs to discuss the features of an informal and a formal letter. If students have any examples of when they have written or received letters, ask them to describe them to their partner. Ask the pairs to imagine the importance of letters 20 years ago (before the internet and mobile phones), then 40 years ago (telephones only in some homes). Explore the differences today and how our expectations about communication have changed.

Then turn to **Q1** and look at two letters that might be written today. Use **PPT 3.6a–b** to work as a class, annotating the letters to identify the features (have students close the Student's Book if you do this, so they cannot refer to the highlighted sections there).

Extra support: Give students **Worksheet 3.6a**, to support comparison of the features of a formal and informal letter in answer to **Q1**.

During class feedback, draw out the different layout, forms of address, tone and use of objective/personal language. Highlight similarities in structure and purpose.

BUILD THE SKILLS

Show students the 'Checklist for success' on **PPT 3.6c**. Discuss the features of letter-writing that are similar to features in other forms of writing they have studied. **PAF** (Purpose, Audience, Form) and **CSS** (Content, Structure, Style) are useful acronyms.

Support students with detailed scrutiny of the features of the letters, drawing attention to the use of vocabulary, sentences, punctuation and opening/closing.

Responses might include:

- **Vocabulary:** The first letter is informal, using words such as 'Anyway', and 'sucks her thumb and snores'. The second is formal using language such as 'delighted to accept'.
- **Abbreviations:** The first letter uses contractions such as 'I'm', 'it's', 'don't', 'can't'. The second letter does not use any contractions
- **Sentence types:** The first uses short, simple sentences such as 'I miss you so much'. The second uses one complex and one compound sentence.
- **Punctuation:** There is an exclamation mark in the first letter. The second letter uses minimal punctuation with just one comma.
- **Openings and closings:** Davina is casual with her friend Jo in the first letter, signing off with 'Love to you and the rest of the gang'. Davina Kahn is formal in the second letter, using 'Yours sincerely' to sign off.

Chapter 3: Key writing forms

Extra support: Give students **Worksheet 3.6b** to focus their ideas and help them structure a response to **Q2**.

DEVELOP THE SKILLS

For **Q3**, students consider a letter with a different purpose – a complaint that continues shop assistant Davina's story. Run through the annotations on the letter to show that letters can be a vehicle for developing ideas as well as for relating events and expressing feelings. Ensure that students grasp how the ideas are developed and how paragraph cohesion is established. Also draw out students' thoughts on the level of formality and what language creates this.

Extra challenge: Ask students to look in more detail at the language that creates the level of formality in the letter opening. They should identify the use of 'expect' and 'expectations', which balance the second paragraph nicely, as does 'high levels of courtesy and advice'. They should also recognise the authority in 'As you are aware' and 'did not meet my expectations in either regard'. Compare this last example with the more informal and less precise 'did not give me either'.

For **Q4**, ask students to make notes on how the customer feels using the bullet points on page 97. They should look at the first problem, the second problem, then at the requested actions. Students' ideas might include:

- Davina using her mobile phone and ignoring the customer
- Davina letting one customer dominate her attention when there was a queue building up
- Davina not knowing the whereabouts of key items in the shop
- Davina giving the incorrect change at the checkout
- Davina should write a letter of apology explaining how she has learned from this experience
- Davina should be retrained on basic customer service.

TAKING IT FURTHER	Letter-writing often allows students to show shades of meaning in their writing because it invites the creation of a distinct personality and voice. It is important that they develop sympathetic understanding of audience and purpose together with an original perspective about the context. Support students in writing letters that convey personality despite considerable constraints. Letters from soldiers serving in the World Wars and Vietnam, which are readily available on the internet, demonstrate the way that personality can withstand unimaginable pressures.

Chapter 4: Writing for purpose

4.1 Writing to inform and explain

Resources:
- Student's Book: 4.1, pp. 100–101
- Workbook: 4.1, pp. 83–84 can be set as homework
- PowerPoint slides 4.1a–g

Assessment objectives:

W2 Organise and structure ideas and opinions for deliberate effect

W4 Use register appropriate to context

EXPLORE THE SKILLS

Introduce writing to inform and explain as a way of communicating information – a vital life skill. Read through the opening section in the Student's Book and go through the list of features of informative writing (which can be displayed on **PPT 4.1a**). Discuss briefly where students may have encountered the features before and how they have proved to be useful (for example, they may note the use of precise vocabulary when writing a speech, from Chapter 3).

As a class, read through the information text on page 100, about grey wolves, and discuss **Q1**. Ensure that students interpret 'text as a whole' correctly from the question – they must ask themselves whether wolves have always been presented negatively. Take feedback, eliciting examples of the threat they are believed to pose (to livestock now that their natural prey is declining), the pack (prepared to act together to get what they want) and the historical perspective (was viewed as a caring parent in the 3rd century BC).

Ask students to work through **Q2–4** in pairs, making notes on their answers. Take feedback. Students should have noted the following:

- ➤ **Q2** The reference to 1812 fairy tales and the fact that wolves are a real threat to livestock emphasises the frightening elements of wolves.
- ➤ **Q3** Yes, the information is presented logically in that it begins by describing the general way in which wolves are currently regarded, and then looks at whether this has always been the case. The final sentence could not be swapped with the first, because it refers to the previous sentence.
- ➤ **Q4** The second paragraph focuses on the caring side of wolves and questions how the reputation of wolves changed.

BUILD THE SKILLS

Read the introductory information in this section and make sure that students are clear about what a topic sentence is – the sentence that sums up the focus of the paragraph. As a class, decide on the answer to **Q5** (*All in all, they seem to be the ultimate hunting beast*).

To reinforce this learning, display **PPT 4.1b** to emphasise the difference between the content of a topic sentence (the focus of the paragraph) and a sentence that simply contains interesting/additional information. Try to make a paragraph without the topic sentence and see whether the missing summary hinders understanding. There is an example of this on **PPT 4.1c**.

Extra support: PPT 4.1d gives a further example of sentences from a paragraph for students to identify the topic sentence. Investigate how the paragraph can be ordered, where the topic sentence best fits and why. The correct arrangement might be:

➤ *Many cultures celebrate springtime. It is traditional for gifts to be hung on trees. They are made of chocolate. Eggs represent fertility and rebirth.*

Explain to students that without the first sentence (topic), the other three do not fit together smoothly.

Chapter 4: Writing for purpose

DEVELOP THE SKILLS

Read through the information at the start of this section on page 101 of the Student's Book. Make sure that students understand what connectives are and how they can be used to link sentences and develop information.

Put students in pairs to answer **Q6**. They should identify that the common thread between the statements is collaboration and how wolves work as a team. We can see that *act together* links to *packs of 3–30* which links to *useful for killing larger animals* which links to *usually led by an 'alpha' male and female whose offspring comprise the pack*. This is mentioned in the first article, when the writer talks about *pack mentality*.

Extra challenge: Display **PPT 4.1e**, which contains an example informative paragraph. Then show **PPT 4.1f**, which shows the same paragraph with connectives added. Ask students to evaluate the use of connectives, then display **PPT 4.1g** and ask them to add connectives to the paragraph on Dragon Hunter King 2020 in the same way.

APPLY THE SKILLS

For **Q7**, recap on the list of features of writing explained at the start of the lesson. Encourage evaluation of their use of the features so far by linking *topic sentences* that students used when building the skills, and *connectives* that they used when developing the skills. Discuss the word bank on page 101 and how students might use the words and phrases in their paragraph. Students could write the sentences for their paragraph first, then trial the use of different connectives and prompts from the word bank as part of drafting.

When they have finished, spend some time reflecting on how different students have approached writing their paragraph, and the merits of each.

TAKING IT FURTHER	Informative writing at the highest level has a logical order and sense of clarity throughout. Encourage students to avoid including unnecessary information when writing by setting strict word limits in practice assignments and by regularly modelling concision. You could ask students to write an information text about their school in three paragraphs, each containing three sentences (one simple, one compound, one complex).

© HarperCollins *Publishers* Ltd 2018

4.2 Structuring informative writing

Resources:
- Student's Book: 4.2, pp. 102–103
- Workbook: 4.1, pp. 83–84 can be set as homework
- Worksheet 4.2
- PowerPoint slides 4.2a–h

Assessment objectives:

W2 Organise and structure ideas and opinions for deliberate effect

EXPLORE THE SKILLS

Begin by explaining to students that paragraphs and tenses help to order texts logically and help the reader's understanding. Then read **Q1**. Ensure that students understand what the question is asking: they need to work out the main focus in each paragraph by identifying a topic sentence and then the wider content.

Work through **Q1** as a class, by reading the text together and encouraging students to work out the focus of each paragraph. The easiest way might be to remove sentences and see how this affects understanding and reading flow. For example, read the first paragraph without the sentence 'Falconry is a centuries-old activity, and it is still revered today'. Discuss how difficult it is to read the second sentence without the initial topic sentence. The focus of the first paragraph is, therefore, what falconry is. Responses to the rest of the text may include:

➢ The second paragraph starts with 'The process of training hawks is highly skilled'. Further details follow starting with 'It begins with' and continues to relate the chronological process of the skilled training of a hawk.

➢ The third paragraph, contains the topic sentence at the start ('These specialised words go back many, many years') then goes on to give an example of how Shakespeare compared training a hawk to taming a wife.

➢ The final paragraph describes how 'Nowadays, falconry is used for more pleasant purposes'. It then goes on to provide evidence of how they are used at 'fairs, exhibitions and even weddings'.

Discuss how the topic sentence is first in all four paragraphs but this may not always be the case.

Extra support: Instead of asking students to identify the topic sentences themselves, show **PPT 4.2a** and **4.2b**, which highlight the topic sentences, and ask students what it is about these sentences that makes them the topic sentence.

BUILD THE SKILLS

Ask students to read through paragraph 2 again and identify the five-step process used to train a hawk:

➢ **1** getting a hawk used to its handler by being close by
➢ **2** feeding from your hand
➢ **3** feeding when attached to a line (creance)
➢ **4** feeding on a line from a distance of 50–100 metres
➢ **5** flying freely, coming to you for food attached to a line

Put students in pairs to answer **Q2**. When pairs are ready, take feedback. Display **PPT 4.2c** and **4.2d** to demonstrate how tenses are used and for what purpose.

The present tense is used in the first two paragraphs to show that the practice is current. Then the tense shifts to the past to discuss use of hawk training back in Shakespeare's time. Then it reverts to the present tense to show that the training still goes on.

Chapter 4: Writing for purpose

Use **PPT 4.2e** and **4.2f** to show how the writer has used time to mark the order of events. Focus on 'It begins with', 'Once,' 'Now', 'First', 'Then', 'To start with', 'After a few days', which show the order that training follows. Readers can see how much time and effort goes in to making falconry displays work. Students should be aware of how the order emphasises the steps and details that training involves.

DEVELOP THE SKILLS

Experiment with putting the paragraphs in a different order using **Worksheet 4.2** and draw out the effect of losing the focus on the topic at the start. By not beginning with an explanation of what falconry is, we are in danger of losing track of what is being trained and why. Together, work out the reasons why careful ordering of a text is so important:

- to maintain overall focus
- so that paragraphs can give details about different aspects of the topic
- to allow the reader to skim and scan the text to find facts easily.

Students should then answer **Q3** in pairs. Their experience of trying the paragraphs in different orders should enable the completion of part **a)** with comments such as *If we do not explain what falconry is at the start, the reader could get confused about how the different aspects are linked.* For part **b)** students should identify the connectives 'It begins with', 'First', 'Then', 'To start with', 'When', 'Nowadays' and how these make the information flow.

Read through the information about whaling together and discuss briefly the ways in which the information could be ordered. Put students in pairs to answer **Q4** and create a paragraph plan. When everyone has finished, take feedback and compare the different plans students have come up with. If more support is needed, display **PPT 4.2g**, which shows a sample paragraph plan for the whaling article and **PPT 4.2h**, which contains an example of how the first paragraph might be structured.

Extra challenge: Ask students to research and make notes on the future for whaling – positive or negative – by directing them to relevant websites.

Students should use the website material to create three topic sentences to make an article supporting or campaigning against whaling. Remind them to use connectives to link sentences within the three paragraphs.

APPLY THE SKILLS

Refer students to the 'Checklist for success' in the Student's Book. Then ask students to complete **Q5** independently. Encourage students to use the bullet points to structure their response and to use the plan the constructed in **Q4**.

TAKING IT FURTHER	Planning needs to be inventive and unrestricted by formulae, so advise students to work with a simple planning structure to begin with as on **PPT 4.2g**, but to move away from this as soon as they feel confident enough to do so. For example, they might consider structuring the whaling articles in the following way:
	<table><tr><th>Vision of the future</th><th>Past controversy</th><th>Current campaigns</th></tr><tr><td>Positive outcomes for whales.</td><td>Battles between whalers and environmentalists.</td><td>Headlines directly instructing trade to stop.</td></tr></table>
	Set students the task of finding another structure for the whaling article. They could use the research they did in the Extra challenge activity in this topic.

© HarperCollins *Publishers* Ltd 2018

Chapter 4: Writing for purpose

4.3 Writing to persuade

Resources:
- Student's Book: 4.3, pp. 104–105
- Workbook: 4.2, pp. 85–86 can be set as homework
- Worksheet 4.3
- PowerPoint slides 4.3a–b

Assessment objectives:

W2 Organise and structure ideas and opinions for deliberate effect

EXPLORE THE SKILLS

Display **PPT 4.3a** and run through the features of persuasive writing with students. Discuss the types of writing they studied earlier where they may have come across these features. Explain that the purpose of persuasion is to change someone's mind. There are three key elements that contribute to this: ideas, language and structure. Read the information about this at the start of the 'Explore the skills' section on page 104 of the Student's Book. Ask students where they have seen persuasive writing – for example, in an advertising campaign either on television or on billboards.

Read the opening to an extract about driverless cars on page 104. Explore what is happening in the text using the annotations in the Student's Book and students' own ideas. Try to draw out the negativity of the vocabulary choices and discuss what language choices the writer might have made if the overall point of view had been more positive. What is the effect of the following vocabulary changes?

- 'minds of their own' → 'independence'
- 'appals' → 'excites'
- 'chaos' → 'freedom'.

Put students in pairs to answer **Q1** and **Q2**. For **Q1**, they should note the powerful nature of 'appals', 'nasty' and 'absolute'. For **Q2**, they should identify that 'robotic machines with minds of their own' in the first paragraph become the cause of a 'nasty attack' in the second. The structure is logical and the text flows because further details are added to topics mentioned at the start.

BUILD THE SKILLS

Return to the list of features of persuasive writing on **PPT 4.3a** and explain how emotive language is used to prompt a 'call to action' (the last bullet point). You could give real-life examples of this by citing persuasive advertising campaigns such as Barnardos 'Believe in me' or the Brazilian Salvation Army's 'Warm Clothing Also Saves Lives'. In the former, three paragraphs outlining Barnardos' work end with 'Help us to continue our vital work: Donate.' In the latter, the life-saving image and message are followed by a phone number and 'Donate'.

Read the extract from a parent to a head teacher on page 105 of the Student's Book, and make sure students can make the connection between the emotive language used in the charity campaigns and the language in the parent's letter. Drill down to the meanings and implications of 'metal monsters' contrasted with 'happy chatter'. Look at the use of alliteration and assonance in the letter. Have a brief class discussion about what effect this language might have on the head teacher.

Ask students to complete **Q3** in pairs.

a) The parent wants the council to ban cars from the road outside their children's school.

b) The parent paints a happy picture of chattering children with their parents walking along in safety.

DEVELOP THE SKILLS

Recap on how language can have powerful impact on readers. Introduce the table in the Student's Book and review the effects of powerful vocabulary, rhetorical questions and pattern of three, then ask students to

Chapter 4: Writing for purpose

respond individually to **Q4**, choosing the verbs that have a particularly powerful impact ('belching', 'grinding', 'skidding'). Take feedback on what comes to mind when students read these words.

Move on to **Q5**, which students could answer as a paired discussion. Again, take class feedback, noting down their thoughts on why the opening sentence is especially effective. They should identify that it makes the outcome clear from the start – the council should be asked to ban cars from the street outside the school.

> **Extra support:** Display **PPT 4.3b**, which contains a list of the verbs in the letter, and ask students to choose the three most powerful. Once they feel confident with this, you could ask them to add to the list of verbs by imagining what else the parent might say in the letter.
>
> **Extra challenge:** Ask students to work in groups of three to role-play the discussion between the school principal and two senior teachers as they open the letter from the parent. What might they say to each other and what might they do about it?

APPLY THE SKILLS

Point out that it is important to consider both sides of an argument when persuading an audience to agree with a point of view. One good technique is to outline the opposing point of view in order to completely destroy its argument.

Ask students to complete **Q6** independently. Remind them that they need to come up with a persuasive point of view in favour of driverless cars. Ensure that they use at least one effective technique they have learned in this topic.

When everyone has completed the paragraph, they could swap with a partner and assess the effectiveness of each other's work.

> **Extra challenge:** Ask students to complete **Worksheet 4.3**, which further explores how rhetorical devices improve speech.

TAKING IT FURTHER	When writing to persuade, students should not only present a clear view from the start, they should also weave a complex argument that considers all sides, and offer evidence. They should offer a discerning judgement about which features are appropriate to purpose and audience. To practise this, set students the following task:
	Persuade your reader that a ban on students from the local cinema would be a good thing.
	Your audience is the local community.
	Your purpose is to persuade local people that the cinema will be less rowdy without school children dominating the entrance, the sweet shop, the exit.
	Your task is to write an article that will change minds.

Chapter 4: Writing for purpose

4.4 Structuring persuasion

Resources:
- Student's Book: 4.4, pp. 106–107
- Workbook: 4.2, pp. 85–86 can be set as homework
- Worksheet 4.4
- PowerPoint slides 4.4a–e

Assessment objectives:

W2 Organise and structure ideas and opinions for deliberate effect

EXPLORE THE SKILLS

Read the introduction to this topic on page 106 of the Student's Book, emphasising the importance of organising or structuring persuasive writing to have the best effect. As a warm-up, put students in groups of three and hand out **Worksheet 4.4**. This contains three pieces of information about fizzy drinks. Ask students to cut up the pieces of information and experiment with the reading order. They should also read the text aloud in their groups and experiment with delivery of the information.

Once each group has experimented with different structures, work as a whole class to answer the following questions:

- How is the argument presented best?
- How are the three sentences best delivered?
- What techniques can be used to emphasise powerful words and phrases?
- What else might you say to make this argument more persuasive?

Students should stay in their groups to complete **Q1** and **Q2**. Answers are:

Q1 Walking to school will also benefit parents.

Q2 This is the only logical place: it begins with 'Furthermore', and it presents a secondary benefit – the primary one being children's health.

BUILD THE SKILLS

Explain that structure is essential for an effective persuasive text, so it is important to consider this when planning persuasive writing. Students could tackle **Q3** in small groups, making notes on their ideas. Then take feedback, drawing out some of the following ideas:

- Social benefits: parents and young children walking to school together will have a chance to talk; parents will be able to teach children road safety.
- Financial benefits: parents could save money on petrol or public transport fares.
- School environment: pollution around the school will be reduced.

Extra challenge: Use **PPT 4.4a** to demonstrate how points can be turned into paragraphs by the addition of evidence and summing up, and support students using the structure independently on further points in **PPT 4.4b**. If necessary, as an example, demonstrate how the following paragraph works:

Think about how much money you could save by not having to drive children to and from school. What could that money be spent on? A typical car journey to school has been calculated to cost up to approximately $7. Multiply this by five and then double it for the two journeys, if you do not have a neighbour willing to share transport costs. This means $70 a week could be saved.

Chapter 4: Writing for purpose

DEVELOP THE SKILLS

Discuss how different verb forms can have different effects on the reader, and how important tone can be in persuasion. As an example of different tones, use **PPT 4.4c**. Then hold a class vote on which sentence in this PowerPoint slide is most likely to achieve success. See below for some ideas:

- Stand up now! (a straightforward order)
- If you want to go to lunch on time today, stand up and clear your desks now. (Gives an apparent choice, with an element of reasoning.)
- Could you all please stand up because we need to clear our desks and join the lunch queue as soon as possible? (Framed as a polite question – and gives a more persuasive reason.)

Discuss the outcome of the vote. There is no right answer: it will depend on the character of the teacher and the class. However, point out that getting the right tone is, nonetheless, important.

Introduce modal verbs using the table on page 107. Explain their association with polite forms, then encourage students to practise using them by looking at the sentences in **PPT 4.4d** as a starting point. Ask them to give new versions of each sentence that uses modal verbs in the same way but with different subjects, such as:

- *If you sing songs, you will feel more cheerful.*

Students should then complete **Q4** and **Q5**. The answers to **Q4** are 'would be' and 'might be'. The **Q5** sentences are included at the end of **PPT 4.4d**, but students should now think of their own ways to complete them.

> **Extra support:** Show students how frequently modal verbs are used. Ask students to complete these five sentences (given without example completions) in **PPT 4.4e**.
>
> - Would you mind if…? (*I sat on this chair?*)
> - Could you help me with…? (*putting these invitations on everyone's seat?*)
> - Might you be able to…? (*carry the plate of biscuits through to our guests?*)
> - May I suggest that…? (*we finish by 7:30 so everyone can get home before it gets dark?*)
> - We can always take… (*the bus to get home.*)

APPLY THE SKILLS

As a class, read through the 'Checklist for success', then ask students to complete **Q6** independently. When students have completed their paragraphs, they should swap their writing with a partner and peer assess based on the points in the checklist and any other learning from this lesson.

TAKING IT FURTHER	Students should not just present one piece of evidence to back up a point in their persuasive writing. They should include a broad range so that any objection can be quashed quickly. As an exercise, ask them to find at least three ways to back up the following statement: - *Contactless payment cards are a great benefit to society.* Possible answers could include: - There is no need to remember and insert a PIN. - Disabled people can find them easier to use. - It is quicker and queues at checkouts move faster. - Fears of machines copying card details are allayed. - You still need to authorise payment preventing fraud.

4.5 Writing to argue

> **Resources:**
> - Student's Book: 4.5, pp. 108–109
> - Workbook: 4.3, pp. 87–88 can be set as homework
> - Worksheet 4.5
> - PowerPoint slides 4.5a–c

Assessment objectives:

W2 Organise and structure ideas and opinions for deliberate effect

EXPLORE THE SKILLS

Read through the features of argumentative writing listed on page 108 of the Student's Book. Ask students whether they can identify the differences between writing to argue and writing to persuade. The key difference is that argument generally looks at both sides before drawing a conclusion, whereas persuasion is often one-sided.

As a class, review the example structure at the start of the 'Explore the skills' section, then ask students to answer **Q1** and **Q2** in pairs. Take class feedback.

For **Q1**, they may have their own opinion on whether or not it is effective, but ensure that they can give reasons for their decision. They may feel it is a clear and straightforward way of presenting an argument and that it shows an understanding of both sides. However, some may recognise that there may be points that sit on both sides of the argument. For example, it is healthy to ride a bike to work, but not if you fall off and injure yourself.

For **Q2**, students might come up with a structure that matches a point *for* with a point *against* each time, so that instead of dealing with them in two separate paragraphs, the points are individually balanced. For example, *On the one hand, bike rental schemes can be expensive to set up. But on the other hand, the petrol costs saved far outweigh the initial set-up costs.*

BUILD THE SKILLS

Make sure that students understand what we mean by facts and statistics:

➢ Facts are pieces of information that can be backed up with evidence (as opposed to opinions).

➢ Statistics are numerical data that have been gathered from research and evidence, from which we can draw conclusions.

Ask students to complete **Q3** in pairs. They should identify:

➢ **facts:** they are popular (NB this is not an opinion); they are expensive to build and run

➢ **statistics:** over nine million dollars raised in one year

➢ **witness comments:** the quote from Jon Devani.

Students should have recognised that the extract writer does not cite his or her personal experience. **Q4** asks them to think about how this could be added. Display **PPT 4.5a** to show them an example of a personal experience that could be added to the extract to improve the argument. Then ask them to work in pairs to come up with their own ideas. They do not have to come up with just one idea! Take class feedback and note some of the best ideas on the board.

Extra support: Use **Worksheet 4.5** to help students develop possible examples of personal experience.

Chapter 4: Writing for purpose

DEVELOP THE SKILLS

Discuss how using different structures can wrong-foot the opposition when arguing. All sorts of approaches can be tried, and the most inventive will often be successful.

Ask students to reread the extract, then work in pairs to answer **Q5**. Take feedback, then display **PPT 4.5b**, which shows the arguments in favour of the bike-rental scheme (red) and counter-arguments against it (blue). It should be clear that the structure combines arguments and counter-arguments within each paragraph: the counter-argument is actually given first, then rebutted. To confirm answers to **Q5b**, focus on the blue sections, reading them out to ensure the counter-arguments are clear. Point out how they have been rebutted. For example:

- **Argument:** bike schemes are very popular
- **Counter-argument:** they cost a lot of money to set up
- **Rebuttal:** they raised over nine million dollars in a year.

Read through the rest of the information in this section as a class to make sure that students understand how arguments need to be challenged at every step.

Extra support: Remind students that each paragraph is structured by making a point, then making the argument against that point, together. Use **PPT 4.5c** to show how the structure could work and model making changes.

Extra challenge: Ask students to come up with questions that might help to develop arguments *against* the pro-cycling ones put forward in the extract. Examples are:

- Did Devani really save so much money by hiring a bike?
- How much did he spend on equipment or clothing?
- How much time did he previously spend working on the train that is now lost in cycling?
- What were the details of the accident he had?
- How much rainfall was experienced last year?
- How much time did Devani have to spend changing on arriving at work and before leaving?

APPLY THE SKILLS

Remind students about the complex structure of arguments and the techniques that can be used to present, support and challenge evidence. Focus students on the counter-argument third paragraph required by **Q6**. Advise students to use the bullet points and the plan summary from **Q5**.

TAKING IT FURTHER	Ask students to find argument (A), counter-argument (C) and rebuttal (R) to structure paragraphs for one of the following issues: ➢ Fizzy drinks should reduce their sugar content. ➢ Animals should not be kept as pets. ➢ Plastic bags should be banned.

4.6 Structuring paragraphs in argument texts

Chapter 4: Writing for purpose

Resources:
- Student's Book: 4.6, pp. 110–113
- Workbook: 4.3, pp. 87–88 can be set as homework
- Worksheets 4.6a–b
- PowerPoint slides 4.6a–c

Assessment objectives:

W2 Organise and structure ideas and opinions for deliberate effect

EXPLORE THE SKILLS

Read the introduction to this topic on page 110 of the Student's Book and summarise the importance of using cohesive devices in writing, particularly in argument texts. Then review the information at the start of the 'Explore the skills' section as a class and remind students how to form compound sentences. Discuss the purpose of the conjunction and the conjunctive adverb in the first example. Then ask students to work in pairs to answer **Q1–Q3**. Take class feedback. Answers are:

Q1 'yet'

Q2 The conjunction is there to set up the counter-argument.

Q3 idea + *and* + idea → to give additional information
idea + *so* + idea → to show a result or consequence
idea + *but* + idea → to offer an alternative
idea + *or* + idea → to give a contrast, indicate difference or problem
idea + *because* + idea → to give a reason

Read the information about conjunctive adverbs together before students return to their pairs to answer **Q4**. They should identify that:

- ➢ 'yet' sets up the counter-argument
- ➢ 'in order to' introduces further detail
- ➢ 'however' leads into an opposing view
- ➢ 'as' explains this view.

BUILD THE SKILLS

Explain to students that connectives can contribute more than just cohesion to a paragraph; they can also signpost a developing point of view. Point out how, once they have crafted their topic sentence to introduce the subject, they need to use conjunctions and conjunctive adverbs to start building their argument. As a practice activity, display **PPT 4.6a**, which contains a paragraph with connectives highlighted. Ask students how each of the highlighted words reveal the writer's viewpoint.

Students should discuss **Q5–Q7** in small groups. Afterwards, each group should nominate one person as spokesperson during class feedback. Responses should be:

Q5 The viewpoint expressed is that wind turbines are a good thing. We know this from the phrase 'a wonderful phenomenon'.

Q6 a) 'furthermore'
b) 'even'
c) 'in order to'

Q7 'wonderful', 'inspiring', 'huge and beautiful' and 'otherworldly'

They should then tackle **Q8** independently.

Chapter 4: Writing for purpose

Extra support: Help students plan and write their paragraph by suggesting some arguments that could be made to oppose wind turbines – for example, how noisy they can be, the way they might obstruct a beautiful view or the dangers they pose to birds that might fly into them.

Extra challenge: Give students **Worksheet 4.6a**, which has an extra task for them to practise using connectives to express different viewpoints, based on the paragraph from **PPT 4.6a** (display this for reference during the activity).

DEVELOP THE SKILLS

Introduce the idea that using conjunctive adverbs is not always the best way to structure an argument text, then read the extracts from the article about fracking together. Take questions to ensure that students understand what fracking is. Put students in pairs to respond to **Q9** before taking feedback. They should identify some or all of the following:

➢ **For:** It is cheap; it can be carried out from places where it would normally be uneconomic to do so; it replaces dirty coal; it helps fight climate change.

➢ **Against:** It causes earthquakes and pollution; its emissions are significant; it contributes hugely to global warming.

Students should remain in their pairs to respond to **Q10**, using **Worksheet 4.6b** to complete the table. Their completed tables should look something like the example below.

Sentence	Conjunction or conjunctive adverb	Effect (To contrast? To show an outcome?)
Hailed as… colourful.	or	presents the positive and negative sides
It enables us... price of energy.	but	presents the alternative view
Nevertheless... generation.	and	presents further evidence
Dirty coal… climate change.	so	provides detail
However,… fuel.	However	provides comparison
Its emissions… global warming.	and	gives more evidence

Read the task on page 113 as a class and make sure that everyone understands the key elements of the question: the issue under discussion (the proposed building of a wind farm), the form of the response (a speech) and the viewpoint they must express (opposed to the proposition).

Display the bullet points from the task on **PPT 4.6b** and ask students to discuss, in pairs, any other arguments they can think of against the proposal in response to **Q11**. Take feedback and add convincing ideas to the list. Keep this displayed for the final writing task. Once ideas have been collected, work as a class on **Q12** to decide on a suitable order in which to present these points. For example, you might lead them towards environmental concerns, then costs, then personal inconvenience. Be open to alternative suggestions.

APPLY THE SKILLS

Recap the conventions of speeches outlined in Topic 3.1 if necessary, then ask students to complete **Q13** independently. Refer them to the 'Checklist for success' on page 113, or display it on **PPT 4.6c**. When everyone has completed their speech, they could swap with a partner and use the 'Checklist' to peer asses each other's work.

TAKING IT FURTHER	Students writing to argue should be able to propose unexpected but convincing points. To practise this, they could write another speech about the building of a recycling plant. They should prepare points form the point of view of a local business leader who is afraid that it will reduce their profits. Points might include: how the plant will result in increased traffic on local roads; how the recycling process might lead to pollution; it is not clear that the plant will be economical. Encourage them to come up with ideas that will take the argument in a new direction.

Chapter 4: Writing for purpose

4.7 Writing to explore and discuss

Resources:
- Student's Book: 4.7, pp. 114–115
- Workbook: 4.4, pp. 89–91 can be set as homework
- PowerPoint slides 4.7a–d

Assessment objectives:
W2 Organise and structure ideas and opinions for deliberate effect

EXPLORE THE SKILLS

Display the features of discursive writing on **PPT 4.7a** and go through them as a class. Ask students whether they are familiar with any of these features from other forms of writing they may have come across. Clarify any uncertainty – for example, if students are unsure what a 'measured tone' is.

Read the article about foraged food on page 114. As a class, discuss whether the writer shows an open-minded approach throughout the article. How might the restaurant owners feel if they read it? Put students in pairs to respond to **Q1**, then come back together as a class to discuss the answers:

a) The issue being discussed is the fashion for eating 'found' or foraged food.

b) The writer feels that the fashion for foraged food may be more than a passing fad.

c) 'the idea of going back to nature seems very appealing'; 'it seems likely to remain popular'

BUILD THE SKILLS

Ask students to reread the article and then work in pairs on **Q2**. There are some suggestions on **PPT 4.7b**, which can be displayed either for support while pairs are working, or afterwards during class feedback.

DEVELOP THE SKILLS

Use the annotated example on page 115 to briefly discuss what 'tone' means and how it affects a piece of writing. Then set them to work on **Q3**. They should recognise that the lack of the first person 'I', the more cautious vocabulary such as 'seems' and 'likely', and the balance reflected in words such as 'While…' and 'even if', all contribute to a more measured tone in the article.

Extra support: To consolidate understanding of tone, display **PPT 4.7c** and practise changing the tone by removing or changing the highlighted features. **PPT 4.7d** provides an opportunity for further discussion and analysis of the final sentence in the article.

Extra challenge: Ask students to discuss issues they are not familiar with using a measured tone:
- Should students stay at school until the age of 18?
- Could more effort be put into looking after our elderly relatives?

APPLY THE SKILLS

Look at the new paragraph and give students time to revisit the features explored in the topic before they tackle **Q4**.

| TAKING IT FURTHER | Ask students to collect persuasive articles and then rewrite them, changing the tone so they become more discursive. |

Chapter 4: Writing for purpose

4.8 Structuring content in discursive writing

Resources:
- Student's Book: 4.8, pp. 116–119
- Workbook: 4.4, pp. 89–91 can be set as homework
- Worksheets 4.8a–b
- PowerPoint slides 4.8a–d

Assessment objectives:
W2 Organise and structure ideas and opinions for deliberate effect

EXPLORE THE SKILLS

Recap on the features of discursive writing from the previous lesson: measured tone, acknowledgement of different viewpoints, clear explanations. Then read through the explanatory text and the information about chocolate on page 116 of the Student's Book. Work as a class on **Q1** to discuss ways of organising the information along the lines of the bullet points.

Put students in pairs and hand out Worksheet **4.8a**. Ask them to complete the table with information from the Student's Book, then to use this to help them develop an alternative structure for **Q2**.

BUILD THE SKILLS

Explain how the structure of addressing pros and cons in the same paragraph allows for both balance and development of ideas, using the annotated example. Students should then return to their pairs to work on a paragraph for **Q3**. Show students **PPT 4.8a** as an example of a possible paragraph format. The colour-coding is: red – topic sentences; blue – supporting information; green – writer's viewpoint. Students could also work in threes using **PPT 4.8a** as a model. On separate sheets of paper, they should write a topic sentence on the benefits of chocolate. They then pass their sheet to the next student, who adds supporting information. Finally, they pass their sheets on again, and each student adds an appropriate summary point.

> **Extra support:** Use **Worksheet 4.8b**, which provides ready-drafted sentences. Students should then read each one aloud and allocate it to one of three piles: Topic sentences, Supporting information, and Writer's viewpoint. They should then group the sentences into four possible paragraphs.

DEVELOP THE SKILLS

Review the table of discourse markers on page 118, then read the annotated article below it. Discuss how these features help to create a measured tone.

Students could work alone or in pairs on **Q4**. Display the gap-fill task on **PPT 4.8b** while they are working. When everyone has finished, show **PPT 4.8c** for students to check their answers.

Read through the additional information about the benefits of chocolate, then ask students to complete **Q5** in pairs (the answer is **a)**). During class feedback, discuss **Q6** then ask students to decide where the information should be added. (As the information is largely about sales, and the article is about health, the information should probably go in the middle, or perhaps at the beginning.)

APPLY THE SKILLS

Display the 'Checklist for success' on **PPT 4.8d**. Recap on the conventions of articles in Topic 3.5 if necessary. Then ask students to complete **Q7**.

TAKING IT FURTHER	Ask students to use the skills developed in the chocolate debate in a new topic – social media. Is it a giant leap forward or an unjustifiable waste of time?

© HarperCollins *Publishers* Ltd 2018

Chapter 4: Writing for purpose

| 4.9 | Descriptive writing |

Resources:
- Student's Book: 4.9, pp. 120–123
- Workbook: 4.5, pp. 92–93 can be set as homework
- Worksheet 4.9
- PowerPoint slides 4.9a–f

Assessment objectives:

W2 Organise and structure ideas and opinions for deliberate effect

EXPLORE THE SKILLS

Ask students about their favourite piece of descriptive writing. Try to cover fiction and non-fiction, current and historical writing – mention some of your own favourites if necessary! Ask students what they particularly like about these pieces. What makes the writing memorable? What techniques can they identify that have an especially powerful effect on the reader?

Display **PPT 4.9a** and review the basic advice for successful descriptive writing. Can students think of anything else to add to this list? Next use **PPT 4.9b** to ensure that all students are secure with the key terms.

Read the piece of descriptive writing on page 120 as a class, then work together on **Q1**, identifying any features from the bullet list – for example simile ('like the hair of a giant monster') and personification ('raindrops danced on the forest floor').

For **Q2**, students need to weigh up each possibility offered in the bullet points. They should conclude that the first bullet point describes what the paragraph as a whole is about, because all the other features sit within that subject.

Students could work in pairs on **Q3**, listing all things described within the tendrils:

➤ *the worsening weather*
➤ *sparkling raindrops*
➤ *a tiny tree frog with an orange eye.*

For **Q4**, students should identify that the writer uses senses such as sight (*the tendrils continued to shift and shake to the rhythm of the rain*) You could draw out what is missing from the extract in terms of senses here – Smells? Sounds? Taste? Touch?

Read the information about the importance of deciding what to describe, and the example notes. Students could then return to their pairs to respond to **Q5**. They should identify that the student has not yet used:

➤ *a river setting*
➤ *before and after the storm (and there is no mention of the sun)*
➤ *roots*
➤ *ants*
➤ *python.*

Extra challenge: Divide students into three groups and display **PPT 4.9a** on the whiteboard. Give each group one of the notes from the example on page 121 of the Student's Book. Invite them to experiment with techniques in descriptive writing. For example, the first group might take the idea of a remote place (tropical forest), and take the advice to *use language techniques*, then come up with the description using a simile:

➤ *The tropical forest stood still as if carved out of stone.*

If necessary, guide students by suggesting, for example, that the group focusing on location could think of metaphors for the forest foliage, the group focusing on timing could find similes for the disappearing sun's rays, and the group focusing on 'What?' could find similes for the red ants or the python.

Chapter 4: Writing for purpose

BUILD THE SKILLS

Ask students to look at the way that a trail of vocabulary is created by collecting further verbs to add to the list connected to 'sun's rays' on page 121. For example, they could 'stab', 'gleam' or 'radiate'. Then ask students to work in pairs on **Q6**. Then take feedback from the class, drawing out how *shine* (bright) is different from *glow* (dim) and *sparkle* (flash) is different from *beam* (blinding).

Students could work in pairs on **Q7**, deciding which of the words would best describe the sun's rays through the trees. Take feedback. They will have different ideas so put some of their example sentences on the board and ask the class which they think work best and why. You could remain as a class to brainstorm ideas for the synonyms asked for in **Q8**.

Review the semantic field table on page 122, then hand out **Worksheet 4.9** and ask pairs to complete **Q9** by adding further nouns to the table. They should then decode between them which word or phrase from their table they like best and write one or two sentences using it for **Q10**. Take class feedback and discuss what works well and why.

Extra challenge: If students are confident about the use of semantic fields, ask them to complete the second task on **Worksheet 4.9**, creating a semantic field of verbs they could use in relation to each of the features.

DEVELOP THE SKILLS

Ask students to think about how their work in this topic so far could be shaped into paragraphs. Refer back to the description of the forest at the start of this topic and explain how the features in it have been allocated in the table on page 123. Then ask students to work in their pairs on **Q11**, copying the table and adding their own ideas.

Extra challenge: Invite students to use a range of vocabulary and techniques to explore visual imagery (similes and metaphors) and sound imagery (alliteration and assonance). As a guide, display **PPT 4.9c**, which contains some examples of alliteration, and **PPT 4.9d**, which explores their effects.

When everyone has completed the table, join two pairs and ask them to compare ideas. They should amend their tables in light of this, adding or changing any ideas.

APPLY THE SKILLS

Explain to students that in an exam, they may be asked to describe a person rather than a place, but they can use the same techniques they have explored in this lesson. Share the first paragraph for writing about a lonely person on **PPT 4.9e**. Ask students to work individually to either complete the plan or write a plan of their own based on the structure in **Q11**. They should then write one more paragraph from the plan.

Afterwards, display the 'Checklist for success' on **PPT 4.9f** and ask students to use it to assess their partner's work.

TAKING IT FURTHER	Students need to find the most pertinent method to communicate. This might be focusing on sound in a place with music blaring out. The best way to convey the disruption might be to use assonance, emphasising the *screeching guitar noise repeatedly beating out the same rhythm and blowing our ear drums*.
	Ask students to describe one of the following animals using repeated vowel sounds (assonance) and repeated consonant sounds (alliteration) to emphasise their characteristics: ➤ a three-toed sloth (South and Central America) ➤ water snakes (North America) ➤ duck-billed platypus (eastern Australia).

© HarperCollins *Publishers* Ltd 2018

Chapter 4: Writing for purpose

4.10 Narrative writing

Resources:
- Student's Book: 4.10, pp. 124–127
- Workbook: 4.6, pp. 94–95 can be set as homework
- Worksheet 4.10
- PowerPoint slides 4.10a–d

Assessment objectives:

W2 Organise and structure ideas and opinions for deliberate effect

EXPLORE THE SKILLS

Ask students to think about a favourite story book or film, and share what features and techniques made it stand out for them. Display the list of basic techniques for successful narrative writing on **PPT 4.10a** and see how many the students had already mentioned in their discussion of favourite stories. Work together as a class on **Q1**, identifying other features, such as a 'hook' at the beginning of a story. Add any new ideas to the list.

Carefully review the five-point plan on page 124 as a class. Then help students to consider how it could be applied to the story plan in **PPT 4.10b**. Ask them how well this plan works in terms of engaging interest and providing a potentially satisfying resolution.

Then get students to answer **Q2–3** in pairs. They should discuss the two sub-questions in **Q2** and compare the effectiveness of this story plan with the one in **PPT 4.10b**.

Take feedback, drawing out the following points:

➢ There is a 'situation', with characters described.

➢ There is a 'development' – the announcement of the talent contest, which could challenge the characters, offering opportunities for personal change (rising to the occasion).

➢ The lack of rehearsal time could be seen as a complication, but it would be more interesting if it had consequences, such as one character panicking and dropping out, so that the others then try to persuade him or her.

➢ Having none of the characters winning does not work well as a climax – it is more of an anti-climax; having the person who dropped out re-entering and winning would work.

➢ There is no real resolution in the plan – the final bullet leaves the story open-ended; it would be better to have the characters benefit in some way – perhaps by forming a band!

➢ The plan does not stick to the first advice bullet in 'Explore the skills' – six characters is too many.

➢ It sticks to the second advice bullet; the other bullets relate to whole narratives rather than plans.

BUILD THE SKILLS

Now ask students to think about their favourite characters – for example, James Bond, Doctor Who, Harry Potter, Katniss Everdeen, Goku. Allow a few minutes for class discussion of what makes an appealing character.

Get students to discuss **Q4** in pairs. Then hand out **Worksheet 4.10** and ask students to add notes to develop the characters outlined in the Student's Book.

Students can tackle **Q5** by completing the final row in the worksheet. They could discuss this in pairs, but they should ideally write down their own ideas individually.

Chapter 4: Writing for purpose

Extra support: Help students to consider possible ways to use the bullet points in **Worksheet 4.10**:

- their backstory – they might come from a poor, or wealthy, background, or have got into trouble in a previous school
- their ambitions or motivation – they might want to become famous, or make someone proud
- strengths and/or weaknesses – they could have a great voice, or suffer from stage-fright
- typical behaviour or speech – they could swagger or walk with an unconfident stoop.

DEVELOP THE SKILLS

Read through the information about characterisation at the start of the 'Develop the skills' section. Lead a classroom discussion of how the features in the bullet points could bring a character to life and hint at what they are like. Introduce the 'Show, don't tell' maxim: it is more interesting for a reader to work out what a character is like from clues than to be told what they are like. Show **PPT 4.10c** for examples. Ask students to think of other ways in which they could *show* what a character is like. For example, appearance can suggest character.

Ask students to work through **Q6** on page 126 to develop their characterisation skills. The main factor used in the extract is the first bullet point – Marco behaves in a way suggesting nervous energy, computer skills, focus and fear of authority.

Then look at **Q7** and ask students for *what* Marco might say and *how* he might say it. For example:
'I – I'm just going there now, Sir. I just wanted to check something – er, to do with my homework.'

Q8 looks at the emotional journey that Marco travels along. Students could work on this in pairs but write down their own ideas. Perhaps Marco turns out to have a gift for digitally programming backing tracks and becomes a hero.

Q9 looks at the importance of location. Students should work in pairs or small groups. If they work in groups of five, each could develop ideas for a story in one of the settings. They could then share ideas.

APPLY THE SKILLS

Ask students to read through all of the material they have drawn on in this topic so far. They should then complete **Q10** by starting the narrative. Show **PPT 4.10d** for a checklist of what their story plan and opening should include.

TAKING IT FURTHER	Encourage a ruthless self-checking regime for students so that choice of vocabulary is consistently pertinent, sentence structure is varied and sophisticated and paragraphing creates cohesion and develops narrative in interesting and unpredictable ways. Ask students to select elements of the following extract to improve. How could vocabulary and sentence structure be made better? Words that might be replaced are in bold.
	➢ Marco **walked** through the subway. The wind **battered** discarded newspapers around his ankles. He sighed, **knowing** that this place was always going to remain desolate, deserted and **unloved**. What would make people care about their surroundings?

Chapter 5: Comprehension

5.1 Locating and selecting information

Resources:
- Student's Book: 5.1, pp. 130–133
- Workbook: 5.1, pp. 96–98 can be set as homework
- Worksheet 5.1
- PowerPoint slides 5.1a–d

Assessment objectives:

R1 Demonstrate understanding of explicit meanings

R5 Select and use information for specific purposes

EXPLORE THE SKILLS

Using the Student's Book, start by asking for a definition of *skimming* and *scanning*, before explaining their importance. Refer back to the work that students may have done on these skills in Topics 1.1 and 1.2 of the Student's Book, if they have worked through these already.

For **Q1**, ask students to skim read the text about Kirirom national park. Give them a time limit, such as one minute, depending on the group. Then display the five questions using **PPT 5.1a** and select students at random to provide the answers; extend their learning by questioning how they came to their answers. Responses might include:

a) Non-fiction. Possible reasoning: lots of dates, statistics and proper nouns.

b) To inform. Possible reasoning: lots of facts and suggestions about a holiday destination.

c) Adults (who are adventurous/healthy). Possible reasoning: details about energetic activities, doesn't seem luxurious, lots to do with history, no mention of child-friendly activities.

d) It also includes descriptions. Possible reasoning: descriptions of the mountain, contrasting language to describe the capital and the outdoor activities.

e) The first paragraph focuses on the area's history and what it's like; the second paragraph focuses on what you can do there. Possible reasoning: paragraph 1's reference to the 1940s and its use of past tense compared with paragraph 2's 'Today'; descriptions of scenery compared to description of activities; facts about the past compared with facts about accommodation and food.

Ask students to complete **Q2** individually, using their scanning skills to find the correct answers. Again, give students a time limit such as two and a half minutes (30 seconds per question).

Take answers from students. Responses should include:

a) Moroccan

b) the 1940s

c) two hours' drive

d) the (twenty-feet tall) fireplace

e) 60 US dollars

Note that twenty feet is approximately equal to six metres.

For **Q3**, put students in pairs or small groups to discuss the different strategies they used when scanning the text. Ask for feedback and note similar techniques.

BUILD THE SKILLS

Using **PPT 5.1b**, explain the difference between facts and opinions. Ask students to identify how the examples on the slide match the definitions.

Display **PPT 5.1c**, which contains the text discussed in **Q4**. Ask students to complete the question by scanning the text and identifying two facts and two opinions. Students could be asked to raise their hands

Chapter 5: Comprehension

when they have their answers, in order to emphasise how scanning helps students to speed up in exam conditions. Take feedback and then discuss with the class what they scanned for in order to find their answers. Responses might include:

- dates, statistics, proper nouns (for facts)
- adjectives linked to qualities or judgements, personal pronouns (for opinions).

DEVELOP THE SKILLS

Using the Student's Book, explain that students may be asked to select information about a specific idea. Ask them to reread the text about chocolate and complete **Q5**, finding two ways in which white chocolate is different from other chocolate. Take feedback. Responses should include:

- white chocolate has a different colour (pale yellow or ivory)
- it contains sugar
- it doesn't contain cocoa solids
- it contains a vanilla flavour.

Display **PPT 5.1d** and ask students if anyone had any of the responses listed. Explain that these are typical mistakes that students make, due to misreading the text or misreading the original question. As a class, try to work out what the student did wrong in each response **(Q6)**.

APPLY THE SKILLS

Hand out **Worksheet 5.1** and ask students to complete the three parts of **Q7**, using any scanning strategies that help them (such as highlighting or underlining). Give students a time limit, such as six minutes.

> **Extra support:** Direct students to paragraph 1 for **Q7a**, paragraph 2 for **Q7b**, and paragraph 1 and the end of paragraph 2 for **Q7c**.
>
> **Extra challenge:** Give some students a stricter time limit, such as three minutes. Students who finish first and have all correct answers could also work alongside you as markers, ticking correct answers, writing an improvement question next to incorrect answers (such as 'What feature of the natural landscape is included at the end of paragraph 2?') and making a final comment using the Check your progress section of the Student's Book.

Responses should include:

a) its fireplace is twenty feet tall; it was built in the 1940s; it was built by the king and his acolytes; the palace was destroyed; the fireplace is the only part of the palace that remains; it was built on a mountain top

b) trekking, mountain biking, swimming in waterfalls; look at the scenery

c) alpine or pine forest; mountainous; waterfalls; (green) cardamom forests

Once students have checked their answers, ask them to self-assess using the Check your progress section of the Student's Book.

TAKING IT FURTHER	Encourage students to read a newspaper regularly in order to improve their awareness of non-fiction writing. Working in friendship groups, they could choose articles and set each other six 'locate and select' questions based around facts and opinions or a specific theme.

Chapter 5: Comprehension

5.2 Literal and inferred meanings

Resources:
- Student's Book: 5.2, pp. 134–137
- Workbook: 5.2, pp. 99–101 can be set as homework
- Worksheet 5.2
- PowerPoint slides 5.2a–d
- Dictionaries and thesauruses

Assessment objectives:

R1 Demonstrate understanding of explicit meanings

R2 Demonstrate understanding of implicit meanings and attitudes

R5 Select and use information for specific purposes

EXPLORE THE SKILLS

Using the Student's Book, explain the importance of putting ideas into your own words in order to show full understanding. Read through the extract about canoeing, then use **PPT 5.2a** to model how a phrase from a text can be put into your own words.

Ask students to complete **Q1**, then take suggestions in a class forum.

Extra support: Use **PPT 5.2b–c** to scaffold an answer to the first two phrases in **Q1**.

Extra challenge: To show students the importance and variety of synonyms, ask them to come up with as many different versions of one of the phrases as they can. They could use a thesaurus to help them.

BUILD THE SKILLS

Make sure that students understand the idea of context: information that precedes and follows a word or phrase, which can be used to clarify its meaning.

Read the text about Taiping. As a class, work through **Q2**, scaffolding the ways in which students can work out the meaning of a word from its specific context.

Ask students to work in pairs to complete **Q3**.

Extra support: Allow students to use a dictionary and thesaurus if necessary.

Extra challenge: Encourage students to work without a dictionary or thesaurus and, instead, to think carefully about words and try to come up with their own synonyms.

Take feedback. Responses should include:

a) 'sleepy' = quiet, peaceful, calm and so on

b) 'Taiping is perhaps the most storied of them all' = Taiping has more tales about its past than other towns; of all the local towns, Taiping's past has been the most eventful; compared to other towns, Taiping has a particularly vivid history and so on

c) 'Taiping defies its eventful past' = Taiping is much quieter now; Taiping is no longer a place of violence and chaos; the mood of the town is completely different to how it was years ago and so on

As a class, discuss any successful ways in which students approached the task, as well as anything they found particularly difficult.

Chapter 5: Comprehension

DEVELOP THE SKILLS

Explain to students that, so far, they have been looking at *literal* meanings. They are now going to look at *inferred* meanings. Make sure that everyone understands that these are the meanings that a text suggests or implies, rather than those that are explicitly stated.

Read the text about a beach. Ask students to work in pairs and to complete **Q4** and **Q5** using **Worksheet 5.2**.

> **Extra support:** Help students to complete the literal meanings column by encouraging them to look in the phrase bank for synonyms for *hot*, *busy*, *happy* and *ruined*.

Take feedback. Discuss the specific words that the students felt implied meaning (suggestions are underlined below). The answers are:

a) The weather is hot = the sun was blazing / people were queuing for glasses of iced water.
b) The beach is busy = the crowded beach / searching for a spot.
c) The children are happy = children were happily playing games / smiling faces brightened the scene.
d) The writer feels that tourists have ruined the beach = tourism had spoiled the peace and beauty / this place was once paradise.

Using the Student's Book, reiterate the importance of using your own words. Focus students on the idea of identifying attitudes in a text.

Scaffold how to write about attitudes in a text by using **PPT 5.2d** to answer **Q6** as a class.

Ask students to complete **Q7** in pairs. Response might include:

a) The beach is very busy (from 'the crowded beach' and 'searching for a spot'); people enjoy being at the beach (from 'children were happily playing games' and 'smiling faces brighten the scene'); it's visited by lots of holidaymakers (from 'tourism has spoiled the peace and beauty').
b) Some people might not enjoy visiting the beach because it is far too busy (from 'searching for a spot'), it's not relaxing or attractive (from 'once paradise' and 'spoiled the peace and beauty), and it's uncomfortably hot (from 'queuing for glasses of iced water').

APPLY THE SKILLS

Ask students to reread the text about Taiping and complete **Q8** individually. Response might include:

a) 'drenched' = covered in; soaked by; smothered by, and so on; 'On the fringes of town' = around the edge of Taiping
b) People might go for a run or ride a bicycle around the gardens (from 'attract joggers and cyclists to sprawling green grounds'), explore the jungle and go swimming (from 'head just a bit further towards the jungle and take a dip in the waterfall'), or go hill-trekking (from 'hike up Bukit Larut').
c) People might find Taiping too quiet or dull (from 'settled in the sleepy yet steadfast rhythms of a market town'); it takes a bit of effort to find the most attractive parts of the Lake Gardens (from 'rent a bike to find the most scenic spots'); it takes a long time to reach Taiping (from 'three-hour journey').
d) People might visit Taiping because it's not as busy as other more popular destinations (from 'Penang and Ipoh are now hot tourist destinations in Malaysia. But the road between them is strewn with small towns'); it's an interesting, historical town (from 'the most storied of them all'); it has interesting architecture and sights (from 'churches, gardens and neoclassical buildings'); the marketplace is impressive (from 'what a market it is: two magnificent wooden arcades'); the food at the market is inexpensive and tasty (from 'food is cheap and delicious'); the Lake Gardens are pretty (from 'scenic') and there's lots to do (from 'rent a bike ... head just a bit further towards the jungle and take a dip in the waterfall ... hike up Bukit Larut').

Ask students to use the 'Check your progress' points to assess their work and identify areas for improvement.

TAKING IT FURTHER	In friendship groups, students could set each other a weekly synonym task. Each student is allocated an unfamiliar word. Using a thesaurus and a dictionary, they should make a list of synonyms for that word. They could also use four of their synonyms in a sentence to show how the words might be used in a different context (considering, for example, how and why one of their words might be more suitable than another).

Chapter 5: Comprehension

5.3 Practice questions and sample responses

Resources:
- Student's Book: 5.3, pp. 138–141
- Workbook: 5.3, pp. 102–103 can be set as homework
- Worksheets 5.3a–b
- PowerPoint slides 5.3a–c

Assessment objectives:

R1 Demonstrate understanding of explicit meanings

R2 Demonstrate understanding of implicit meanings and attitudes

R5 Select and use information for specific purposes

YOUR TASK

A sample task has been included to give students an opportunity to practise the style of task set in Paper 1, Question 1. You may decide to set this as a formal assessment or to complete the process in class, with teacher support. **Worksheet 5.3a** reproduces the task should you wish to set it as formal assessment. Please note that some references to non-metric measurements are included in the extract. 216 miles is approximately equal to 348 kilometres, 8.5-mile perimeter is approximately equal to 13-kilometre perimeter, and 22 miles is approximately equal to 35 kilometres. **PPT 5.3a–c** includes the assessment objectives, key skills and the task to share with the class.

If you want to mirror examination conditions, you could allow about 25 minutes for students to complete the task.

EXPLORING RESPONSES

The Student's Book offers two sample responses designed to represent sound achievement (Response 1) and excellent achievement (Response 2). Depending on the ability range of your class, you may want to work with the actual mark scheme for this question, which is available on the Cambridge website. A student-friendly checklist has been provided on page 142 of the Student's Book.

These responses have been reproduced without annotations on **Worksheet 5.3b**, so students could work to add their own annotations before completing **Q6** and looking at the commentaries and feedback provided in the Student's Book.

Having worked with the sample responses, identifying areas for improvement and seeing what each response has done well, students should annotate their own response with similar comments, or – if appropriate – redraft them in light of what they have learned from the process.

Chapter 6: Summary writing

6.1 Identifying and selecting according to the question focus

Resources:
- Student's Book: 6.1, pp. 144–145
- Workbook: 6.1, pp. 104–106 can be set as homework
- PowerPoint slides 6.1a–b

Assessment objectives:

R1   Select and use information for specific purposes.

EXPLORE THE SKILLS

Explain that this lesson focuses on the first things that students should do in addressing the summary task: identifying exactly what the question is asking, and selecting information accordingly. If necessary, recap on the skills of skimming and scanning (using pages 8–13 of the Student's Book).

Address **Q1** with the class. The answer is 'since the start of his career'. You could elaborate by pointing out that although the passage is said to be by a retired footballer, it might have been about sport generally. In this case, part of the focus would be 'how *football* has changed'.

Students could tackle **Q2** and **Q3** in pairs. For **Q2** points **b)**, **c)** and **e)** are relevant. For **Q3** there are various alternative wordings, such as: 'How does the author say soccer has developed since he first became a professional player?'.

BUILD THE SKILLS

Read the text with the class and check that they understand it. Students could continue to work in pairs, writing answers and then feeding back to the class.

For **Q4**, the two aspects are what the wrestlers wear and the ritual of twisting, wrapping and tying the *sundhro*.

Extra support: Use **PPT 6.1a**, which highlights the parts of the text relevant to the two aspects. If you wish to give students only a little help, you could flash it up briefly, and only show it for longer when discussing the answers.

In response to **Q5**, students will need to discuss the wording of the question: '*what* the wrestlers do and *why* they do it'. The description of the wrestlers twisting, wrapping and tying the *sundhro* is relevant (what they do); so too is the fact that this is 'sacrosanct' (why they do it): it is a time-honoured tradition. Actually, there is a practical purpose too, but that is not revealed until the second part of the text in the 'Develop the skills' section. What they wear cannot really be counted as something that the men *do*.

DEVELOP THE SKILLS

Read the continuation of the wrestling account with the class and check that they understand the explanation of the sport. Together, look at the picture in the Student's Book and have a brief class discussion on what it shows. (One bout coming to an end, with two other opponents on the right getting ready by tying each other's *sundhro*.)

Students could work in small groups for **Q6**, listing the rules of Malakhara wrestling. The main point is for them to be selective, sticking to the rules and aims of the sport, which are:

➢ Each man must aim to get his hand inside the back of his opponent's *sundhro*, then throw him to the ground from that position.
➢ The arms may not be used to perform any type of wrestling grip.
➢ The legs may be used to trip and overbalance the opponent.

Chapter 6: Summary writing

You could display these on **PPT 6.1b** to review with the class after groups have answered the question.

APPLY THE SKILLS

Students should test their learning by tackling **Q7** individually. When they have finished, ask them to use the 'Check your progress' points to assess their progress in identifying and selecting information according to the question focus.

> **Extra support:** Point out that the answers are in the final paragraph of the text.
>
> **Extra challenge:** Encourage students to focus on the implied meaning in the wording of the final paragraph. The language is slightly informal, indicating humour: 'no one overly concerned' (like 'not that bothered'; 'slapped him around' (very casual); 'if he didn't die by knock-out it would probably be through drowning' (comically ironic exaggeration).

TAKING IT FURTHER	As an exercise on an alternative focus, students could summarise in their own words 'what the wrestlers wear and how it features in the wrestling'. (They wear a turban, and 'the baggy trousers of their *shalwar kameez*' tucked up, leaving their legs free for grappling with their opponent. The *sundhro* is the only thing they wear that plays an active role in the wrestling – although you could argue that wearing relatively little is also relevant to the wrestling: they would get hot and possibly tear their clothes if they wore more.)

Chapter 6: Summary writing

6.2 Selecting and ordering main points

Resources:
- Student's Book: 6.2, pp. 146–149
- Workbook: 6.2, pp. 107–108 can be set as homework
- Worksheet 6.2
- PowerPoint slides 6.2a–d

Assessment objectives:

R5 Select and use information for specific purposes

EXPLORE THE SKILLS

Explain that the 'main point' of this lesson is for students to learn what a 'main point' is. With this in mind, read through the *Rough Guide* text with students. Ask them to pick out a main point in each paragraph, then go on to read the 'Remember' bullet points with them. Alternatively, show them the bullet points on **PPT 6.2a**.

Students should consider the bullet points in pairs. Discuss any issues over the given answer (the third bullet point is the main one).

Check that students understand the paragraph which precedes **Q1** on page 147 of the Student's Book, commenting on how less important details are sometimes included as subordinate clauses, within commas. Something within parentheses would be even more clearly a less important point – perhaps an explanatory one.

Students could work on **Q1** and **Q2** in pairs. For **Q1**, they should conclude that 'deep, slender fjords gouged by glaciers' is not relevant to what attracts tourists (unless they have a special interest in geology). For **Q2**, they should choose 'characterful old villages'.

Extra support: Ask students whether the north–south orientation of the lakes or the narrowness of their beaches would attract tourists. (Answer: no.)

BUILD THE SKILLS

The next stage consists of summarising details within a main point, and asking whether a particular explanation is important enough to be a main point.

Read the continuation of the text with students. Students could then tackle **Q3** and **Q4** in pairs. The answers for **Q3** are a) 'other cities' and b) 'the many cultural variations/distinctions'.

Extra challenge: Ask students to think of other details that might have been included in the account and that could be grouped together in a summary. For example: types of bird or other wildlife; types of boat on the lake; individual types of Italian food in the restaurants. 'Fishing, boating, water-skiing and swimming' could be grouped together as 'leisure pursuits'.

For **Q4**, students should conclude that people feeling 'more loyalty to their home town than to the nation as a whole' is unlikely to qualify as a main point, in that it will probably not attract visitors, whereas 'cuisines, dialects and outlooks' is more likely to do so.

DEVELOP THE SKILLS

Read out the introduction to this section and check that students grasp the idea. It may not be obvious at first that there could be a better order in which to summarise an aspect of the text than the order of the text itself.

Chapter 6: Summary writing

Extra support: It is worth emphasising that students should 'aim to demonstrate an overview… not just summarise one bit at a time'. Students could even practise summarising from memory, as this will get them away from the 'one line at a time' approach.

Q5 is a good task for students to work on in small groups. One approach would be to write the items on separate slips of paper and attempt to arrange them physically into groupings, then write down the words or phrases to do so.

Below is one possible way to group items. Some could be summarised by a generic term. For example, 'beautiful landscapes, beautiful lakes, lush vegetation' could become 'natural beauty'. Others could be combined in a concise sentence, as in, 'Good weather makes it possible to enjoy a variety of outdoor activities'.

- lots of play areas, theme parks, variety of watersports, good weather
- food and drink, local variations
- beautiful landscapes, beautiful lakes, lush vegetation
- ferries, possible to avoid crowds, horse-riding and cycling routes through woodland
- city–country contrast, art and architecture, interesting villages.

Students could continue in groups to work on **Q6**. The order of importance for families might be:

1. lots of play areas
2. variety of watersports
3. good weather
4. theme parks
5. horse-riding and cycling routes through woodland
6. food and drink
7. beautiful lakes
8. beautiful landscapes
9. possible to avoid crowds
10. ferries
11. interesting villages
12. art and architecture
13. city–country contrast
14. local variations
15. lush vegetation

APPLY THE SKILLS

Read the text with the class, or ask students to read it on their own as more of a test of their skills. Students could then work individually or in pairs on **Q7** and **Q8**.

If students choose to follow the suggestion of addressing 'enjoyable' and 'interesting' in turn, the points, in order, could be:

- varied and ruggedly beautiful landscape
- good locally varied cuisine
- music
- festivals
- interesting people
- evidence of long history
- many cultural influences.

Extra support: Students could begin by establishing what each paragraph is broadly about.

Extra challenge: Ask students to write a 100-word summary based on their ordered points.

TAKING IT FURTHER	Students could undertake **Worksheet 6.2**, summarising a text about tourism in Tokyo. **PPT 6.2b–d** provides unsorted main points, a completed summary, and a rationale for ordering the summary. For further challenge, you could ask students to devise and justify a different order, and then rewrite the summary.

Chapter 6: Summary writing

6.3 Writing a summary

Resources:
- Student's Book: 6.3, pp. 150–153
- Workbook: 6.3, pp. 109–111 can be set as homework
- Worksheet 6.3
- PowerPoint slides 6.3a–d

Assessment objectives:
R1 Demonstrate understanding of explicit meanings
R2 Demonstrate understanding of implicit meanings and attitudes
W2 Organise and structure ideas and opinions for deliberate effect
W3 Use a range of vocabulary and sentence structures appropriate to context

EXPLORE THE SKILLS

Begin by showing a video clip of Laura Dekker, such as the *National Geographic* excerpt (4 m 53 s) from a documentary on YouTube. This will serve as an introduction to the text in the Student's Book. Then read the text with the class. See whether there are any reactions to the story from the class, before moving on.

Extra support: If there are words that some students do not understand, rather than just explaining them, encourage students to work out their meaning from the context. They can do this by thinking of what word or phrase could be substituted in the sentence for the one they do not understand, and then reading the whole sentence to see how likely this possible meaning is. For example, in the first sentence, 'chronicles' has to be a verb. From the rest of the sentence, it could not mean 'criticises', and, as the film is a documentary, it is likely to mean 'tells the story of'.

Students should work in pairs to answer **Q1**, which is about working out meaning from context. The correct answer is 'entangled'. Explain why the other meanings could not be right.

Students could then apply their contextual skills to further words and phrases, such as:

➢ 'rite of passage' (a ceremony, test or ordeal marking a move from one stage of life to the next, especially childhood to adulthood)
➢ 'montage' (in a film, a section composed of several shots and short sequences collectively representing a whole period of time)
➢ 'traverse' (cross)
➢ 'succinctly' (they should definitely understand this in order to write summaries!)

Focus on what kinds of meanings these might have, perhaps using a process of elimination. For example, bearing in mind that the text is a film review, and Schlesinger is the director, 'montage' is likely to be a part of the film that could last five minutes.

Read out the explanatory text and the exam-style question on page 151. You could get students to shut their books at this point and ask them to think of points that could be made in response to this question. Write them on the board, then tell students to reopen their books and read the suggested list and compare theirs with it.

Next, consider the sentence 'At 14 Dekker became the youngest ever solo circumnavigator'. Give students a minute or so to work out answers to **Q2** in pairs (**a**) it combines the first two points; **b**) a 'circumnavigator' is someone who sails round the world). You could also point out that 'solo' replaces 'alone'. You could show students **PPT 6.3a** which displays the text in colour-coded form to help explain this.

© HarperCollins *Publishers* Ltd 2018

Chapter 6: Summary writing

BUILD THE SKILLS

This section looks at two keys ways to write more concisely: omission or replacement of words, and grouping together of examples. Students could work in pairs and then feed back to the class. Answers are as follows:

Q3 'ten-month' could be replaced by 'long', or lengthy, or just left out; 'before the trip' could become 'pre-trip' ('pre-trip legal battle').

Q4 The fourth bullet point could become **a)** 'She received insults and ill wishes online'; **b)** 'She received online abuse'.

> **Extra challenge:** Give students **Worksheet 6.3**, or show **PPT 6.3b** and **6.3c** to tackle the worksheet sentences as a class.

DEVELOP THE SKILLS

Remind students what a complex sentence is. Point out that a complex sentence can often make two or three points in fewer words than two or three simple sentences. Read the bullet points as a class and compare them. Point out that the second two are both shorter (14 words each), but the third bullet point is more fluent because it is a single sentence, with its smooth flow only interrupted by one comma.

Students could work in small groups to experiment with different ways to combine all the points in a sentence for **Q5**. (Suggested answer: *We learn that at 16, after overcoming legal issues and online abuse, and spending two years at sea, Laura Dekker became the youngest ever solo circumnavigator.*)

> **Extra support:** Tell students to look back at the text to see what two things Laura Dekker had to overcome, what she spent (it was not money) and what she became by breaking the record.
>
> **Extra challenge:** Ask students to try to combine the five bullet points in **Q5** without using the gap-filling sentence provided.

APPLY THE SKILLS

Draw students' attention to the focus of the question: 'What do we learn about Laura Dekker?'. They could undertake the whole task individually, or work in pairs or groups to make a list of points, then write their summaries individually. Possible points:

- youngest ever solo circumnavigator
- determined (overcomes obstacles; completes trip)
- independent outsider
- open-hearted
- confident
- critical of conventional life
- interested in other cultures
- technically capable
- prone to loneliness
- sensitive
- learns to be alone
- becomes attuned to the sea.

At the end of the lesson, get students to assess their progress using the 'Check your progress' bullets.

> **Extra support:** Show students the **PPT 6.3d**, which provides the points above.

TAKING IT FURTHER	To write effective summaries, students need to select information accurately and thoroughly, then summarise it in a concise manner. For further practice in selecting information, students could write a 60–100-word summary based on the review, this time focusing on 'what we learn about the film *Maidentrip* and the reviewer's views on it'. The aim should be to exclude information that is just about Laura Dekker.

Chapter 6: Summary writing

6.4 Practice questions and sample responses

Resources:
- Student's Book: 6.4, pp. 154–157
- Workbook: 6.4, p. 112 can be set as homework
- Worksheet 6.4
- PowerPoint slides 6.4a–b

Assessment objectives:
R1 Demonstrate understanding of explicit meanings
R2 Demonstrate understanding of implicit meanings and attitudes
R5 Select and use information for specific purposes
W2 Organise and structure ideas and opinions for deliberate effect
W3 Use a range of vocabulary and sentence structures appropriate to context
W5 Make accurate use of spelling, punctuation and grammar

YOUR TASK

A sample task has been included to give your students an opportunity to practise the style of task set in Paper 1, Question 1. You may decide to set this as a formal assessment or to complete the process in class, with teacher support. **Worksheet 6.4** reproduces the task should you wish to set it as formal assessment. **PPT 6.4a–b** include the Assessment objectives and the tasks to share with the class.

Remind students of the key skills tested by this question (the relevant Assessment objectives).

If you want to mirror examination conditions, you could allow about 25 minutes for students to complete the task.

Extra support: Emphasise to students that there are two parts to the question – the plans for reintroduction, and the arguments in favour. Note that they do not need to include arguments *against* reintroduction, or indeed their own views on either side.

EXPLORING RESPONSES

The Student's Book offers two sample responses designed to represent sound achievement (Response 1) and excellent achievement (Response 2) for this question. Depending on the ability range of your class, you may want to work with the actual mark scheme for this question, which is available on the Cambridge website. A student-friendly checklist has been provided on page 158 of the Student's Book.

Students could work to add their own annotations to these responses before completing **Q1** and looking at the commentaries and feedback provided in the Student's Book.

Having worked with the sample responses, identifying areas for improvement and seeing what each response has done well, students should annotate their own response with similar comments, or – if appropriate – redraft it in light of what they have learned from the process.

Chapter 7: Analysing language

7.1 Identifying synonyms and literal meanings

Resources:
- Student's Book: 7.1, pp.160–161
- Workbook: 7.1, pp. 113–114 can be set as homework
- Worksheet 7.1
- PowerPoint slide 7.1

Assessment objectives:

R1   Demonstrate understanding of explicit meanings

EXPLORE THE SKILLS

Using the Student's Book, explain the importance of using synonyms to help show understanding of a text.

> **Extra support:** Give students **Worksheet 7.1**, which contains some extra activities to consolidate understanding of synonyms.

Read the text and answer **Q1** as a class, referring to the 'Top tip' to explore how mistakes could be made.

Using **PPT 7.1**, go through the scaffolded example of how to work out the meaning of the word 'dodging'. Then ask students to work in pairs on **Q2**, using a similar process. Take responses, which might include: 'continually', 'regularly', 'repeatedly' and so on.

BUILD THE SKILLS

Ask students to complete **Q3** individually, then take feedback as a class. The answers are:

a) 'glancing backwards'   b) 'determinedly'   c) 'sped up'   d) 'paused momentarily'

DEVELOP THE SKILLS

Using the Student's Book example of the word 'tapping', explore the importance of precision when explaining the meaning of words.

Ask students to complete **Q4** in pairs, then take feedback. Responses might include:

a) with difficulty, he got around (the defenders); he worked hard to get by (the defenders), and so on
b) (the ball) moved at speed; (the ball) moved quickly, and so on.

> **Extra challenge:** Ask students to come up with more than one phrase. Discuss which one they feel is the most precise and why.

APPLY THE SKILLS

Ask students to complete **Q5** individually, then take feedback as a class. Responses might include:

a) immediately; straightaway and so on   b) ran as fast as he could
c) closing in, threateningly; getting dangerously near

Ask students to use the 'Check your progress' points to assess their work and identify areas for improvement.

TAKING IT FURTHER	Each week, students could text each other a sentence of a book they are reading, and challenge the recipient to explain a specific word or phrase in it.

Chapter 7: Analysing language

7.2 Explaining the suggestions that words can create

Resources:
- Student's Book: 7.2, pp. 162–163
- Workbook: 7.2, pp. 115–116 can be set as homework
- PowerPoint slides 7.2a–b
- Dictionaries and thesauruses

Assessment objectives:
R2 Demonstrate understanding of implicit meanings and attitudes
R4 Demonstrate understanding of how writers achieve effects and influence readers

EXPLORE THE SKILLS

Read the extract in the Student's Book, followed by the exploration of the phrase 'punched the air in triumph'. Remind students how important it is to use their own words when writing about language. As a class, complete **Q1**. The final response might read: *The phrase shows that Etebo felt excited and proud so he wanted to celebrate.*

BUILD THE SKILLS

Using **PPT 7.2a–b**, complete **Q2** as a class (the answers are **a)** first bullet point and **b)** second bullet point). Highlight the fact that in both parts, the third bullet points are technically correct, but they repeat words from the original phrase.

Extra challenge: During feedback, ask students to justify their choices through reference to specific words and their meanings.

DEVELOP THE SKILLS

Ask students to complete **Q3** and **Q4** in pairs before taking feedback. Answers might include:

➢ Etebo took pleasure from everyone's recognition; Etebo enjoyed being in the spotlight and so on.
➢ Etebo was determined to stop the efforts of the other team; Etebo was resolved that their rivals wouldn't succeed, and so on.

Extra support: Allow some pairs to use a dictionary or thesaurus to aid their understanding.

APPLY THE SKILLS

Ask students to complete **Q5** independently and then take feedback. Reponses might include:

a) they were full of anticipation; the crowd were astonished by the shot and so on
b) the spectators were overjoyed; the crowd went wild with happiness and so on
c) they eagerly shouted encouragement; they roared passionately with approval

TAKING IT FURTHER	Students could select, at random, a page of a fictional book that they are reading, choose a quotation about a character, and then – using their own words – explain what that character is feeling.

© HarperCollins Publishers Ltd 2018

Chapter 7: Analysing language

7.3 Identifying the writer's craft

Resources:
- Student's Book: 7.3, pp. 164–167
- Workbook: 7.3, pp. 117–119 could be set as homework
- Worksheet 7.3a–b
- PowerPoint slides 7.3a–d

Assessment objectives:

R1 Demonstrate understanding of explicit meanings

R2 Demonstrate understanding of implicit meanings and attitudes

R4 Demonstrate understanding of how writers achieve effects and influence readers

EXPLORE THE SKILLS

Using the Student's Book, explore what we mean by the 'writer's craft'.

Students should read the extract from *The Beach* and complete **Q1**, **Q2** and **Q3**. **Worksheet 7.3a** contains the text and questions for students to annotate if they need to. Please note that reference is made to a non-metric measurement in the extract. Ten feet is approximately equal to three metres.

Extra support: Direct students to particular sections of the text: 1a) paragraph 1; 1b) paragraph 3; 2a) paragraphs 1 and 2; 2b) paragraph 1.

Extra challenge: Encourage students to evaluate their findings in **Q1** and **Q2** (not just **Q3**), considering which of their verbs, nouns, adjectives and adverbs has the most impact and why.

Take feedback from the class. Encourage students to explain their choices by verbalising what each word adds to the overall scene being described in the extract. Responses might include:

1. a) coast, cliffs, gorges, barrier, peaks, jungle, razors, spray (These words give a clear picture of the landscape, particularly its size and the obstacles that the travellers will face when exploring.)
    b) jagged, strange, dense, Jurassic, exotic, tiny, brown; strangely, suitably (Many of these words emphasise how unusual the landscape is.)
2. a) hoping, tried, wasting, picked, sliced, push, stopped (These words suggest difficulty through a sense of effort, disappointment, and physical challenge.)
    b) impassable, hardest, dense (These words emphasise the difficulty by suggesting physical barriers and effort.)
3. a) picked; b) barrier; c) precious; d) goal

BUILD THE SKILLS

Remind students of the three main types of imagery, showing them **PPT 7.3a–b**, if necessary. These include definitions and a task identifying simile, metaphor or personification.

Put students in pairs to work on **Q4**. Use **PPT 7.3c** to display the task. Gather feedback from pairs, then display the answers on **PPT 7.3d**.

DEVELOP THE SKILLS

Ask students to work individually on **Q5**, using the four parts of the task to explore the effect of the phrase 'trees like rusted, ivy-choked space rockets'.

Chapter 7: Analysing language

Take feedback as a class. Responses should include:

a) simile (and some personification)
b) the size; the trees' height and width; the narrator is impressed or awed
c) 'rusted' describes the colour and texture of the bark as well as suggesting how old the trees are
d) the ivy seems to be abundant and is smothering the trees; the personification makes it seem threatening

As a class, reread the second paragraph of the extract from *The Beach*. Using **Worksheet 7.3b**, students should complete **Q6** in pairs.

Take feedback. There are a variety of possible answers, but responses might include:

- The superlative adjective 'hardest' shows how difficult their journey was.
- The simile 'sliced like razors' makes the surrounding vegetation sound dangerous and shows that the narrator's journey is, at times, painful.
- The verb phrase 'push through' shows that the travellers had to put a lot of effort into exploring the island; the verb 'push' shows that they had to physically withstand the sharp leaves of the bushes.
- The simile 'fanned from the trunk like stabiliser fins' emphasises how large and impressive the trees are; the verb 'fanned' shows how the roots spread out across the ground, creating another obstacle.
- The noun 'canopy' suggests that the branches overhead are creating a roof of vegetation which would make the jungle seem darker and more sinister.
- The noun phrase 'dense spray' shows how the bamboo spread outwards to create another obstacle.

APPLY THE SKILLS

As a class, reread the last paragraph of the extract from *The Beach*, then ask students to work independently completing **Q7**.

> **Extra support:** Encourage students to use their notes on **Worksheet 7.3b** as a model to help scaffold their four answers. Ensure that students focus on the last paragraph; perhaps begin by directing them to the first two sentences of the last paragraph.
>
> **Extra challenge:** Suggest that students choose words and phrases that allow them to comment on different techniques used by the writer.

Ask students to get into small groups to share their work. As a group, they should agree on the most effective word and the most effective phrase to describe the narrator's emotions before feeding back to the rest of the class. Possible responses might include:

- The verb 'disappointed' shows that the jungle wasn't quite as impressive as he expected.
- The simile 'like I was walking through an English forest' helps to explain his disappointment that the jungle doesn't look really unusual.
- The metaphor 'shrunk to a tenth of my normal size' shows he is impressed by the scale of the jungle.
- The adjective 'exotic' suggests that he liked that some features of the jungle were strange to him.
- The noun phrase 'Tarzan-style lianas' suggests that the plant life made the jungle exciting because he felt like he was in a movie.
- The pattern of three verbs 'dripped... flattened... stuck' shows that the dripping water made him uncomfortable.
- The alliterated noun phrase 'good gulps' suggests that he was very thirsty and enjoyed taking a drink.

Ask students to use the 'Check your progress' points to evaluate their work.

TAKING IT FURTHER	Encourage students to choose a page from any fictional book that they have enjoyed reading and to pick out words and phrases that are effective in setting the scene or showing what characters are feeling. Emphasise how students should select what they feel are the most effective words and phrases, apply subject terminology and explain their choices.

Chapter 7: Analysing language

7.4 Analysing the writer's craft

Resources:
- Student's Book: 7.4, pp. 168–169
- Workbook: 7.4, pp. 120–123 can be set as homework
- Worksheet 7.4
- PowerPoint slides 7.4a–b

Assessment objectives:
R2 Demonstrate understanding of implicit meanings and attitudes
R4 Demonstrate understanding of how writers achieve effects and influence readers

EXPLORE THE SKILLS

Reread the extract from *The Beach* on page 164 of the Student's Book. Then, as a class, read through the 'Top tip' on page 168 to establish how to effectively analyse the writer's craft.

Use **PPT 7.4a–b** to complete **Q1** together, exploring how the example of analytical writing has been structured using point, evidence, analysis and further development.

BUILD THE SKILLS

Highlight the importance of specificity when analysing. Explain to students that they need to focus on the *effect* of individual words and phrases, rather than just explaining the *meaning* of a quotation or describing what it is about. Although meanings are a part of this explanation, they are not enough on their own.

Students then complete **Q2** in pairs. **Worksheet 7.4** could be used to allow students to annotate and assess the two examples of analytical writing, as well as to secure the concepts of point, evidence, analysis and further development.

Take feedback as a class. Responses might include:

➢ Although the first example is shorter, it is the strongest response. While more concise, it is also more detailed in terms of analysis.

➢ The first example uses specific terminology (such as 'verb phrase' instead of simply 'the words') as part of the analysis.

➢ The effect of the language used is much more specific in the first example (such as 'suggests he is getting frustrated' rather than just 'to show how he feels').

➢ Both examples contain some development by focusing on a different word from the quotation and considering its effect.

➢ However, while the first example uses the development successfully, the second example does not maintain its focus on how language is conveying the narrator's feelings (explaining how 'precious' describes the hours of the day, as opposed to exploring the mood of urgency that it creates in order to show the narrator feels that time is running out).

DEVELOP THE SKILLS

Referring to the Student's Book, ask the class to look back on the work they did in Topic 7.3 exploring the description 'trees like rusted, ivy-choked space rockets'. Then ask students to work independently, completing **Q3** with the help of the four key prompts for successful analysis.

Extra support: Students could work collaboratively in pairs, using **PPT 7.4b** as a model to help scaffold their work.

Extra challenge: Encourage students to develop their paragraph further by selecting and analysing another quotation about the trees in the extract from *The Beach*.

Chapter 7: Analysing language

Once their responses are complete, students should get into pairs or small groups to peer assess their paragraphs. Ask them to look back at **Worksheet 7.4** to remind themselves what made the first example better. Students should make a constructive comment about each other's work, considering:

➢ conciseness, focus and specificity
➢ analytical detail
➢ use of subject terminology.

Ask each pair or small group to decide whose paragraph was the most successful and share it with the rest of the class.

APPLY THE SKILLS

Reread the last paragraph of the extract on page 164. Then ask students to complete **Q4** independently, making sure that at least one of their three choices is an example of imagery.

Take feedback as a class. There are lots of possible choices, but responses might include:

➢ 'Jurassic' is a powerful adjective, suggesting how the narrator expected ancient, lush, and possibly huge vegetation.
➢ The metaphor 'shrunk to a tenth of my normal size' emphasises the massive scale of the jungle and how the narrator feels almost intimidated by his surroundings.
➢ 'Exotic' is a powerful adjective to show how parts of the jungle seems wonderfully strange and foreign.
➢ 'Scurrying' is a powerful verb to convey how the small limbs of the monkeys move so quickly.
➢ The simile 'like stalactites' is a good way to show how the lianas hang from the canopy of the jungle and seem particularly strong.
➢ 'Soaked' is a powerful verb to get across how much water collected in the trees of the jungle and was dripping onto the narrator.

Ask students to use the 'Check your progress' points to evaluate their work.

TAKING IT FURTHER	Each week, encourage students to select a random page from a fiction book that they are reading and to identify its most powerful individual word and its most powerful use of imagery. They should practise writing up their findings up in a paragraph, clearly identifying and analysing the effects achieved by their chosen word and phrase.

Chapter 7: Analysing language

7.5 Practice questions and sample responses

Resources:
- Student's Book: 7.5, pp. 170–175
- Workbook: 7.5 pp 124–126
- Worksheets 7.5a–b
- PowerPoint slides 7.5a–d

Assessment objectives:

R1 Demonstrate understanding of explicit meanings

R2 Demonstrate understanding of implicit meanings and attitudes

R4 Demonstrate understanding of how writers achieve effects and influence readers

YOUR TASK

A sample task has been included to give your students an opportunity to practise the style of task set in Paper 1, Question 2. You may decide to set this as a formal assessment or to complete the process in class, with teacher support. **Worksheet 7.5a** reproduces the task should you wish to set it as formal assessment. **PPT 7.5a–d** include the assessment objectives, key skills and the task to share with the class.

If you wanted to mirror examination conditions, you could allow about 40 minutes for students to complete the task.

EXPLORING RESPONSES

The Student's Book offers two sample responses designed to represent sound achievement (Response 1) and high achievement (Response 2) for this question. Depending on the ability range of your class, you may want to work with the actual mark scheme for this question, which is available on the Cambridge website. A student-friendly checklist has been provided on page 176 of the Student's Book.

The first set of responses have been reproduced without annotations on **Worksheet 7.5b**, so students could work to add their own annotations before completing **Q5–Q8** and looking at the commentaries and feedback provided in the Student's Book.

Having worked with the sample responses, identifying areas for improvement and seeing what each response has done well, students should annotate their own response with similar comments. If appropriate, they could redraft them in the light of what they have learned from the process.

Chapter 8: Extended response to reading and directed writing

8.1 Understanding extended response to reading questions

Resources:
- Student's Book: 8.1, pp. 178–181
- Workbook: 8.1, pp. 127–131 can be set as homework
- Worksheet 8.1
- PowerPoint slides 8.1a–f

Assessment objectives:
R1 Demonstrate understanding of explicit meanings
R2 Demonstrate understanding of implicit meanings and attitudes
R3 Analyse, evaluate and develop facts, ideas and opinions, using appropriate support from the text

EXPLORE THE SKILLS

Read through the example extended response to reading question from page 178 of the Student's Book. Draw attention to the **who** you are as the writer of the task (Alfredo), **what** you are creating (persuasive letter to business partner) and **why** you are writing (to persuade your business partner that a guided tour is a good idea).

Q1 asks for the key information missing from the annotations. Display **PPT 8.1a**, which highlights the important information and point out that the annotations have missed the word count and marks for the quality of writing. Explain to students that they need to be aware of how much they must write, and that they need to manage their time carefully in order to do this. They also need to be aware of the quality of their writing and constantly be checking their spelling, punctuation and grammar.

Use **PPT 8.1b** to introduce F-PAT – an acronym that can help students check that they have understood what they are being asked to do in an extended to response to reading question. Talk through what each of the words means in general terms and then explain that in case of the specific task they are looking at in the Student's Book:

➢ **Form** is a letter
➢ **Purpose** is to persuade
➢ **Audience** is their business partner
➢ **Tone** is semi-formal (based on the start they have been given).

Hand out **Worksheet 8.1** to give students an opportunity to use F-PAT with a different task, then check that everyone has annotated their worksheet correctly:

➢ Form is an email
➢ Purpose is to persuade their uncle to fund the start-up costs of a new business venture
➢ Audience is their uncle, a local businessman
➢ Tone is semi-formal (they are addressing a family member about an investment opportunity).

DEVELOP THE SKILLS

Read Text A together as a class. Display **PPT 8.1c** and work through the example of F-PAT on it, pointing out how you know the form, purpose, audience and tone for this piece of writing. Then read **Q2** together. Help students identify that the writer is not Alfredo – we know this from the sentence that mentions *the author* is *his friend*. For part **b)** discuss as a class what kind of text this is. You could agree with diary, journal, letter, but draw students to think about travel writing captured as a novel, which gives a vivid picture of a particular place at a particular time.

© HarperCollins *Publishers* Ltd 2018

Chapter 8: Extended response to reading and directed writing

Extra support: Use **PPT 8.1d** to show some quotations from Text A and talk through the tone they create. Help students to see that Alfredo is the expert here and the writer is not very confident, realising that Alfredo knows what he is doing. The writer's tone is such that he acknowledges he is in an unfamiliar situation, and is handing control to Alfredo.

Then display **PPT 8.1e** and go through the highlighted examples in the paragraph, which describes the situation the writer then finds himself in (overwhelmed by the sight of *45,000 people*). He is surprised by the crowd of people and how they looked crammed in to the strange vessel. Support students to see the compliant tone that the writer uses here. He is happy to be guided by his friend through this strange but fascinating place.

APPLY THE SKILLS

Read the task in **Q3** together, then ask students to copy it out and annotate it. Give students 15 minutes to complete their annotations. Display the 'Checklist for success' from page 181 of the Student's Book on **PPT 8.1f** so that students can refer to it while annotating the task.

When everyone has finished, ask students to work with a partner to compare annotations. They should have identified:

➢ Form is an interview
➢ Purpose is to describe the experience of the match
➢ Audience is a reporter
➢ Tone is informal because they need to convey the excitement of being at the match
➢ Word count
➢ Marks available.

TAKING IT FURTHER	Students who are comfortable using text for different purposes should try using increasingly challenging situations. For example:
	You are a cleaner, working in the stadium after the game has finished. Write an email to your boss about the amount of work you had to do when cleaning the different places that you were assigned to:
	➢ *the balcony*
	➢ *the entrance and exit*
	➢ *the Suns*
	➢ *the Shades.*
	Explain what you found difficult in 250 to 300 words.

Chapter 8: Extended response to reading and directed writing

8.2 Extended response to reading: gathering information

Resources:
- Student's Book: 8.2, pp. 182–183
- Workbook: 8.1, pp. 127–131 can be set as homework
- PowerPoint slides 8.2a–b

Assessment objectives:
R1 Demonstrate understanding of explicit meanings
R2 Demonstrate understanding of implicit meanings and attitudes

EXPLORE THE SKILLS

Read the information and the annotated task at the start of the 'Explore the skills' section on page 182 of the Student's Book. Put students into pairs to discuss how the format of the question directs them to key features that they need to include. Most students should identify the bullet points as the main helping feature. Then read through the table and ask pairs to copy and complete it for **Q1**.

BUILD THE SKILLS

Display **PPT 8.2a** to model an analysis for the second bullet point, drawing out the three different experiences:

➢ the Suns (*it was jammed*)
➢ the Shades (*better dressed and almost as crowded*)
➢ the Balcony people (*folding chairs and a good view*)

Ask students to copy the table and add more detail to the boxes with the quotations in response to **Q2**, identifying who the people are and what this means, and how their experiences differ. They should identify the following:

➢ for the Suns, the experience is of being squashed into a small space where thousands experience the match together
➢ for the Shades, there is a bit more space and people are a bit more careful
➢ fhe Balcony people, in contrast, have seats and can see the game clearly.

DEVELOP THE SKILLS

Read the information here, making sure that all students are clear about what 'inference' means using the annotated example. Introduce the idea of making 'educated guesses' when reading and inferring from a text. Then work through each part of **Q3** asking questions to get students thinking about whether or not the inferences are reasonable:

a) How reasonable is it that the balcony people hate the Suns? Could it be 40% likely? Are the balcony people likely to be thinking about the Suns?
b) How reasonable is it that the Suns hate the Balcony people? Is that more likely or less? Decide together 60%.
c) How reasonable is it to think that Balcony people are privileged? Is that 80%?
d) Is it fair to think that Balcony people are excited by watching the Suns more than the football? Does that make it about 20%?
e) Is it likely that the Balcony people don't like football? 0%?

© HarperCollins *Publishers* Ltd 2018

105

Chapter 8: Extended response to reading and directed writing

Extra support: Ask targeted students to make more simple inferences about the text before they tackle the ones in **Q3**. For example:

➢ What does 'We were frisked' imply about security? Answer: *It was taken very seriously and security guards acted like policemen.*

➢ What does 'It was an ant hill' suggest about conditions? Answer: *It looked like they were being forced to act like insects.*

APPLY THE SKILLS

Display the third bullet point from the task on **PPT 8.2b**. Read the introduction to this section in the Student's Book, then discuss briefly what we might be able to infer from the text about what tourists will learn or experience from going to a match, drawing out the following:

➢ the different ways that different people are treated

➢ the costs that some people are able to spend

➢ the excitement and the importance of the 'pristine rectangle of green grass'.

Ask students to write brief notes in the empty boxes as modelled on **PPT 8.2a**.

Then ask students to work in pairs or small groups to find the evidence for the two statements in **Q4**. For **a)** they should look at the descriptions of the people and identify 'a tureen filled with brown screeching faces'. For **b)** they should be looking at the final five lines, which describe the people who watch from outside the stadium.

For **Q5**, support students to read between the lines of 'It was, those 45,000 people, a model of Salvadorean society'. Ask students to think about how Paul Theroux feels about what he sees. Ask whether we can infer that he is:

➢ appalled by the divisions between the different groups of people

➢ pleased to see how excited everyone is waiting for the match to begin

➢ upset by the excesses enjoyed by the privileged members of the Balcony people.

Ask students how the ticket prices ($2000 for a season ticket) emphasise the writer's feelings. ('In a country where the per capita income was $373' highlights the poverty which exists beside the excesses seen at the football game.)

Ask students to review the 'Check your progress' points on page 183 of the Student's Book and decide whether they have made sound progress or excellent progress.

TAKING IT FURTHER	Students with highly developed inference skills can benefit further from reading at greater depth. Support students to stretch their skills by making inferences from the following sentences: ➢ *The multicultural extravaganza made us all proud to be a part of this city.* ➢ *It was so much better when I was a young boy.* ➢ *People were turning up to work with smiles on their faces for the first time.*

Chapter 8: Extended response to reading and directed writing

8.3 Extended response to reading: developing a convincing role

Resources:
- Student's Book: 8.3, pp. 184–187
- Workbook: 8.2, pp. 132–134 can be set as homework
- PowerPoint slides 8.3a–b

Assessment objectives:
R3 Analyse, evaluate and develop facts, ideas and opinions, using appropriate support from the text
W1 Articulate experience and express what is thought, felt and imagined
W3 Use a range of vocabulary and sentence structures appropriate to context
W4 Use register appropriate to context

EXPLORE THE SKILLS

As a class, read through the information in this section, exploring the skills required when adopting a role. Emphasise the difference between behaviour (the way someone acts, often dictated by circumstances) and character (someone's personality and generally consistent traits regardless of the situation they are in).

Explain that role-play is often the first step to creating a convincing role and can be most effective when they 'really get inside the head' of a character that is unlike them. As a class, discuss the roles students may have played either at school or outside it. What did they learn about the character by becoming him/her? Is there a character they have read about that they would like to know more about?

For **Q1**, students could discuss the roles in pairs.

a) Ask students to think about the life of a taxi driver living in a busy city: would he feel stressed, exhilarated, frazzled, or constantly defeated?

b) Would a new young waitress be excited, unsure, embarrassed or enthusiastic? Or all these things?

Extra challenge: Ask students to think about the narrators that could have told the story of the El Salvador football match. Encourage depth and flexibility by creating scenarios such as someone having a bag stolen during the match, or being separated from their friends in the crowd.

BUILD THE SKILLS

Read through the bullet points in this section, getting students to think about the questions that can help build a solid mental image of a character. Introduce the idea of the character of a ticket tout at the football match and review the table on page 185 of the Student's Book, using **PPT 8.3a**, discussing how the notes help develop a rounded, usable character. As a class, talk about the missing inference required for **Q2** and work together to come up with a sentence written in character. For example:

➢ *I feel proud of the fact that hundreds of people see the football game because of me. I do not like the fact that people doubt my honesty.*

Students could work alone or in pairs to copy and complete the stick man and build the character of the ticket tout and his life for **Q3**. Afterwards, they should move on to **Q4**, creating a similar diagram for one of the 'Balcony' people. Draw a stick man on the board and take class feedback, noting information, inferences and ideas. Ensure that all inferences are based on quotations from the text:

➢ *Balcony people had season tickets.*

➢ *Balcony people had small rooms, cupboard sized, about as large as the average Salvadorean hut: I could see wine bottles, the glasses, the plates of food.*

➢ *Balcony people had folding chairs and a good view of the field.*

Chapter 8: Extended response to reading and directed writing

DEVELOP THE SKILLS

Explain to students that the link between voice and character must be clear, and that they must weigh up what is realistic each time that words are spoken. Read the bullet points and the 'Key terms' panel to ensure that students understand what 'jargon' and 'slang' mean and how they relate to informal language.

Students should work on **Q5** in pairs. The answers are (with clues in bold):

- child → 'Can I have a drink? Please, **daddy**! I'm so hot! Please!'
- footballer → 'Well, it was tough but **we** held out – great save by Marco – so **we're** still in with a chance of the Cup, which is great.'
- reporter → 'After an **uneventful** first half, the match **came to life** on 52 minutes when Ribeiro saved the penalty.'
- ticket seller → 'Four for the West Stand? Right, that will be **forty dollars please**.'

For **Q6**, read the extracts together and elicit that although all three extracts match the role of a ticket tout, the third extract most closely matches the character of Alfredo, because it shows the same personality traits we have seen in Paul Theroux's writing.

Moving on to **Q7**, support students to match evidence with inference as below:

- He warns Paul about his security. → He is worried for Paul's safety as a friend and a tourist.
- He 'jumped the queue' and 'elbowed forward' to get the tickets. → He could be seen as a leader or someone who takes responsibility.
- His friends 'marvelled' at his ability to do so. → He is determined, and perhaps slightly ruthless?
- He knows which tickets to get – not the Suns, but the more expensive Shades. → He might not have much money, but considers the event worth the extra cost.
- He tells Paul 'such a match' would never be seen in his own town, Santa Ana. → He is very excited by the experience, which is special for him too.

Students should discuss **Q8** in small groups. Remind them that he uses short, direct sentences, he seems to be confident and he is likely to talk about football games and football players.

APPLY THE SKILLS

Students should work independently to plan and write their response in **Q9** under exam conditions. Display the 'Checklist for success' on **PPT 8.3b** for students to refer to while they are writing.

Ask individuals to review their work and, using the progress criteria from the Student's Book, to consider how well they have done and what they need to do to improve.

TAKING IT FURTHER	Students need to focus on the 'voice' of the character, perhaps using a greater range of punctuation and variety of sentence lengths to demonstrate excitability. Ask students to create a conversation between Alfredo (short, direct sentences) and Paul (longer, more complex sentences) using a full range of punctuation as in Text A.
	Paul: I could not believe there was not an empty seat visible; not anywhere.
	Alfredo: I know. Everyone feels the same. We will never see such a game in Santa Ana.

Chapter 8: Extended response to reading and directed writing

8.4 Extended response to reading: structuring a response

Resources:
- Student's Book: 8.4, pp. 188–191
- Workbook: 8.3, pp. 135–137 can be set as homework
- PowerPoint slides 8.4a–h

Assessment objectives:

W2 Organise and structure ideas and opinions for deliberate effect

W3 Use a range of vocabulary and sentence structures appropriate to context

W4 Use register appropriate to context

EXPLORE THE SKILLS

As a starter, ask students to look at **PPT 8.4a**, which shows the text for an advert in a shop window selling a second-hand bike. Then show them **PPT 8.4b**, which shows the advert with the task. Point out that this task is similar to the 'Extended response to reading' task, in that it involves adapting given information for a particular purpose.

Then run through the questions on **PPT 8.4c** with the class, focusing on the skill of adapting information for a new purpose. Draw out the following ideas:

➢ The main aim of writing would be to thank her.

➢ It would make the grandmother happy to know her money had been spent on something worthwhile.

➢ Perhaps just the fact that the bike is 'beautiful', 'lightweight' and has '16 gears' – these are easy points for a non-specialist to appreciate.

➢ For 'responsive steel frame' you might say 'flexible but strong'; for 'all-season tyres' you might say 'I'll be able to ride it all year'.

Now tell students to refresh their memory of the main task, given in the Student's Book, and of the work they did in Topic 8.2, gathering the information in the bullet points. Explain that they will now need to organise this in letter format, as outlined in the bullet points beginning with the salutation: *Dear Raul*.

Help the class to consider **Q1** as a whole group. Discuss the type of language needed when writing to Raul (informal, but focused on business). Compare this with how they might have written the thank you letter to a grandmother. Ask what sort of phrases they might use in writing to Raul. For example, which of these might they say?

➢ I have a business proposal for your consideration that may be of mutual benefit. (too formal)

➢ I've got this cracking idea for making us both a shed-load of money! (too informal)

➢ I have what I think is a great business idea, and I hope you like it too. (just right!)

BUILD THE SKILLS

You could read the text below **Q2** aloud to the class, then tell students to copy it out and work in pairs to annotate it to show how the bullet points above **Q2** have been achieved.

When all students have finished, show the annotated version on **PPT 8.4d**, and discuss how exactly how the points have been achieved, and what other versions might also work. For example, the final sentence could begin, 'And how amazing it's going to be for them …'.

For **Q3**, students will need to refer to the original text on Student's Book pages 179-80, and the second bullet point in the task: 'the different ways to experience the match'. They could work in pairs or individually and then compare their answers.

Chapter 8: Extended response to reading and directed writing

Take feedback. Compare the students' completed persuasive sentences with these suggested answers, also given in **PPT 8.4e**:

a) Suns tickets – *don't worry, I'll ensure tourists don't have these because… they're too noisy*.

b) Shades tickets – *these are perfect because… they'll be quieter and tourists will prefer to be in the shade – especially those not used to the heat*.

c) Balcony tickets – *these are good, but… they're only available as expensive season tickets*.

For **Q4**, students should work individually to write a further paragraph using the bullet-point model given here.

> **Extra support:** Offer the writing frame on **PPT 8.4f**, and then show the completed version on **PPT 8.4g**.

DEVELOP THE SKILLS

The third bullet still needs to be dealt with, and it is the most demanding in some ways because there are not many links to draw out of the text. For **Q5**, students need to reread the text carefully and use their inference skills. They will need plain paper to copy out and complete the spidergram. They could tackle this individually, but another good option is to have them work in groups with a sheet of A3 paper, each adding ideas in turn. Stress that the ideas should be inferred from the text – not just made up.

Use **PPT 8.4h** to show what can be inferred from just a little given information. Encourage students to find more examples – draw out that the tourists will be in among a huge cross-section of Salvadorean society, seeing how it is divided socially and how Salvadoreans behave on an occasion like this. There is no mention of other tourists. One can infer from this that tourists will get an authentic, truly Savadorean experience, not one prepared specially for the tourist trade.

> **Extra challenge:** Ask what the tourists might learn about Salvadorean society, based on phrases such as 'it looked like a kettle' and 'about as large as the average Salvadorean hut'.

APPLY THE SKILLS

Students should now individually write a full plan and draft their response, referring to the 'Checklist for success' and 'Check your progress' boxes on Student's Book page 191. When all have finished, students could peer-assess using these boxes.

TAKING IT FURTHER	Students will give a more effective response by making use of appropriate conventions from writing to argue/persuade, but must also show evidence of using inference based on the given material to shape their own response.
	Ask students to draft a letter to the chairman of the football club, persuading him to invite disadvantaged children to the next big game, providing them with balcony seats – perhaps sponsored by their usual occupants.

Chapter 8: Extended response to reading and directed writing

8.5 Understanding directed writing questions

Resources:
- Student's Book: 8.5, pp. 191–195
- PowerPoint slides 8.5a–d

Assessment objectives:

R1 Demonstrate understanding of explicit meanings

R2 Demonstrate understanding of implicit meanings and attitudes

R5 Select and use information for specific purposes

EXPLORE THE SKILLS

Referring back to the sample extended response to reading task in Topic 8.1, remind students of the importance of annotating the task to identify all the key elements. Recap on F-PAT (Form, Purpose, Audience and Tone) and how this helps keep the response to the task focused while writing. For **Q1**, model matching the key elements of the question to the essential features, shown in **PPT 8.5a**.

BUILD THE SKILLS

Draw students' attention to the focus of Paper 2's approach to directed writing – for example, the fact that they will have to integrate information from more than one text, and also transpose ideas and content from the stimulus texts into a different writing form.

Look at the extract from Text A in the Student's Book with the class and check that they all understand the significance of the highlighted parts. Define, with examples: 'viewpoint', 'alternative points' and 'evidence'.

Explain that they might find it helpful to use three different colours to highlight each element in this way. They should highlight the parts of the text that they will use. The starts of the extracts are on **PPT 8.5b–c**, which colour-code viewpoint (red), alternative view (blue), and evidence (green).

Read through the two stimulus texts provided ('Pandas – worth saving?' and 'A love affair with nature') with the class. Pause after each to get the class's initial reactions to them, and for some ideas about the main ways in which the two texts differ. Students should then read the texts silently and make their own notes on them as they go, following the model ('The writer believes …').

Extra challenge: Use strict time limits, such as two minutes for each extract in the Student's Book, to really hone the use of skills under pressure.

DEVELOP THE SKILLS

Tell students to work in pairs to complete the table for **Q3**, comparing the key points from each text. This is a good opportunity for them to compare their notes for each paragraph in the two passages and help each other to find contrasting points.

Use **PPT 8.5d** to show example comparisons. Ask students what views or ideas can be inferred from any of these points. For example:

➢ Conservation has 'limited resources': there must be pragmatic choices; there is not enough money available to save every species.

➢ I don't want the panda to die out: but it may be inevitable, or even a lesser evil than the losses of habitat or other species that could be saved by spending less on pandas.

➢ We spend millions and millions of pounds on pretty much this one species: perhaps we spend too much on pandas at the expense of other animals.

The key point here is that it is not possible to respond at a high level without drawing inferences from the texts of the kind dealt with earlier in the chapter.

Chapter 8: Extended response to reading and directed writing

> **Extra support:** Help students to develop their skills of inference by asking what the statements given above might mean. For example:
>
> ➢ Conservation has 'limited resources': if he is saying we spend millions on pandas, what is this statement likely to mean?
>
> ➢ I don't want the panda to die out: this on its own would be a very obvious thing for a conservationist to say, so perhaps he is implying a 'but ...',
>
> ➢ We spend millions and millions of pounds on pretty much this one species: what does his wording imply – that it is not enough?

APPLY THE SKILLS

Allow students a few minutes for further discussion of the conservation issues in the passages before they complete **Q4** individually, producing just one paragraph summarising *their* viewpoint. Advise students to collect evidence from the text first then shape *their* viewpoint from the evidence using the table.

Point out to them that the original task did not indicate whether the campaign was good or bad, and so this is something they will need to decide on before they plan and write their answer.

Ask pairs to compare their completed paragraphs.

You may then wish to set completion of either one further paragraph, or the whole article, for homework.

TAKING IT FURTHER	Students could research, plan and write another piece exploring two sides of a controversy, perhaps an animal-related one, such as the question of whether zoos benefit animals or are simply for the entertainment of human beings, or the controversy of whether animals such as the lynx should be reintroduced to habitats in which they lived before being made locally extinct: see Student's Book page 154.

Chapter 8: Extended response to reading and directed writing

| 8.6 | **Directed writing: analysing and evaluating texts** |

Resources:
- Student's Book: 8.6, pp. 196–197
- Workbook: 8.5, pp. 139–142 can be set as homework
- Worksheet 8.6
- PowerPoint slides 8.6a–e

Assessment objectives:

R1 Demonstrate understanding of explicit meanings

R2 Demonstrate understanding of implicit meanings and attitudes

R3 Analyse, evaluate and develop facts, ideas and opinions, using appropriate support from the text

R5 Select and use information for specific purposes

EXPLORE THE SKILLS

Ask students to discuss, in pairs, what it means when a writer *implies* something, and what is meant by *inferring*. When students have had a chance to think about this, take feedback. Draw out that to 'imply' is to hint at or suggest a meaning, and 'inferring' is deducing (working out) what that meaning is.

Focus students on the sentence under 'Explore the skills'. Check that students understand the concept of an 'intensifier' and ask what other words could have been used instead of 'extraordinarily' (really, vastly, hugely). Ask the class why they think the writer begins the sentence with 'The truth is'. Possible answers:

➢ He wants to flag up that this is an uncomfortable truth that conservationists do not want to hear.

➢ He wants to focus the reader on this fact.

➢ He wants to suggest that pandas are not worth all that money.

Ask students to work in pairs on the two examples in the table, drawing out the effect of 'Of course' and 'fluffy' then 'entranced' and 'gentle'. Point out that they should say whether they agree or disagree with what is *implied*, not just the basic statement.

Take feedback, drawing out:

➢ Text A implies a criticism of people who are led to donate to save an animal just because it is looks appealing: the word 'fluffy' suggests that they are childish.

➢ Text B implies that there is something wonderful and therefore valuable in the child's fascination with the panda, and that this makes saving pandas worthwhile.

BUILD THE SKILLS

Synthesis is about combining, summarising, and drawing out a new point from this. For **Q2**, discuss the process with the class using **PPT 8.6a** and ask for further examples of ideas from the two texts that could be synthesised.

One possible pair of statements to compare and synthesise is:

➢ Text A: 'I think pandas have had a valuable role in raising the profile of conservation, but perhaps 'had' is the right word.'

➢ Text B: '… if it is a cuddly panda that grabs my attention, then what's wrong with that?'

Extra support: Use **Worksheet 8.6** to go over the three steps to synthesis. Students could work in groups of three, with individuals focusing on one of the 'combine', 'summarise' or 'create' stages.

© HarperCollins *Publishers* Ltd 2018

Chapter 8: Extended response to reading and directed writing

DEVELOP THE SKILLS

Explain to students that evaluation means weighing up the worth or validity of something – in this case an argument or part of one. Does it make sense? Is there any evidence to support it? Once these questions have been answered, you can make a judgement.

Read the paragraph about tiger conservation to the class with appropriate emphasis and check that they understand the significance of the annotations. One way to do this is to see whether they can provide alternative words or phrases that achieve similar effects. For example:

➢ captivated – seduced, impressed, won over
➢ proud tiger – the majestic tiger
➢ unique – unmistakable
➢ honest judgements – realistic/unsentimental judgements
➢ visual appeal – good looks

These are shown on **PPT 8.6b**.

You could also see whether students can think of other ways of saying 'I agree' or 'I disagree'. For example:

➢ I wholeheartedly/completely/entirely agree.
➢ I believe that he is right to say…
➢ I cannot agree that…
➢ I utterly disagree
➢ I dispute the view that…
➢ The view that… makes no sense.

These are shown on **PPT 8.6c**.

Ask students to attempt **Q3** individually and then compare their attempts in pairs. They should peer-assess to see whether a) they have shown clear disagreement, and b) they have used at least two of the given 'disagreement' phrases.

Display **PPT 8.6d**, which shows the paragraph agreeing with Packham, then **PPT 8.6e** to show how the change in focus can be made. Note how:

➢ 'I disagree with Chris Packham' is used
➢ 'visual appeal' becomes 'iconic appearance'
➢ 'surely' is again used in a rhetorical question.

APPLY THE SKILLS

For **Q4**, ask students to revisit the notes they made they made on Texts A and B in Topic 8.5. They should have a number of paired sentences from the two texts, which they should now turn into evaluative sentences.

Encourage all to aim for at least five evaluative sentences.

They should then revisit the 'Check your progress' box on Student's Book page 197.

You may then wish to allow some students to complete the whole article for homework, if they feel confident.

TAKING IT FURTHER	Students could research other conservation controversies, such as whether it is right to kill off successful invasive species in order to protect native species.
	One example is the grey squirrel (introduced to the UK from North America) and the native red squirrel. Grey squirrels are trapped and killed in areas of northern England to protect the red squirrel population. Another example might be wild boar in the Forest of Dean Gloucestershire, in England. If your school is not in the UK, you will probably have your own examples.
	Students should attempt to find opposing viewpoints and synthesise them, leading to them concluding with their own view.

Chapter 8: Extended response to reading and directed writing

8.7 Directed writing: structuring your response

Resources:
- Student's Book: 8.7, pp. 198–201
- Workbook: 8.6, p. 143 can be set as homework
- Worksheet 8.7
- PowerPoint slides 8.7a–d

Assessment objectives:
W2 Organise and structure ideas and opinions for deliberate effect

EXPLORE THE SKILLS

Tell students to read the task again, reproduced under 'Explore the skills'. Challenge them to find elements of it that they had forgotten, or about which they do not yet feel confident.

Remind students of the lists of points that they made in Task 3 of Topic 8.5. If any student does not have this list with them for any reason, they could work in a pair and use someone else's list as a starting point, but they will still need to refer back to Texts A and B (Student's Book pages 193-195).

Explain that they are now at the point of deciding how to organise their points into an integrated piece of extended writing, and that there are three main ways in which they could do this. They should read the three options carefully. Then organise students into groups of three. Tell them to take it in turns to take one method and attempt to explain to the other two students exactly how it would work, and what its advantages might be.

Take feedback on this. Draw out that:

➢ *Option 1* divides the points up into two – agree and disagree. It requires the student to make a clear distinction between the two. This might be a problem if they feel very undecided.

➢ *Option 2* is the most integrated approach, requiring the student to identify from the start what views the writers have in common – for example, that they both love animals and want species to survive.

➢ *Option 3* is probably the most straightforward as it allows the student to work through Text A, then Text B. However, this will not necessarily lead to the best piece of writing.

Ask students to read the plan in **Q1** in their groups and try to decide which approach it follows. After a couple of minutes, share with them that it uses Option 2, starting with the most important common area. Take feedback on how well they think it would work for them. They should now make an initial decision on which approach to take. Reassure them that they can still change it later.

BUILD THE SKILLS

Students should read the introductory text and the colour-coded paragraph and annotations. Tell them to look back at Text B and see whether they can find where the writer makes the point summarised in this paragraph. Take feedback, inviting one or more students to read out what they think is relevant. Confirm that this point is made in paragraph 3 of Text B.

Students should work on **Q2** individually but allow them to compare their ideas. Note: they should copy the paragraph in the order that they think works – not copy it as it is and then try to organise it (though they could do this if working on a computer). Then show them one possible restructured version of the paragraph in **PPT 8.7a**. Get students to identify how it conforms to the structure in the colour-coded and annotated paragraph.

Extra support: Hand out **Worksheet 8.7** and some scissors. This enables students to cut up the four sentences and reorder them, so they will not need to copy them out. (There are two identical sets on the sheet.) Invite them to finish the sentence: *They need to know the reality about...* in their own way.

© HarperCollins *Publishers* Ltd 2018

115

Chapter 8: Extended response to reading and directed writing

DEVELOP THE SKILLS

Point out that this section looks at the *form* of the writing required by the task: it is for a speech, and the way that a speech is worded differs from the way an article is worded. Ask students for ideas about how and why this is the case. Draw out that when people listen, they only have one chance to take in what is being said, and cannot reread a sentence they missed or did not understand. Also, the speaker is addressing the audience in person, so there is more reason to give a personal anecdote, or use the first person more obviously ('In my opinion…') or address the audience directly ('You're all intelligent people…').

For **Q3**, students should work individually and then compare their ideas in small groups. This will give them a chance to try out some of their sentences on a small audience and see how they sound and how well they are received.

When students have finished, share **PPT 8.7b**. This uses direct address ('We all know that…'), personal perspective ('I watched my own children…'), imagery ('the zoo's new royalty'), and an intensifier ('vehemently').

> **Extra challenge:** Ask students to use one of the following to further improve their paragraph, then ask for peer assessment:
> - personification
> - simile
> - alliteration
> - onomatopoeia
> - rhetorical questions
> - assonance.

APPLY THE SKILLS

Students should now make a final choice as to which method of organisation they will use (see under 'Explore the skills'). **Q4** asks them to choose a point from Texts A and B not yet covered in the topic and write a paragraph based on it, with the help of the reminders in the bullet points given here.

As an example of points from the texts that they could use, show students **PPT 8.7c** (taken from **PPT 8.5c–d**). When they have completed their paragraphs, have some students read theirs out. Then show **PPT 8.7d** and discuss with them how effective they think it is.

TAKING IT FURTHER	Students could build on the writing they have done so far for this topic to produce a complete speech. You could organise a time for some or all students to deliver their speeches to the class. They could even be used in a formal debate.

Chapter 8: Extended response to reading and directed writing

8.8 Practice questions and sample responses: extended response to reading

Resources:
- Student's Book: 8.8, pp. 202–207
- Workbook: 8.4, p. 138 can be set as homework
- Worksheets 8.8a–b
- PowerPoint slides 8.8a–b

Assessment objectives:

R1 Demonstrate understanding of explicit meanings

R2 Demonstrate understanding of implicit meanings and attitudes

R3 Analyse, evaluate and develop facts, ideas and opinions, using appropriate support from the text

W1 Articulate experience and express what is thought, felt and imagined

W2 Organise and structure ideas and opinions for deliberate effect

W3 Use a range of vocabulary and sentence structures appropriate to context

W4 Use register appropriate to context

W5 Make accurate use of spelling, punctuation and grammar

YOUR TASK

A sample task has been included to give your students an opportunity to practise the style of task set in Paper 1, Question 3. You may decide to set this as a formal assessment or to complete the process in class, with teacher support. **Worksheet 8.8a** reproduces the task should you wish to set it as formal assessment. **PPT 8.8a–b** include the Assessment objectives and the task to share with the class.

Remind the class of the key skills tested by this question (the relevant Assessment objectives).

If you wanted to mirror examination conditions, you could allow about 40 minutes for students to complete the task.

EXPLORING RESPONSES

The Student's Book offers two sample responses designed to represent sound achievement (Response 1) and excellent achievement (Response 2) for this question. Depending on the ability range of your class, you may want to work with the actual mark scheme for this question, which is available on the Cambridge website. A student-friendly checklist has been provided on page 214 of the Student's Book.

These responses have been reproduced without annotations on **Worksheet 8.8b**, so students could work to add their own annotations before completing **Q2** and looking at the commentaries and feedback provided in the Student's Book.

Having worked with the sample responses, identifying areas for improvement and seeing what each response has done well, students should annotate their own response with similar comments, or – if appropriate – redraft them in light of what they have learned from the process.

Chapter 8: Extended response to reading and directed writing

8.9 Exam-style questions and sample responses: directed writing

Resources:
- Student's Book: 8.9, pp. 208–213
- Workbook: 8.7, p. 144 can be set as homework
- Worksheets 8.9a–b
- PowerPoint slides 8.9a–b

Assessment objectives:

R1 Demonstrate understanding of explicit meanings

R2 Demonstrate understanding of implicit meanings and attitudes

R3 Analyse, evaluate and develop facts, ideas and opinions, using appropriate support from the text

R5 Select and use information for specific purposes

W1 Articulate experience and express what is thought, felt and imagined

W2 Organise and structure ideas and opinions for deliberate effect

W3 Use a range of vocabulary and sentence structures appropriate to context

W4 Use register appropriate to context

W5 Make accurate use of spelling, punctuation and grammar

YOUR TASK

A sample task has been included to give your students an opportunity to practise the style of task set in Paper 2, Section A. You may decide to set this as a formal assessment or to complete the process in class, with teacher support. **Worksheet 8.9a** reproduces the task should you wish to set it as formal assessment. **PPT 8.9a–b** include the Assessment Objectives and the task to share with the class.

Remind the class of the key skills tested by this question (the relevant Assessment objectives).

If you wanted to mirror examination conditions, you could allow about one hour for students to complete the task.

EXPLORING RESPONSES

The Student's Book offers two sample responses designed to represent sound achievement (Response 1) and excellent achievement (Response 2) for this question. Depending on the ability range of your class, you may want to work with the actual mark scheme for this question, which is available on the Cambridge website. A student-friendly checklist has been provided on page 214 of the Student's Book.

These responses have been reproduced without annotations on **Worksheet 8.9b**, so students could work to add their own annotations before completing **Q2** and looking at the commentaries and feedback provided in the Student's Book.

Having worked with the sample responses, identifying areas for improvement and seeing what each response has done well, students should annotate their own response with similar comments, or – if appropriate – redraft them in light of what they have learned from the process.

Chapter 9: Composition

9.1 Understanding composition tasks

Resources:
- Student's Book: 9.1, pp. 216–217
- Worksheet 9.1
- PowerPoint slides 9.1a–b
- Coloured pencils or highlighters
- Optional: mini whiteboards

Assessment objectives:

W1 Articulate experience and express what is thought, felt and imagined

W2 Organise and structure ideas and opinions for deliberate effect

W3 Use a range of vocabulary and sentence structures appropriate to context

W4 Use register appropriate to context

W5 Make accurate use of spelling, punctuation and grammar

EXPLORE THE SKILLS

Read through the opening paragraph on Student's Book page 216 carefully with the class, making sure that everyone is clear about the requirements of a composition task. In particular, ensure that students understand that they have only to write in response to **one** task from the total of four tasks on offer (two writing forms with two choices in each).

As a starter activity, put students into pairs and display **PPT 9.1a**, which gives suggestions for identifying a descriptive or a narrative task. Go through these together, then display the two paragraphs on **PPT 9.1b** and ask students to identify whether they are likely to be responses to a descriptive task or a narrative one. Encourage students to justify their answers, giving examples of language that helped them decide. They should then complete **Q1** in their pairs. They should identify that a) is descriptive (contains the word 'describe') and b) is narrative (contains the word 'story').

BUILD THE SKILLS

Ask students to comment on which writing style they prefer. They may like to pick one area to focus on. The key thing is to choose the task that will best allow them to express their ideas and 'show off' their language skills. Explain that this does not necessarily mean picking the 'easiest' task – they may have difficulty if they find they have nothing relevant to write about.

Remind students that different types of writing have different conventions. Review the relevant information in Chapter 4 if necessary. Ask students to complete **Q2** in pairs. Answers for 'good descriptive writing' might include:

- **Structure:** detail is organised and precise, paragraphs follow a logical and engaging sequence; includes a gripping surprise or shocking first section; starts with the ending in a flashback sequence or referring to memory; central character may become the protagonist; the storyline may take a surprising turn.

- **Style:** stylistic devices used to create vivid imagery; focus on the small details of a character's face as well as the larger details such as setting to create a clear and imaginative image in the readers mind.

Extra challenge: Ask a student to describe a chair in the classroom. Then you describe it:

> *The chair looked simple enough but the wood knew stories you wouldn't believe.*

Ask students how the two descriptions compared. Discuss how you can come at a description from a different angle to make it more interesting to the reader.

Chapter 9: Composition

DEVELOP THE SKILLS

Review the information in Topics 4.9 and 4.10 to recap on the key features of descriptive and narrative writing if you think it would be helpful at this point. As a class, read through the process described in the panel on page 217 of the Student's Book. Focus on Stage 2 in particular, exploring why it is important that they choose the question that will best show off their skills.

Refer back to the questions in Task 1:

- Describe an occasion when two people meet for the first time.
- 'Although it was almost midnight, I heard the sound of footsteps approaching our house. I opened the door…'. Use these two sentences to start a story.

> **Extra support:** Explain to students that they need to think creatively about the opportunities the tasks give to include original ideas, language and thinking. They should not just look for what appears to be the most straightforward task. They may be able to write most effectively about an event that has happened to them. Have a brief class discussion to exemplify this. Imagine the task was: 'Although it was almost midnight, I heard the sound of footsteps approaching our house. I opened the door…'. Ask students whether they can draw inspiration from a time in which they themselves were scared. Get them to describe those feelings.

For **Q3**, put students into small groups and ask them to discuss which of these tasks they would choose. They should be able to justify their choice to other members of the group, referring to the criteria in the process panel.

APPLY THE SKILLS

Once they have selected their task, students need to ensure that they have fully understood what it involves before they start planning their answer. Explain that they should allocate a small amount of time to reviewing the talk by highlighting the key words. This will help focus their planning and, ultimately, their full written answer.

As a class, look at the highlighted example in the Student's Book, and the annotations that unpick the key elements in the task. Remind them that they are looking for instruction and context: *what* they have to do and *how*. Then give students **Worksheet 9.1** and ask them to highlight and annotate their selected task in the same way. They should identify the following key features:

- **Descriptive:** Describe an occasion when two people meet for the first time
- **Narrative:** 'Although it was almost midnight, I heard the sound of footsteps approaching our house. I opened the door…' Use these two sentences to start a story.

When they have practised on the tasks they looked at earlier in this topic, ask students to use **Worksheet 9.1** to complete **Q4** individually.

Ask students to assess their progress using the 'Check your progress' points in the Student's Book.

TAKING IT FURTHER	Show students old exam papers and ask them to highlight the key terms and explain to a partner how they would respond to the question. Generate discussion of ideas for responses. Do students prefer to continue a sentence or be given a topic? Why? Consolidate the lesson by ensuring that all students would be able to respond to an exam-style question.

Chapter 9: Composition

9.2 Planning ideas for a descriptive task

Resources:
- Student's Book: 9.2, pp. 218–219
- Workbook: 9.1 pp. 145–147 can be set as homework
- PowerPoint slides 9.2a–d

Assessment objectives:

W1 Articulate experience and express what is thought, felt and imagined

W2 Organise and structure ideas and opinions for deliberate effect

W3 Use a range of vocabulary and sentence structures appropriate to context

W4 Use register appropriate to context

W5 Make accurate use of spelling, punctuation and grammar

EXPLORE THE SKILLS

Building on the examples from the last lesson, students will now begin to plan ideas for a descriptive task and order them effectively. When presented with an exam-style question, it is important that they know exactly what they are being asked to do. Using **PPT 9.2a**, remind students of the work completed last lesson by reviewing the task and the highlighted key terms. Ensure that students remember that they need to demonstrate:

- an understanding of conventions
- a good range of ideas
- complex and sophisticated writing.

Remind them that good descriptive writing is lively, engaging and detailed. So in this task, for example, they may like to think about the perspective of the customer and the manager, or how other customers are responding to the situation as it unfolds.

Ask students to complete **Q1** individually. You could display **PPT 9.2b**, which shows the task and some tips to get them started.

For **Q2**, students should work individually to develop their ideas using the spider diagrams in the Student's Book as a starting point. Remind students that this task requires them to focus on the descriptive elements. If they are struggling to come up with additional points for the diagrams, give them some direction:

- Unhappy customer: harassed-looking mother, perhaps, with child in buggy; tense, disappointed, ready to argue
- Sights and sounds: the shop could be dirty and disorganised; boxes everywhere

Ask students to copy and complete the table in **Q3** to develop their ideas further. As students are creating their tables, circulate and offer advice where necessary to ensure that their second paragraph develops the ideas from the first suitably.

Extra support: Use **PPT 9.2c–d** here for support. Explain that visualising a scene will help them describe it in more detail. Review the rules for role-plays on **PPT 9.2c**, then put students in groups of three. Two students should quickly role-play a situation in which a customer complains about a digital camera that has broken. He/she has already had to have it replaced once. However, it is out of warranty and the assistant won't replace it. The third member of the group should make notes about the body language of the customer and the shop manager that could be used in a piece of descriptive writing. Their task will be to observe closely (hands, face, position of body and tone of voice). **PPT 9.2d** provides a starting point for their role-play if they need it.

Chapter 9: Composition

For the role-play to work, and to help students focus on details, the 'performers' will need to use:

- variety of tone, pitch, and speed when speaking
- gesture and movement that fits the situation and their role.

Ask the class how role-playing the situation makes writing a response easier. What did they notice?

BUILD THE SKILLS

Move on to the new descriptive task in **Q4**: 'Describe a summer afternoon in the park'. Ask students for their initial thoughts about such a scene and note them on the whiteboard. Many students will come up with ideas for a warm, idyllic scene. Remind them that the best responses are original and creative, and ask them to consider alternative responses to this task – for example:

- a summer afternoon that turns into a thunder storm of epic proportions
- a scene involving a runaway goat
- a description of the dinner table at a family gathering
- the scene in the sick room at school on a busy day.

Ask students to discuss their ideas further in pairs, then complete **Q4** on their own.

DEVELOP THE SKILLS

Read the text about word associations and explain that this can be used as a planning tool. In groups of four, students should come up with word associations for **Q5**. They should add one word each. More able students might like to choose their own descriptions. Responses might include:

a) children with football – shouting – angry faces – ball goes over the wall – beyond the wall is magical garden

b) water fountain – bright sunlight – coin dropped in to make a wish

c) old men playing chess – leaves fall from trees – quiet – beautiful, hand carved pieces – old speckled hand

Now ask students to consider how they could make their description more interesting, considering the bullet points in **Q6**. They should make notes, which will help them decide which idea they want to select and develop in response to **Q7**.

Remind them to 'think outside of the box' – for example, it is important to use adventurous and engaging language. Think about the example of a plain brick. Is this an exciting thing? Point out that a more interesting description would be: 'a slab of stone as cold and as hard as the fossilised shopkeeper himself'. This example is both engaging, unexpected and has the added bonus of using a language device. Can students think of their own example in order to make a plain, old door more interesting?

APPLY THE SKILLS

Students should now read **Q8** and begin generating ideas for a response in the form of a spider diagram or the method they find most useful for planning.

Extra challenge: Go back to the original question: Describe a scene in which a customer complains to a shop manager about an item he or she has bought. Drawing on the skills students have acquired so far, ask them to spend 15 minutes writing a response at home. A creative response to this could be a sketch of the shop as students see it in their mind, labelled with interesting descriptions.

TAKING IT FURTHER	Ask students to analyse examples of descriptive writing. Travel writing examples can be found on the internet.

9.3 Structuring description creatively

Resources:
- Student's Book: 9.3, pp. 220–223
- Workbook: 9.3, pp. 150–152 can be set as homework
- Worksheet 9.3
- PowerPoint slides 9.3a–b

Assessment objectives:
W1 Articulate experience and express what is thought, felt and imagined
W2 Organise and structure ideas and opinions for deliberate effect
W3 Use a range of vocabulary and sentence structures appropriate to context
W4 Use register appropriate to context
W5 Make accurate use of spelling, punctuation and grammar

EXPLORE THE SKILLS

Ask students to look at the task: 'Describe someone's impressions of a new town or city', then ask them what the key words are. As a class, read through each bullet point so that students understand they can approach their answer through time or place. Ask students to discuss each point with a partner in order to generate ideas. Stop students for feedback or visit pairs and ask for their responses. Note ideas that show flair or use of language devices on the board for other students to refer to.

Ask students to read the plan at the bottom of page 220, then work in pairs to answer **Q1**. They should recognise that it follows a chronological sequencing pattern. Ask students what the benefits of such a structure might be, and elicit the ideas that it is logical, interesting, easy to follow and makes the description easy to visualise.

Students should now use the skills built to respond to **Q2**. They should be able to identify that the next paragraph would be in the evening.

BUILD THE SKILLS

Read the opening to the 'Build the skills' section, which discusses how structure relates to the focus of a piece of descriptive writing. For example, students could move from focusing on a whole scene to zooming in on a small detail. To illustrate this, you could discuss the following technique:

➢ person from a distance → close up of arm → close up of hand → close-up of fingerprint

To get students thinking about the focus of descriptive writing, have a class discussion. Display **PPT 9.3a**, which contains two descriptions. Ask two students to read them aloud, then build the discussion around the following questions:

➢ Which focus do you prefer here and why?
➢ How does focusing on specific details engage the reader?
➢ From the details given, what do you assume about the woman being described?
➢ Which description paints her more negatively and why?
➢ Why is changing around detail and sequences a useful tool in descriptive writing?
➢ What three things could you take from this description to make your descriptions more interesting?

Hand out **Worksheet 9.3** and ask students to complete it in light of the discussion.

Now return to the Student's Book and review the annotated example paragraph on page 221 together, making sure that students understand the effect of the annotated features. Ask students to work in pairs to write a paragraph following a similar structure for **Q3**.

Chapter 9: Composition

They should move on to **Q4** in their pairs, reading the paragraph and identifying the listed features (1a, 2b, 3c, 4d, 5e).

Display **PPT 9.3b** as a visual aid for **Q5**, then ask students to answer the question in their pairs. They should find that the can of fizzy drink is zooming in, the student on the bike is panning from one side to another and that sun coming up is the long shot framing one thing.

> **Extra challenge:** To focus students' minds on the camera technique, ask them to stand up and imagine they are holding a camera. Call out camera shots and ask them to physically demonstrate the angle or move. Give them 'scenes' to choose suitable shots for:
> - a tear falling from an eye
> - a bird in the sky
> - a scene in a busy café
> - a prison guard taking in a new inmate
> - water running from a shower head, down a wall to the drain.

For **Q6**, students need to put together their ideas to create their own paragraph. They may like to plan it out visually first by folding a piece of paper into eight and adding a camera angle and description for each section.

DEVELOP THE SKILLS

Read the prepositions in the table to the class, explaining how they help us to identify time and place, then ask students to answer **Q7** (**a**) 'through'; **b**) 'in' and 'at; **c**) 'before') and **Q8**.

Read the information about the use of conjunctions in descriptive writing on page 223. Explain how they can help prevent a piece of descriptive writing drifting into narrative. Ask students to rewrite the two sentences in **Q9**, adding conjunctions (for **a**) they may choose 'and' or 'but'; for **b**) 'as').

APPLY THE SKILLS

Refer students to the 'Checklist for success' before they start writing in response to **Q10** to help them plan their description. Give students a few minutes to read back through their work from the previous three lessons. You may like to set this as an exam-style task, written in silence.

> **Extra support:** Students may like to work in groups for the final activity, and plan responses together.
>
> **Extra challenge:** When completing the descriptive task, encourage students to include metaphor, simile or emotive language.

TAKING IT FURTHER	Ask students to look again at the description they wrote for **Q10**. Can they now add more focus? Can they play around with the order and time to make the description more engaging to the audience? Ask students to cut up their examples and reorder the description. They can add additional sentences and conjunctions on another sheet of paper and stick the description back together like a jigsaw. This method helps visual learners as well as actively demonstrating how descriptions need planning carefully. Remind students to use the *'camera method'* technique. Stick examples on the wall as they are finished and encourage students to get up and walk around to read these examples. Which description was their favourite and why?

Chapter 9: Composition

9.4 Using the senses and imagery in descriptive writing

Resources:
- Student's Book: 9.4, pp. 224–225
- Workbook: 9.2, pp. 148–149 can be set as homework
- Worksheet 9.4
- PowerPoint slides 9.4a–d

Assessment objectives:

W1 Articulate experience and express what is thought, felt and imagined

W2 Organise and structure ideas and opinions for deliberate effect

W3 Use a range of vocabulary and sentence structures appropriate to context

W4 Use register appropriate to context

W5 Make accurate use of spelling, punctuation and grammar

EXPLORE THE SKILLS

Using the information on page 224 of the Student's Book, introduce students to the idea of imagery and how to use simile and metaphor to create pictures in the reader's mind. Read the examples of simile and metaphor and then set **Q1** for students to discuss in pairs. Take class feedback. To get students thinking about using similes themselves, display **PPT 9.4a** and ask for ideas to complete the four similes. Note down some of the most creative ideas. Have a brief class discussion about the effect of using similes and other imagery. How might they improve a narrative? How might the reader respond to these images? Elicit the idea that they create a more vivid image in the reader's mind, engaging them and making them want to read.

Extra challenge: Ask students to come up with some of their own similes and add them to the list on **PPT 9.4a**.

BUILD THE SKILLS

Ask students to look at the example of poor imagery at the start of this section in the Student's Book. Discuss why the simile here does not work – 'hoarse' and 'flowing like honey' are contradictory. Display **PPT 9.4b–c** and discuss as a class which option works best for the simile and the metaphor (for the simile it is 'golden waterfall' and for the metaphor, it is 'dagger'). Then put students in pairs to answer **Q2**:

a) The customer's angry words hit the manager like a *sharp whip*.

b) His powerful serve crossed the net like a *missile*.

For **Q3**, Students should discuss options for completing the imagery and come up with an option for each. Take feedback and note some of the best examples on the board for reference during the writing task at the end of the lesson.

DEVELOP THE SKILLS

Using the Student's Book, explain that good writers link their images in a fluid and convincing way to create an overall effect. Read the extract on page 225 as a class, then ask students to complete **Q4** in pairs. The answers are:

a) Similes: 'like a huge, silver brooch', 'like miniature diamonds', 'like the richest prince on earth'; metaphors: 'The moon… was an enormous locket', 'the sky's dark neck'.

b) The images appeal mainly to the sense of sight, but the passage also appeals to the sense of touch ('a cool mist').

c) The overall comparison links the night scene to jewellery and precious stones.

Chapter 9: Composition

Read the next descriptive paragraph and, as a class, agree on the answer to **Q5** ('I was like a tiny leaf swept up in a huge, unstoppable storm').

Extra challenge: Give students **Worksheet 9.4** and ask them to complete the table. This asks them to identify techniques, come up with suitable imagery and comment on its effects.

APPLY THE SKILLS

For **Q6**, students need to write their own description of 100–125 words. You may want to break this task up into stages:

➢ Put students in pairs and ask them to describe a delicious feast to each other verbally (for example, *bowls of warm, dark chocolate with tiny biscuits on the side*).

➢ Through discussion, students could think of an image from an unknown town or city to link with this (for example, *a lake surrounded by houses*).

➢ They could then connect the setting with the feast on paper to start developing the description independently (for example, *It was late, the moon shone on the lake reflecting its light and reminding him of the bowls of dark chocolate he'd eat with his Grandma, the houses like the tiny biscuits he'd used to dip. He approached the lake with caution…*).

Remind students of the work they did on perspective in Topics 9.2 and 9.3 to ensure they make their writing as interesting as possible.

When students have finished writing, ask them to swap their books with their partner and peer assess each other's work using the 'Checklist for success' on **PPT 9.5d**.

Extra support: Students could create a word bank to be used in lessons following the '**good, better, best**' ideology. This can then be used to the advantage of all students. It also models a more effective way of describing detail. For example:

➢ **good** – *warm*

➢ **better** – *as warm as bath water* (use of simile here)

➢ **best** – *warmed her skin like unexpected late afternoon sunlight breaking through a cloudy day* (use of metaphor here).

TAKING IT FURTHER	Students can be referred to lyrical poetry or even song lyrics to identify the language devices used there. A good classroom activity is to have students bring in their favourite song lyrics. These can then be photocopied and handed out to students to highlight key language devices, and to discuss the structure and its impact.

Chapter 9: Composition

9.5 Narrative writing: structure and detail

Resources:
- Student's Book: 9.5, pp. 226–229
- Workbook: 9.4, pp. 153–156
- Worksheet 9.5a–b
- PowerPoint slides 9.5a–b

Assessment objectives:

W1 Articulate experience and express what is thought, felt and imagined

W2 Organise and structure ideas and opinions for deliberate effect

W3 Use a range of vocabulary and sentence structures appropriate to context

W4 Use register appropriate to context

W5 Make accurate use of spelling, punctuation and grammar

EXPLORE THE SKILLS

This lesson moves on from descriptive to narrative writing, focusing on structure and detail. Students will learn how to plan, develop and write an engaging narrative. Before opening the Student's Book, ask students what they think are the features of good narrative writing. Write down suggestions on the board. When all ideas have been exhausted, ask students to open their books and review the list at the top of page 226. Do the ideas match those that students came up with? Discuss any that were missing.

Remind students that the start of a good story or the 'hook' sets the tone for the narrative and draws in the reader. Ask students to complete **Q1**, filling in the table with further ideas on **Worksheet 9.5a**. Then focus their attention on **Q2**. Ensure that students have made their key decisions and know how their opening narrative will develop. Listen to examples as a class, and encourage students to give input into each other's ideas.

Extra support: Allow students who may find **Q1** difficult to work in pairs or small groups, so they can bounce ideas off each other and their narrative.

BUILD THE SKILLS

Read the information at the start of this section as a class, then read through the two examples in **Q3**, and ask students to decide which one uses the technique outlined in the bullet points (the second one).

Display **PPT 9.5a** so students can refer to the text, then ask them to work independently on **Q4**, writing down their own ideas about what may have happened to the brother, considering the ideas listed. Encourage students to answer directly from the text provided using point, evidence and explanation in their answers. For example:

➢ *I don't think the brother ran away and got lost, I think he ran away because he was in trouble. He seems aggressive ('grabbed my shirt') and he scares his brother, 'I gasped'. This leads me to think that the brothers are not going to be happily reunited.*

Q5 asks students to continue the flashback themselves.

When everyone has completed their continuation of the flashback, put students in pairs and ask them to compare their work for **Q6**. Can they identify what their partner has done well?

Students should remain in their pairs to discuss **Q7**, coming up with some reasons for the brother's return – for example, he is in trouble and needs help. Take class feedback and note some of the best ideas on the board.

© HarperCollins *Publishers* Ltd 2018

Chapter 9: Composition

DEVELOP THE SKILLS

Students need to grasp the concept of climax and how important it is in creating a dramatic moment. A resolution, good or bad, must always follow.

> **Extra support:** If students struggle to understand the concept of a story climax, an interesting and effective way to teach this is through students listening to a piece of classical music. Ask them to close their eyes and raise their hands at the point where they feel the climax is reached. Pause the music and allow them to justify their choice, as well as explain their answers. For example: more able pupils may have been able to identify crescendo, others may have been able to determine the answer through the rise in volume or beat. Play the music again so that students can identify the resolution – what are their thoughts on this?

Read through the introductory text and the table as a class, before asking students to discuss **Q8** in small groups. Take feedback and record some of the best ideas on the board.

Before tackling **Q9**, look at the two examples as a class. Read the question and ask students to think about whether they want to complete one of them with a final twist, and if so, which one they would choose, or whether they would like to write an alternative ending. Then allow five minutes for students to respond to the task individually.

Read the information about tenses with the class and review the annotated example. Discuss the effect that the change in tenses has here. Then ask students to pair up and complete **Q10**. They should identify that **a)** fits both grammatically and in terms of making sense (it uses the past perfect tense).

Students should then work individually to write the next paragraph for **Q11**. Display **PPT 9.5b**, which contains some tips to help them when they are writing.

APPLY THE SKILLS

Students can now be given the option to the return to the original task or create an entirely new story of their own for **Q12**. Give students **Worksheet 9.5b**, which contains a grid with the five-part structure discussed earlier in the Student's Book for them to use to help plan and write their narrative.

TAKING IT FURTHER	Photocopy examples of students' work from today for the next lesson, ready for the class to analyse and discuss. You may like to share the mark scheme for this question and have students peer assess. In order to differentiate, allow students to peer assess examples that are a level above their own in order for them to identify ways to improve and build on their skills.

Chapter 9: Composition

9.6 Narrative writing: characterisation

Resources:
- Student's Book: 9.6, pp. 230–231
- Workbook: 9.5, pp. 157–160 can be set as homework
- PowerPoint slides 9.6a–c

Assessment objectives:

W1 Articulate experience and express what is thought, felt and imagined

W2 Organise and structure ideas and opinions for deliberate effect

W3 Use a range of vocabulary and sentence structures appropriate to context

W4 Use register appropriate to context

W5 Make accurate use of spelling, punctuation and grammar

EXPLORE THE SKILLS

The focus of this lesson is to be precise and effective in storytelling, using dialogue and description as well as language devices to reveal interesting characters

When looking at **Q1**, students should discuss which example they believe *shows* rather than *tells* us about Mina, as well as which they find most interesting. For example, the second description includes lots of small but interesting details that help to illustrate how bored Mina is (for example, how she *counted the rows of dull, fading flowers on her wallpaper*). This shows the reader how desperate she is for something to entertain her. Students should include the following in their responses to **Q1**:

a) Mina is lying on her bed, bored and restless. She pays attention to the wallpaper, reads her book three times and listens to the clock ticking. She can't think of anything to do with her day.

b) Mina is acting restlessly and seems bored, she sighs and listens to time ticking away. She reads a tattered book suggesting she's read it several times already but reads it again as she has nothing better to do. Also reward answers such as she is wasting her time or she is being lazy, 'lying down' and unproductive – 'clock ticked'.

Extra challenge: Q1 shows that Mina is bored in her room. Ask students to now create an opening sentence with a different perspective for the following situations for Mina:

➢ a stranger watching Mina through the key hole

➢ Mina remembering back when she was a child, bored to tears in her room

➢ Mina's last day in foster care before being adopted, anxiously waiting in her room.

BUILD THE SKILLS

Before starting on this section, allow students to use drama to cascade ideas around a written piece. The purpose of this exercise is to gather ideas and think about how characterisation makes a written piece more interesting. Display **PPT 9.6a–c**, which supports this exercise:

➢ **PPT 9.6a** is a warm-up exercise

➢ **PPT 9.6b** introduces the idea of adding more detail, by trying out ideas in drama – for example, rather than simply saying 'Mina was bored', students could try out poses that suggest boredom such as looking bored, flicking their hair, or looking at their watches then sighing, and then recreating these in their writing.

➢ **PPT 9.6c:** Ask students to work in pairs to return to the creative element of the piece of narrative they are about to write, adding similes and metaphors to the piece. An example is given on the slide.

Read through the information and the example plan at the start of the 'Build the skills' section in the Student's Book. Guide students through each section or allow them to discuss it in pairs, making notes as

Chapter 9: Composition

they go. Students should note the suggested outline for how to plan their stories in order to achieve balance before moving on to **Q2** and completing the section about Mina.

> **Extra support:** Seating plan the lesson before beginning so that students who are more confident in drama activities are in small groups or pairs with less confident students in order to support them in this activity. Allow students one 'pass' during the drama session so that they may choose not to perform in front of the whole class if it makes them nervous. You may prefer quieter students to perform to each other in small groups rather than to the class as a whole.

DEVELOP THE SKILLS

Introduce the idea of dialogue being a way to bring characters to life in narrative writing. Put students into pairs to read through the two examples in the Student's Book, in role as Mina and Mina's mother. Remind them that Mina is stubborn and her mother is angry with her.

Ask for volunteers to perform to the class in order to support weaker students and give ideas to the class as a whole. This will allow students to see different perspectives and garner a variety of ideas. It also allows them to see a character coming to life so that they can imagine this character in their piece of narrative.

Return to the first and improved versions. Ask students the following questions:

> - **What is the first difference you notice between the two extracts?** (The first extract has lot of unnecessary detail that uses up your word count. The second extract is precise and to the point. The first extract has a lot of dialogue used ineffectively whereas the second uses little but still gets the same point across.)
> - **What qualities in the improved version do you need to bear in mind when continuing with the exchange?** (Dialogue should be precise and effective – this also helps with the balance of the story. Remember your word count and use dialogue to move the story on, 'I have to be going now' rather than 'Mina put on her shoes and found her coat before telling her mother she was sorry and will be back in an hour').

Students should then complete the improved version for **Q3**, working individually or in pairs for additional support

APPLY THE SKILLS

In response to **Q4**, students have two options:

They can complete the story about Mina, perhaps using the plan in **Q2** as an outline. For this, they may like to mind-map their ideas or even continue to act out the events in their version of the story before writing down their final version.

They can write a narrative with the title 'The Escape'. To begin this task, students may like to refer to the plan outline in **Q2** as support or mind-map ideas around each component: introduction, development and complication, climax and resolution.

Refer students to the 'Checklist for success' or use peer assessment against these criteria, asking students to comment on ways in which their partner could improve.

| TAKING IT FURTHER | Students can impress by having a clear idea of how they are guiding the reader's response through careful choice of plot, language and structure. By 'playing with the reader' (as long as this is done appropriately), they can show they are in control of their writing. They can also manipulate by using surprise in terms of what information they reveal and when, or by who tells the story – perhaps through an unusual or original viewpoint. See 'Extra challenge' for examples. |

Chapter 9: Composition

9.7 Practice questions and sample responses: composition tasks

Resources:
- Student's Book: 9.7, pp. 232–239
- Worksheet 9.7
- PowerPoint slides 9.7a–b

Assessment objectives:

W1 Articulate experience and express what is thought, felt and imagined

W2 Organise and structure ideas and opinions for deliberate effect

W3 Use a range of vocabulary and sentence structures appropriate to context

W4 Use register appropriate to context

W5 Make accurate use of spelling, punctuation and grammar

EXPLORE THE SKILLS

A sample task has been included to give your students an opportunity to practise the style of task set in Paper 2, Section B. You may decide to set this as a formal assessment or to complete the process in class, with teacher support. **PPT 9.7a–b** includes the task and Assessment objectives to share with the class.

Remind the class of the key skills tested by this question (the relevant Assessment objectives).

If you wanted to mirror examination conditions, you could allow about one hour for students to complete the task. Remind students of their word count. It is helpful for them to know how many words they write in a line on average, in order to estimate how many words are required for different sections. This will then help them with their responses as they will know that their ending will need to be no more than eight lines, for example, or that their story should be no more than a side and a half in the answer book. You should also give them a few minutes to look at their exercise books to refresh their memory of structure.

EXPLORING RESPONSES

The Student's Book offers two sample responses designed to represent sound achievement (Response 1) and excellent achievement (Response 2) for this question. Depending on the ability range of your class, you may want to work with the actual mark scheme for this question, which is available on the Cambridge website. A student-friendly checklist has been provided on page 240 of the Student's Book.

These responses have been reproduced without annotations on **Worksheet 9.7** so students could work to add their own annotations before looking at the commentaries and feedback provided in the Student's Book.

Having worked with the sample responses, identifying areas for improvement and seeing what each response has done well, students should annotate their own response with similar comments, or – if appropriate – redraft them in light of what they have learned from the process.

Chapter 10: Approaching written coursework

10.1 Developing personal writing

Resources:
- Student's Book pp. 242–243
- Worksheets 10.1a–c
- PowerPoint slides 10.1a–e
- Sticky notes
- Mini-whiteboards or plain paper

Assessment objectives:

W1 Articulate experience and express what is thought, felt and imagined

W2 Organise and structure ideas and opinions for deliberate effect

EXPLORE THE SKILLS

This chapter provides a range of opportunities for students to explore a variety of texts and ideas, giving them a foundation from which to explore, develop and apply the skills required for successful completion of the coursework portfolio that makes up Component 3.

As students enter the lesson, display **PPT 10.1a** on the board. Ask them what impression they get of the boy, using the questions on the slide to promote reflection. Allow for sharing of ideas before a short session of whole-class feedback. Explain the relevance of this task: they are going to focus on creating a personal impression.

Introduce students to the learning objectives for this lesson: to draw on their own experiences in order to write originally and personally.

As a class, read the two texts 'The Thought Tree' and 'The Worst School Bus Ride Ever'. Allow time for individual reading and thinking time, then put students into pairs to discuss the tasks in **Q1**, before taking whole-class feedback.

Extra challenge: More able students could prepare a written explanation of the similarities and differences in style between the two pieces. **Worksheet 10.1a** contains a scaffold to assist with this. When they have completed their comparison, students could read them aloud to peers following the whole-class feedback. What aspects of language and tone contribute to the overall style in each piece?

BUILD THE SKILLS

After students have shared their initial ideas about the two extracts, they should use the table on **Worksheet 10.1b** to answer **Q2**.

Extra support: Display **PPT 10.1b** and model for students how the impression has been formed by inferring meaning from a particular part of the text. Circulate while students are working, and direct those who need extra support to key words and phrases from the text.

Allow time for a short session of whole-class feedback, while displaying the extracts on **PPT 10.1c**. Ensure that the focus is on the methods the writer has used to convey an impression, rather than students' ability to infer meaning (remember that they are working towards a writing task).

When students have completed their impressions of the extracts (and perhaps while waiting for others to finish), draw their attention to **Q3** and ask them to write their childhood memory on a sticky note and save it for later.

Chapter 10: Approaching written coursework

DEVELOP THE SKILLS

Explain that in order to create a convincing piece of writing, students will have to develop and sustain ideas throughout their work. This means considering how to add detail to ideas, then change the direction of their writing to move it forward.

Read through the plan for Example A with the class and stress the importance of planning and considering overall structure before beginning any piece of writing. In pairs, students should discuss the tasks in **Q4** and make notes in their workbooks, ready to feed back to the class. Responses might include:

a) The child has made friends, not having the time or need to sit under the tree anymore. They have moved away so they can no longer visit the tree.

b) The child has grown up, becoming more mature.

> **Extra challenge:** Ask more able students to consider the changes the writer has included in their plan, and think about the emotions they might be experiencing at these points of change. Why might the writer be feeling this way? What sorts of language might be used in the final piece to express these emotions?

Before students start on **Q5**, display the question 'How does the use of social media influence children and young people' on **PPT 10.1d**. Explain that the first idea has been added already – 'My memories of my first mobile phone and how I felt'. Students should copy the layout on the slide and make notes on how further detail could be added. If possible, give students mini-whiteboards or sheets of plain paper to first write down their own ideas, then:

➢ share ideas as a pair, taking current ideas and trying to develop them further

➢ share ideas as a group of four, interrogating and challenging the ideas of others. Which ideas are the most effective and will be shared with the class?

➢ one student from each group should be nominated to give feedback and, where possible, write some of their group's ideas on the whiteboard.

Students may come up with some of the following ideas:

➢ providing a sense of freedom and independence from parents

➢ feeling trusted and responsible, having to take care of something valuable

➢ allowing them to manage their own social life, contacting friends and making arrangements

➢ growing older, allowing more worldly awareness, with access to news from around the globe

➢ coming into contact with some of the more frightening aspects of the world they may have previously been sheltered from.

APPLY THE SKILLS

Students should now return to the childhood memory they made a note of on the sticky note earlier, to complete **Q6**. This should be stuck onto the top of **Worksheet 10.1c** as they fill it in, to keep them on task. Students should complete a plan for a piece of personal writing based on their childhood memory.

> **Extra support:** Display **PPT 10.1e** while students are working. Draw their attention to the comments and questions in the thoughts bubbles to help them come up with ideas. If students are really struggling, give examples from a different context (for example, *If I was writing about my first pet, I might write about a particularly funny occasion, such as…*). This will encourage independent thinking and transfer of skills.

| TAKING IT FURTHER | Students may wish to complete the piece of writing they have planned as homework. This could be swapped for peer reflection in a future lesson, or you could mark it yourself, giving strength and target comments in relation to the lesson objectives. |

© HarperCollins *Publishers* Ltd 2018

10.2 Approaching Assignment 1: Writing to discuss, argue and/or persuade

Resources:
- Student's Book pp. 244–245
- Worksheet 10.2
- PowerPoint slides 10.2a–d
- Large sheets of paper
- Sticky notes

Assessment objectives:

W2 Organise and structure ideas and opinions for deliberate effect

R3 Analyse, evaluate and develop facts, ideas and opinions, using appropriate support from the text

EXPLORE THE SKILLS

Display **PPT 10.2a** and distribute sticky notes. Ask the question: *Do you prefer ebooks or printed books. Why?* Students should stick their reasons to the picture of their choice. Following on from this, ask students which purpose/type of writing they think this task could lead to, and encourage them to guess the topic for today's lesson.

Explain that, for Assignment 1 of their coursework portfolio, students will write a response to a text or selection of texts that they have read, and that they will have to write a text giving a discussion, argument or persuasive response to the topic. They will need to:

➢ explore the ideas in the text/s

➢ express their own views on the information and ideas they have read about

➢ write in a particular format (such as a news article, a speech or a letter) and for a particular purpose.

Turn to the Student's Book and read through **Q1** and **Q2**. Ask students to think of topics or issues that matter to them. Give out **Worksheet 10.2** and draw their attention to the examples at the top, then allow time for students to mind-map their ideas. They should then choose one or two topics and consider how they could:

➢ find articles or other forms of writing about them

➢ research information (facts, statistics and other ideas) about them.

Use 'no hands up' or a random name generator to select students to share their ideas for topics and thoughts about how they could find out more. Make a list of topics on flipchart paper and pin this to the classroom wall. You could return to this later to provide topics for extra writing practice.

Students should work in pairs on **Q2**, using the table on **Worksheet 10.2** to list ways they could find other articles/writing and how they could conduct research to find further information such as facts and statistics.

Extra challenge: Encourage students to create a scrapbook of information from various sources on a topic of their choice. This could include clippings from newspapers/magazines, web pages, blogs, leaflets and so on.

BUILD THE SKILLS

Explain the importance of being able to evaluate a text and the arguments or ideas it contains. Look at **Q3** and make the link from the previous task: once information has been gathered, the next step is to evaluate it. Display **PPT 10.2b** and pose the question: *What does the term 'evaluate' mean to you?* Encourage students to consider the clue 'e-valu-ate'. Allow time for reflection and discussion before taking a class vote on the correct meaning.

Chapter 10: Approaching written coursework

> **Extra challenge:** If students have found this an easy concept to grasp, display **PPT 10.2c** and set up a group to take part in an evaluative discussion, using the reflection questions on the slide to stimulate the debate.

DEVELOP THE SKILLS

Once students have identified the correct definition of 'evaluate', explain that they will need to respond to texts in a specific form. Remind students that the 'form' means the type of text, and talk through the examples on **PPT 10.2d**.

Look at **Q4**. Ask students whether they can think of any other forms of writing that might be suitable for their response. Use 'pose, pause, pounce, bounce' to generate discussion here:

➢ **Pose the question:** What other forms of writing could we use for this task?

➢ **Pause:** Give students 30 seconds of thinking time.

➢ **Pounce:** Ask a student to name one other form of writing.

➢ **Bounce:** Bounce this form to another student and ask them a question about this form of writing (for example, *What layout would you use for this? What sort of tone would you expect to use here?*)

Other forms that students may come up with include:

➢ online blogs posts (offering a livelier approach)

➢ a more formal report (considering advantages and disadvantages).

For **Q4**, explain to students that they need to explore the conventions of the three text types provided to them. Explain that this means the expectations we have of these texts as standard, using the examples provided in the Student's Book to illustrate this. In pairs, ask students to complete a table like the one in the Student's Book, listing the conventions of a letter, a speech and a newspaper article.

> **Extra support:** Refer students back to Topic 3.1, 3.5 and 3.6 to remind themselves of the conventions of these texts. It may also help to have available some examples of formal letters, speech transcripts and articles that students can explore and discuss to support their prior knowledge.

APPLY THE SKILLS

Students should now return to their worksheets and the ideas for topics that interested them. Give them a further few minutes to decide on a topic that they wish to write about. Move around the class and ensure that the topics they have chosen are both appropriate and will offer sufficient depth and challenge for development of their ideas. Students should make notes on:

➢ the topic they wish to write about

➢ ideas for texts that they could respond to

➢ the form of text they will write in response

➢ the conventions required for that form of text.

TAKING IT FURTHER	Encourage students to write the first paragraph of their text, introducing the issue at hand. They could then swap these to be reviewed by a friend, considering: ➢ whether the conventions have been met ➢ whether the tone is suitable ➢ whether vocabulary and device choices are effective.

10.3 Assignment 1: Responding to a text

Resources:
- Student's Book pp. 246–251
- Worksheet 10.3
- PowerPoint slides 10.3a–e

Assessment objectives:

R3 Analyse, evaluate and develop facts, ideas and opinions, using appropriate support from the text

W2 Organise and structure ideas and opinions for deliberate effect

EXPLORE THE SKILLS

Display **PPT 10.3a**, showing the quotation 'Sugary sweets are dangerous to health and should be banned'. Give students three minutes to prepare an explanation of what this means and to say whether they agree or disagree. Ask for volunteers to respond (there should be plenty!). Explain to students that this activity is a starting point for developing the skills of responding to a text and forming their own opinion, which is essential for writing well in Assignment 1.

Organise students into groups of four, display **PPT 10.3b** and allocate roles:

- **1:** Clarify (finds out the meaning of difficult words)
- **2:** Summarise (produce a 50-word summary of the text)
- **3:** Analyse (select five key quotations and analyse what the writer's opinion is)
- **4:** Question (think of questions about the text to pose to the class).

Give students 10 minutes to read the article about the revival of printed books and make notes according to their role. Hold a class feedback session, giving each group two minutes to present their findings.

Once groups have presented, ask them to return to the text and bullet point six or seven key points from the article in response to **Q1**. Other points they may come up with include:

- Many independent bookshops have closed over the last decade.
- However, sales of ebooks are falling, while sales of printed books are increasing.
- Some people prefer printed books as a break from looking at a screen/using digital media.
- People appreciate the attractive look and feel of a real book; they offer a variety you don't get with ebooks.
- Displaying books on shelves is in fashion. It makes people seem intelligent.
- People are willing to spend more money on hardback books than other forms.

Extra support: Encourage students to collaborate and help each other, comparing points to give a full range of ideas. Draw their attention to the example given in the Student's Book.

BUILD THE SKILLS

Explain the process of E, E + E (explain, evaluate, express) using the example in the Student's Book as a model. To make this three-step approach clear, nominate three students to stand and read the example aloud to the class, each taking one step of the model.

Extra challenge: Display **PPT 10.3a** again and ask students to work in threes to produce an E, E + E paragraph in response to the argument against sugar. This could be delivered to the class in the same manner as the above.

Chapter 10: Approaching written coursework

Working individually, students should copy and complete the table in response to **Q2**. Emphasise that they should aim to either agree *or* disagree. Use **PPT 10.3c** to model levels of response to this task, focusing on how the student expresses their own opinion. Encourage class discussion on the merits of each response and take a vote on which is better.

DEVELOP THE SKILLS

Read through the points listed in this section of the Student's Book as a class. Check understanding of the key term 'register' as well as recapping 'conventions'.

> **Extra support:** To develop understanding of the key term 'register', number students 1 or 2 and give them the following scenario
>
> ➤ *You are emailing someone to thank them for a gift. Write a paragraph to begin your email.*
>
> Students in group 1 should write in informal register and students in group 2 should use formal register.

Allow students time to consider the two assignment options in **Q3** and decide which to pursue. It may help if you direct them to annotate the task with ideas or produce a brief spider diagram to assess which task they find more approachable.

> **Extra challenge:** Ask students to prepare a 30-second presentation on why they have chosen their topic, outlining three key ideas they will include. This could be delivered incidentally to you as you circulate, or formally to the class.

For **Q4**, students must develop a plan for their response. Draw their attention to the bullet points and 'Top tip' in the Student's Book. They should complete this task using the planning grid on **Worksheet 10.3**. (You may need to provide extra paper if they require additional planning space.)

While students are planning, circulate the room to ensure they are following the E, E + E structure appropriately. Question students about their ideas and encourage them to probe deeper into reasons and arguments.

> **Extra support:** Before students begin writing, ask them to work in groups to devise two useful phrases that could be included in their writing. Check their ideas, then nominate one student from each group to write their phrases into the speech bubbles on **PPT 10.3d**. This will act as a co-constructed scaffold while they write their drafts.

APPLY THE SKILLS

When their plans are complete (and you are satisfied they are ready to begin), students should begin writing their drafts for **Q5**.

Encourage students to check their progress. You could leave them to work independently until the task is complete, then reflect using the 'Check your progress' points on page 251 of the Student's Book. Alternatively, students could peer assess, either at the end of the task or periodically throughout (for example, after their first paragraph is complete). If so, peers should give 'strength' and 'target' comments. Student-friendly criteria (linked to sound progress) is provided on **PPT 10.3e** to assist with this.

TAKING IT FURTHER	To develop students' writing, challenge their vocabulary. Circulate the room and, using a pen or highlighter, select words/phrases that could be developed to produce a more sophisticated response. Students should change their work or produce a list of edits that could be added to a redraft.

10.4 Approaching Assignment 2: Writing to describe

Chapter 10: Approaching written coursework

Resources:
- Student's Book: 10.4, pp. 252–253
- Worksheet 10.4
- PowerPoint slides 10.4a–e
- Large sheets of paper
- Visualiser/webcam (if possible)

Assessment objectives:

W1 Articulate experience and express what is thought, felt and imagined

W2 Organise and structure ideas and experience for deliberate effect

W3 Use a range of vocabulary and sentence structures appropriate to context

EXPLORE THE SKILLS

Around the room, on tables or pinned to walls, place large sheets of paper with the following information in the centre:

➢ a particular setting or building
➢ weather or natural event
➢ an event or experience
➢ a person or group of people
➢ a combination of all of these.

As a carousel task, give students two minutes with each sheet to add ideas for subjects they could write about.

Extra challenge: Encourage students to begin to add sentences of description along with their ideas for subjects. They could use a different-coloured pen for these sentences.

Pin the paper to the wall/board for students to use as a bank of inspiration later in the lesson. Select students to explain their ideas, then discuss the merits/limitations of some ideas. Encourage students to think deeply about which topics they would find the most effective and why. Students should then decide which of the overall topics (from the bullet points) they might choose to describe for **Q1**.

BUILD THE SKILLS

Hand out **Worksheet 10.4** for students to use when completing **Q2**. For each of the descriptive writing skills listed, students should discuss with a partner and explain what they think this means in the middle column. This could take the form of instructions to themselves. Refer students to the example given on the sheet.

Extra support: Use **PPT 10.4a–c** to give examples of what the skills might look like in a piece of writing. Encourage students to reflect on what the 'green' example does that the 'red' does not. This will help students understand what is required for each skill.

DEVELOP THE SKILLS

Ask students to read the three extracts in the Student's Book. For **Q3**, they should work in groups to note where the skills from the table feature in each text. Students should then choose one example of each skill to add to their tables.

Hold whole-class feedback on this task, discussing the different examples of each skill that students have added to their tables and considering the effects of each on the reader. Use **PPT 10.4d** to give examples.

Chapter 10: Approaching written coursework

Students should use a 'think, pair, share' approach to complete the tasks in **Q4**, noting down ideas, discussing them with a partner, then sharing them in groups of four. What is distinctive about each of the texts in terms of:

- the narrative viewpoint – who (if anyone) seems to be speaking or giving the account
- the use of tenses or time
- the mood or atmosphere created?

Some possible responses include:

My Own True Ghost Story:

- Written in the first person singular – the speaker appears to have visited the setting alone.
- Written in past tense to convey a previous experience (befits the title).
- A lonely and dramatic atmosphere / sense of foreboding.

In Praise of Gardens:

- Written in the first person plural – has visited with someone else.
- Written in past tense to convey a previous experience.
- A calm and tranquil mood and atmosphere.

From Stepney to St Tropez:

- Written in the first person – conveying personal memories.
- Past tense – use of 'was' suggests that she has passed away.
- A reflective yet warm mood – fond memories.

Extra challenge: Nominate a more able student from each group to give feedback on their findings to the rest of the class. This student should refer to evidence from the texts to support their ideas.

APPLY THE SKILLS

Use **PPT 10.4e** to give students an opportunity to develop some of the descriptive writing skills they have studied in the lesson. Remind them to apply the skills covered in **Q2** and **Q3**, and to focus on the idea of 'show not tell'. Students should choose a 'tell' statement given on the slide, then use this to produce a short passage of description that 'shows' the same mood or feeling.

Where possible, examples of students' work should be shared at this point using a visualiser or webcam. If not available, responses can simply be read aloud to the class. Encourage reflection on what skills have been applied and where they feature in the students' writing.

At the end of the lesson, students should produce a mind-map detailing their idea for the assignment, for **Q5**. They should identify one special or distinctive person, one memorable place and one memorable event, then choose one to write about. Their mind-map should include as much detail about their choice as possible. Remind students to consider how they can include the writing skills they have learned throughout the lesson.

TAKING IT FURTHER	Encourage students to consider the skills addressed as ingredients, rather than tools. Help them to identify how the skills combine in writing, with many often being used at once, rather than thinking of them as discreet items or a checklist of things to do. They could be asked to continue their 'show not tell' task as homework, applying this idea.

Chapter 10: Approaching written coursework

10.5 Assignment 2: Writing a descriptive text

Resources:
- Student's Book: 10.5, pp. 254–257
- Worksheet 10.5a–b
- PowerPoint slides 10.5a–d
- Thesauruses
- Mini-whiteboard or plain paper

Assessment objectives:

W1 Articulate experience and express what is thought, felt and imagined

W2 Organise and structure ideas and experience for deliberate effect

W3 Use a range of vocabulary and sentence structures appropriate to context

W4 Use register appropriate to context

W5 Make accurate use of spelling, punctuation and grammar

EXPLORE THE SKILLS

Display **PPT 10.5a**, which shows an image of people watching a soccer match. Ask students to take a board pen and jot down key words and phrases they associate with the image on the whiteboard. Lead a discussion about the importance of choosing ambitious vocabulary in descriptive writing. Students could use a thesaurus to search for alternative and more effective words to use to describe the image. For example: 'bright', 'crisp', 'exciting', 'tense', 'friendly'.

Put students into pairs. Students should read the information in the table on page 254 of the Student's Book, then discuss **Q1** and **Q2**. Display the prompts on **PPT 10.5b** to aid ideas. Students should write ideas down, copying the table at the bottom of the slide, making notes ready for whole-class feedback.

Working on their own, students should complete **Q3**, recording and developing ideas for their own writing in their exercise books.

Extra support: Offer targeted students help with their ideas. It may be helpful to distribute tips on sticky notes to aid their thinking and avoid interrupting others working. For example, for a student focusing mainly on what they would see, you could pass a note saying: 'Have you thought about your other senses?'.

BUILD THE SKILLS

Explain to students that they are now going to focus on developing their own ideas for a description of an exciting event or experience. Use the spider diagram on page 255 of the Student's Book to model this method of planning, and remind students that they can find additional support in Chapter 4 and Topic 9.2.

For **Q4**, students should work on their own sense diagrams, developing ideas for their descriptive piece on an exciting event or experience. Remind them that they will need at least seven or eight well-developed ideas to fulfil the demands of the task.

When everyone has completed their sense diagram, read the passage about the football stadium. In pairs, students should consider how the description of the floodlights has been developed, in response to **Q5**.

Chapter 10: Approaching written coursework

> **Extra support:** Display **PPT 10.5c** and direct responses to the questions. Some suggestions might be:
> - The floodlights lead to the idea of rain – as if we are following the drops as they fall. 'Lines' suggests heavy rain/bad weather.
> - The writer moves the image downwards like a camera panning, to focus on the messy surface of the pitch, emphasising the bad weather.
> - The words 'slid' and 'crashed' use onomatopoeia to illustrate the poor conditions, furthered by the simile of 'slipped over, like clowns'.

Students should then take one aspect of their chosen exciting experience and write a three-step description like the one given in the Student's Book, in response to **Q6**.

Once they have finished their work, ask students to swap their book with a partner for peer review. When reviewing, students should identify where each image begins and ends, then make suggestions for further improvements. These suggestions should be specific, and refer to the 'sound' and 'excellent' criteria for Assignment 2 from the 'Check your progress' section at the end of the chapter.

Students should then reflect on how their work could be improved.

DEVELOP THE SKILLS

Students should work in pairs to analyse examples A–D in **Q7**, using **Worksheet 10.5a** to record their ideas regarding form, structure and language. In feedback, encourage students to consider the differences between the examples and explore their effectiveness. Display **PPT 10.5d** to show some possible responses.

Students should use **Q8** of the Student's Book to help develop their own ideas in **Q9**, then complete the planning grid on **Worksheet 10.5b**.

> **Extra challenge:** Direct students to the descriptive writing skills developed in the previous lesson. They should refer back to **Worksheet 10.4** and build these skills into their plans, considering how/where they will be included.

APPLY THE SKILLS

For **Q10**, students should complete a first draft of their response, although it is likely that this will take place in a separate, standalone lesson. Remind students that their draft will be handed in with their final piece, so they must use it thoughtfully to improve their work.

TAKING IT FURTHER	Students should make very specific and deliberate choices regarding the order of their ideas. They should consider their whole-text structure, making choices about the transitions between different ideas and images. Ask students to write a piece describing a building with a time contrast – when it was first built, and in a derelict state. Students should make choices about structure – should it be chronological, or use flashbacks to move between the two perspectives? How will they indicate these changes?

Chapter 10: Approaching written coursework

10.6 Approaching Assignment 3: Narrative writing

Resources:
- Student's Book: 10.6, pp. 258–259
- Worksheet 10.6
- PowerPoint slides 10.6a–d
- Sticky notes
- Large pieces of paper or card

Assessment objectives:

W1 Articulate experience and express what is thought, felt and imagined

W2 Organise and structure ideas and experience for deliberate effect

W3 Use a range of vocabulary and sentence structures appropriate to context

W4 Use register appropriate to context

EXPLORE THE SKILLS

As a starter activity, either bring in a series of objects or props that could be used to inspire a story, or display **PPT 10.6a**, which shows some objects (a sea shell, a crumpled map and a compass). Put students into groups and ask them to invent ideas for a story based on the objects. Share these ideas and discuss their strengths and limitations as inspiration for their writing in Assignment 3. Students should compare their ideas to the criteria on **PPT 10.6b** to make judgements about their successes and targets.

For **Q1**, draw students' attention to the palette of characters, locations and plot ideas in the Student's Book. Explain that they need to come up with three story ideas inspired by these details:

➢ Distribute three sticky notes to each student.
➢ Allow three minutes for discussion of ideas – ringing a bell or signalling time is up at one-minute intervals. In this time, students should add ideas to each sticky note.
➢ Allow further time for students to refine their ideas.

Afterwards, display **PPT 10.6c** and ask students to share their ideas with a critical friend. They should record what they have learned through listening to their partner's ideas, and what their partner suggested about their own ideas.

BUILD THE SKILLS

As a class, read the example task in the Student's Book:

➢ *Write a fictional or autobiographical account of a secret that is revealed with an effect on others.*

Explain to students the importance of making narrative choices to engage the reader, then read through the information given in the table.

On pieces of card or paper, write down the three possibilities for form, narrative voice and style/mood given in the Student's Book. Distribute these to students in groups, and ask them to add ideas to the card about why this option might be chosen and the advantages they would bring to the writing. Examples include:

➢ **short story:** enables the tale to be told from beginning to end in a short space of time, keeping the reader engaged
➢ **diary:** gives a personal insight into the speaker's life and builds a close bond with the reader
➢ **letter:** gives understanding of the writer, but also creates intrigue about the person receiving the letter
➢ **first person:** can be more personal, coming across as honest and open
➢ **third person:** allows insight into the thoughts of many characters
➢ **multiple narrators:** allows a shift in perspective, bringing variation
➢ **formal style:** makes the writing appear serious and allows more ambitious vocabulary choices

Chapter 10: Approaching written coursework

- **informal style:** can be more appealing to the reader and can make characters seem more 'real'
- **reflective:** allows for more use of descriptive devices, and encourages the reader themselves to reflect
- **dramatic:** more striking, often requiring clever use of punctuation and sentence structure for effect

After feedback on these ideas, instruct students to work in pairs to complete **Q2**, reminding them to look back at Topics 4.10, 9.5 and 9.6 for more information about narrative writing.

Extra support: Display **PPT 10.6d** and direct students to the explanations of the key terms *form*, *narrative voice*, *style/mood*. This will clarify what they are being asked to do.

DEVELOP THE SKILLS

Students should consider the example choices given here. They should work in pairs to consider why these choices are made. Some questions to develop discussion, and possible answers, are:

- Why choose to have the characters communicate via letter, not speak? The division between the characters could help create a sense of distance and mystery.
- Why do we need two narrators? The letters going back and forth form a 'conversation' which tells both sides of the story. The writer also shows they can write in different styles.
- Why do they narrators have different styles? This reflects their position in the story – they will not think about the secret in the same way, so this is reflected in the style and language used.

For **Q3**, students should choose an idea generated at the beginning of the lesson and jot down ideas for appropriate narrative choices. Display **PPT 10.6b** again to draw students' attention to some ideas for successful narratives. Encourage students to consider whether their idea will meet these criteria, or how they will have to adapt their idea to ensure that it is effective.

Extra challenge: Ask more able students to consider why these success criteria matter, and to lead a class discussion into this. Some suggestions include:

- Characters and locations/settings should be limited to allow the writer time to describe these in sufficient detail/avoid 'spreading the story too thinly'.
- Including a problem creates a structure that builds tension to a climax then releases it, encouraging the reader to stay engaged.
- In a short story, complex twists or sub-plots will detract from the above/there is not enough time to have too much going on.
- You need to 'hook' the reader in and engage them from the start.
- The ending must be satisfying in some way – answering questions and curiosity.

APPLY THE SKILLS

Individually, students should complete a fully structured plan for their story, using **Worksheet 10.6**.

Extra support: Try phrasing your support through questions rather than statements:

- *Have you considered…?*
- *Could you try…?*
- *What would happen if…?*

TAKING IT FURTHER	Ask students to identify opportunities for description in their stories, and refer back to Topics 10.4 and 10.5 to help them develop detailed ideas for these sections. Ask them to consider the function of direct speech and how this can be used (sparingly) to invigorate the storyline.

Chapter 10: Approaching written coursework

10.7 Assignment 3: Developing narrative writing

Resources:
- Student's Book: 10.7, pp. 260–263
- Worksheet 10.7
- PowerPoint slides 10.7a–e
- Sticky notes

Assessment objectives:
W1 Articulate experience and express what is thought, felt and imagined
W2 Organise and structure ideas and experience for deliberate effect
W3 Use a range of vocabulary and sentence structures appropriate to context
W4 Use register appropriate to context

EXPLORE THE SKILLS

Display **PPT 10.7a** and ask students to categorise the terms from the word wall under one of the three headings. Remind students that they studied this in Topic 10.6 and can turn back to their notes to help them in they need to.

Extra challenge: Challenge students to define or explain the meanings of some of the terms on **PPT 10.7a**.

Explain that the passage in the Student's Book gives advice to writers by showing them what *not* to do. Draw attention to the unanswered questions in the passage. Students should work in pairs to respond to **Q1**, discussing the advice in the passage and compiling a list of 'should' statements (for example, 'A good writer should…'). Some suggestions are listed on **PPT 10.7b** for use during feedback.

Extra support: If students are finding it difficult to come up with ideas, click to reveal just one or two ideas on **PPT 10.7b**, to give an idea of the kinds of things they are looking for.

BUILD THE SKILLS

Read the information at the start of this section in the Student's Book, and remind students of the importance to 'show not tell'. (You could refer back to **PPT 10.4d** to recap previous learning on this during preparation for the description task.)

Using the first table on **Worksheet 10.7**, students should respond to **Q2** by making a list of things they learn about the characters from the passage. They should then swap with a partner and challenge them to find supporting evidence for each point, before swapping back and comparing responses. Some ideas students might think of are:

➤ Antonia is frightened/surprised – *I heard Antonia scream*
➤ Jimmy panics when he hears her scream – *I whirled round*
➤ Jimmy hates the snake – *somehow made me sick / I struck now from hate*
➤ Jimmy is overtaken by shock at first – *I didn't run because I didn't think of it / cornered*
➤ Jimmy is brave – *I ran up and drove at his head with my spade*
➤ Jimmy is in a state of shock afterwards – *I felt seasick*
➤ Antonia is worried about him – *O Jimmy, he not bite you? You sure?*
➤ Antonia thinks he was foolish – *Why you not run when I say?*

In pairs, students should use their ideas so far to respond to **Q3** in their exercise books.

Chapter 10: Approaching written coursework

> **Extra challenge:** Press students on **Q3c**. Challenge them to select and explain particular words and phrases from the text, commenting on the techniques/devices used by the writer.

Students should use the second table on **Worksheet 10.7** to prepare their answer to **Q4**. To help them think about how 'The snake and Antonia' is effective, they should consider the effective parts of the text against the 'should' statements recorded earlier in the lesson, then think about how this affects the reader. Display **PPT 10.7b** as a reminder of the features of good writing.

DEVELOP THE SKILLS

Before they tackle **Q5**, read the example task to students:

> *Write a narrative piece in which the following words appear: 'I knew we didn't have long…'*

Individually, students should consider their plan, making notes using the bullet points in the Student's Book.

> **Extra support:** Display **PPT 10.7c**. Distribute sticky notes to students and ask them to add one of their best ideas to the note and stick it into the appropriate box on the board. This will form a bank of ideas to help struggling students form a plan.

Students should work individually to answer **Q6**, then discuss their ideas with a partner. Moving on to **Q7**, students should copy and complete the first two columns of the table in the Student's Book to aid their planning. Remind students that they can come back and change some ideas later, using the third column.

Students should start **Q8** by considering the choices they have made against the 'should' statements generated earlier and advice given by Braine. Following this, display **PPT 10.7d**, which contains the checklist they studied last lesson. Hold a short whole-class feedback session, selecting students to respond and challenging them on a particular element – for example, 'How many characters does your story have?'. Students should then complete the final column of their table, ensuring that they are happy with their plan.

APPLY THE SKILLS

Students should write their first draft in response to **Q9**. Remind them to use Braine's advice and the extract as a model of how to write well, emphasising that they must not copy from this.

For **Q10**, students should use the success criteria from the 'Check your progress' section to assess their work. To help them with this, display **PPT 10.7e**, encouraging them to think specifically about what they have done well and what they could do to improve.

TAKING IT FURTHER	Ask students to refer to the 'Excellent progress' criteria and consider how their work does or does not reflect this. For each point given, students should be encouraged to make detailed notes on what could be done better next time. Encourage them to consider the example extracts given in the Student's Book for both narrative and description. Is there anything more that they can learn from them?

Chapter 10: Approaching written coursework

10.8 Drafting and improving your work

Resources:
- Student's Book: 10.8, pp. 264–265
- Worksheet 10.8a–b
- PowerPoint slides 10.8a–d

Assessment objectives:
W1 Articulate experience and express what is thought, felt and imagined
W2 Organise and structure ideas and experience for deliberate effect
W3 Use a range of vocabulary and sentence structures appropriate to context
W4 Use register appropriate to context
W5 Make accurate use of spelling, punctuation and grammar

EXPLORE THE SKILLS

Explain to students that this lesson will focus on the development of their redrafting skills, helping them to evaluate and improve their own work. Ask them to consider the biggest challenges they will face when writing their coursework assignments, thinking about what they have previously done well, or found challenging. Use a 'think, pair, share' format for this.

When taking feedback, note down students' ideas on the board, using **PPT 10.8a**. Ask the class which challenges they think pose the greatest barrier to doing well in their coursework, and take a vote to establish a rank order of the class's challenges from least serious to most serious. Following this, explain to students that there are separate marks for content/structure and for style/accuracy: content is worth up to 10 marks, while accuracy is worth up to 15 marks. Stress the importance of accurate writing, which includes choice of vocabulary, sentence structure, register, punctuation, grammar and spelling.

For **Q1**, students should copy and complete the self-evaluation checklist from the Student's Book. Encourage them to reflect on each element and consider the level of confidence they feel in this area. Read through the statements together and use **PPT 10.8b** to build a student-friendly version of each skill. The following may help explain the terms to students:

➢ **Basic conventions:** these are the ways in which things are usually done, not only for texts but other things in life. Give some real-life analogies – for example, the conventions of a school are that there will be classrooms and lessons; the conventions of driving are that you take care and abide by the law; the conventions of a funeral are that people wear black and behave in a sombre manner. Now explore some textual conventions: letters have dates and addresses; speeches begin by greeting an audience and end by thanking them; news articles have headings and subheadings.

➢ **Using a variety and range of vocabulary:** students should be reminded that this does not mean writing in 'posh' language, but instead choosing words that convey the precise meaning they need. For example, write the word 'quiet' on the bored and ask students to think of three degrees of quietness from least to most (for example, hushed, peaceful, silent). Emphasise that they have similar meanings but convey very different moods.

➢ **Basic grammar:** remind students of common errors with tense agreement and subject–verb agreement.

➢ **Paragraphing:** you could use the 'TIPTOP' rule to remind students to start a new paragraph if there is a change in time, place, topic or person.

➢ **Punctuation:** emphasise that punctuation can be accurate but not effective. They need to think about how the different marks will affect the meaning of what they are saying.

➢ **Spelling:** errors are emphasised when students are trying out new vocabulary. Encourage dictionary use for new words and suggest that they create lists of words they know they often get wrong and refer to this when writing.

Chapter 10: Approaching written coursework

Using their completed tables, students should complete **Q2**, reflecting on the areas they are most likely to struggle with in the coursework. Ask students to visually identify their problem areas by highlighting or circling them. Alternatively, you could take a hands-up vote to identify how many students struggle with each area, providing you with information to inform future planning or interventions to deal with the biggest challenges.

> **Extra challenge:** Display **PPT 10.8c**, which contains an edited version of the skills table. Students who feel strong in these areas could be asked to identify and write down suggested strategies for dealing with these challenges.

BUILD THE SKILLS

Explain the three-step approach to proofreading, as described in the Student's Book. Read the first draft of the example work and draw students' attention to the annotations. Ask them to identify which 'step' of the process the annotations relate to. **Worksheet 10.8a** contains some tasks to help students focus on the first step in the redrafting process.

Put students in pairs to work on **Q3** to think about any other changes that have been made between the first draft and final versions of the student's work. Some suggestions might be:

➢ The visual detail added when 'changed themselves' is redrafted as 'forming and re-forming' – the use of present tense 'ing' instead of past tense 'ed' suggesting how it kept happening without stopping.

➢ The separation of 'this is the place where my dreams and hopes began' creates a reflective pause. The reader imagines the stillness and calm atmosphere of the setting and the narrator's quiet reflection.

For **Q4**, display **PPT 10.8d** and explain the task: students should imagine they are reviewing this work for a friend. They should write their friend a short email, explaining what they think of the improved version. They should think about what has changed and why this works better than the first draft.

APPLY THE SKILLS

Students should now review the three-stage proofreading process outlined in more detail in Topic 2.8, making notes to ensure that they are clear about what to do for **Q5**.

> **Extra support:** Students who need further practice should use **Worksheet 10.8b** to develop their proofreading skills, using the initial three-step process and additional prompt questions to develop their ideas. If required, the students could be asked to then redraft this extract, applying their suggestions for improvement.

Remind students that their first drafts will be submitted with the final version of their work, making the process of revising and improving all the more important.

| TAKING IT FURTHER | Students should consider how they may need to adapt their checklist according the particular demands of Assignment 1, 2 and 3, given the very different nature of each piece. |

Chapter 10: Approaching written coursework

10.9a Coursework-style tasks and responses: Assignment 1

Resources:
- Student's Book: 10.9, pp. 266–269
- Worksheet 10.9a
- PowerPoint slides 10.9.1a–f

Assessment objectives:

R1 Demonstrate understanding of explicit meanings

R2 Demonstrate understanding of implicit meanings and attitudes

R3 Analyse, evaluate and develop facts, ideas and opinions, using appropriate support from the text

R5 Select and use information for specific purposes

W1 Articulate experience and express what is thought, felt and imagined

W2 Organise and structure ideas and opinions for deliberate effect

W3 Use a range of vocabulary and sentence structures appropriate to context

W4 Use register appropriate to context

W5 Make accurate use of spelling, punctuation and grammar

YOUR TASK

A sample task has been included to give your students an opportunity to practise the style of task set for Assignment 1 of the Coursework Portfolio. You may decide to set this as a formal assessment or to complete the process in class, with teacher support. **Worksheet 10.9a** reproduces the task should you wish to set it as formal assessment. **PPT 10.9.1a–c** include the Assessment objectives and the task to share with the class.

EXPLORING RESPONSES

The Student's Book offers two sample responses designed to represent sound achievement (Response 1) and excellent achievement (Response 2) for this question. Depending on the ability range of your class, you may want to work with the actual mark scheme for this question, which is available on the Cambridge website. A student-friendly checklist has been provided on page 275 of the Student's Book.

Q1: Students should read the question on the worksheet and consider the key requirements. They should select the key words in the question and annotate them with ideas about what these key words require of the student. Take feedback, leading students towards the words 'response,' 'giving your views' and 'arguing your case.' Explore what this means as a class.

Q2: Students should annotate the sample response with their ideas for improvements. They could add their ideas to the copy of the sample on **PPT 10.9.1c**. They should then work in pairs to write three comments on how the student could improve their ideas. These should be compared to the annotations on page 267.

Q3: Students should redraft the final paragraph of the response so that it works more persuasively. Encourage them to think about how the student expresses their opinion, the language used to do so and the support given to their opinion, using **PPT 10.9.1d** to guide students to key parts of the text.

Students should next read and annotate Response 2 in pairs. Again, they could add their annotations to create a class version on the board. Students should work in pairs to consider what makes this a better response than Response 1.

Q4: Finally, students should look back to their response to this task from Topic 10.3. Using what they have learned in this lesson, then should evaluate their responses and make improvements where possible.

Chapter 10: Approaching written coursework

10.9b Coursework-style tasks and responses: Assignment 2

Resources:
- Student's Book: 10.9, pp. 269–271
- Worksheet 10.9b
- PowerPoint slides 10.9.2g–k
- Sticky notes

Assessment objectives:

W1 Articulate experience and express what is thought, felt and imagined

W2 Organise and structure ideas and opinions for deliberate effect

W3 Use a range of vocabulary and sentence structures appropriate to context

W4 Use register appropriate to context

W5 Make accurate use of spelling, punctuation and grammar

YOUR TASK

A sample task has been included to give your students an opportunity to practise the style of task set for Assignment 2 of the Coursework Portfolio. You may decide to set this as a formal assessment or to complete the process in class, with teacher support. **Worksheet 10.9b** reproduces the task should you wish to set it as formal assessment. **PPT 10.9.2g** includes the Assessment objectives and the task to share with the class.

EXPLORING RESPONSES

The Student's Book offers two sample responses designed to represent sound achievement (Response 1) and excellent achievement (Response 2) for this question. Depending on the ability range of your class, you may want to work with the actual mark scheme for this question, which is available on the Cambridge website. A student-friendly checklist has been provided on page 276 of the Student's Book.

Ask students to recap the descriptive writing skills they were introduced to in Topic 10.4. Take whole-class feedback to see what they can recall, then allow them to refresh their memories from **Worksheet 10.4**. Introduce the topic and task using **PPT 10.9.2h**.

Q1: Students should read Response 1 and then compare the response to the skills from **Worksheet 10.4**. (Reproduced on **PPT 10.9.2i**). Students should decide which skills have been used in the response and annotate to show where they feature. These could be added to **PPT 10.10.2j**. Students should then work in pairs, using the Student's Book annotations, to write three pieces of advice on sticky notes. Each pair should be called to stick their comments to a wall/board and explain their ideas to the class.

Students should now read and annotate Response 2 in pairs. Again, you could ask students to add their annotations to create a class version on the board, **PPT 10.9.2k**. Students should work in pairs to consider whether this is an improvement on Response 1, again considering the descriptive writing skills learned in Topic 10.4.

Students could now be asked to study the annotations of Response 2 from the Student's Book and use them to write an email to the student who wrote the response, suggesting advice for further improvement.

Q2: Students should now look back to their response to this task from Topic 10.5. Using what they have learned in this lesson, they should evaluate their responses and make improvements where possible.

Chapter 10: Approaching written coursework

10.9c Coursework-style tasks and responses: Assignment 3

Resources:
- Student's Book: 10.9, pp. 272–274
- Worksheet 10.9c
- PowerPoint slides 10.9.3l–q

Assessment objectives:

W1 Articulate experience and express what is thought, felt and imagined

W2 Organise and structure ideas and opinions for deliberate effect

W3 Use a range of vocabulary and sentence structures appropriate to context

W4 Use register appropriate to context

W5 Make accurate use of spelling, punctuation and grammar

YOUR TASK

A sample task has been included to give your students an opportunity to practise the style of task set for Assignment 3 of the Coursework Portfolio. You may decide to set this as a formal assessment or to complete the process in class, with teacher support. **Worksheet 10.9c** reproduces the task should you wish to set it as formal assessment. **PPT 10.9.3l–m** includes the task and Assessment objectives to share with the class.

EXPLORING RESPONSES

The Student's Book offers two sample responses designed to represent sound achievement (Response 1) and excellent achievement (Response 2) for this question. Depending on the ability range of your class, you may want to work with the actual mark scheme for this question, which is available on the Cambridge website. A student-friendly checklist has been provided on page 276 of the Student's Book.

Ask students to study the progress indicators for Assignment 3 given on the 'Check your progress' page. Students should think about what they have to do to move from 'sound' progress to 'excellent' progress. Using **PPT 10.9.3n**, take feedback from the class, adding ideas about each given category.

Q1: Students should work in pairs to consider Response 1 on **Worksheet 10.9c**, in relation to the 'excellent progress' indicators in the Student's Book and the feedback taken from the starter task. Following this, students could be asked to add their annotations to the board on **PPT 10.9.3o**. Students should be encouraged to look for specific phrases/sections of the text that exhibit the skills indicated and comment closely on how successful the student is in meeting expectations. Stress that this is the ending to the story – do students feel it is effective?

Students should read the feedback given in the Student's Book, then write down the three things they think need most attention in order to improve the response.

Response 2: Students should now read Response 2 on the worksheet, working in pairs to assess this student's progress and compare it to Response 1. Take feedback from students and collate ideas on **PPT 10.9.3p**.

Following this, read through the annotations and feedback for Response 2 in the Student's Book. Ask students what further specific comments they could add to the feedback to help the student improve.

Q2: Students should now use what they have learned to return to their task from Topic 10.7, evaluating their performance and identifying ways to improve. Display **PPT 10.9.3q** to give students a framework for reflection and self-evaluation.

Chapter 11: Approaching speaking and listening

11.1 Using the right language

Resources:
- Student's Book: 11.1, pp. 278–281
- PowerPoint slides 11.1a–j

Assessment objectives:
S4 Use language and register appropriate to audience and context

EXPLORE THE SKILLS

Begin with a short discussion of the following terms to establish students' understanding:

➤ 'audience': whoever is listening to the speaker
➤ 'appropriate language and tone': accurate standard English is normally expected.

It will be useful at this point to introduce the concept of tone. Allow five minutes to go through **PPT 11.1a–d**, to allow students to see and hear which factors contribute to tone. This could be a class activity, or students could work in pairs, ending with a short feedback session to the class.

Extra challenge: Encourage students to identify and explain how the three aspects work in the example sentences on **PPT 11.1c**:

➤ the top left bubble uses vocabulary that features 't', 'd', which helps emphasise annoyance or disgust
➤ the top right uses soft 's' sounds and long vowels to create a peaceful mood
➤ the bottom speech bubble uses straightforward vocabulary and grammar to avoid emotion, and concentrate on method in the instructions.

Explain that tone is created not just by how we use the voice itself, but by all features of speech – vocabulary, grammar, content – and should always suit the audience.

In **Q1**, persuasion is a major purpose of the talk, so vocabulary and grammar that create a conciliatory tone should be selected. Allow two minutes for each audience, plus two minutes for a brief plenary. **PPT 11.1e–j** contain suggested responses with a brief explanation for each presentation scenario in **Q1**.

Start **Q2** as a class activity, with a volunteer reading out the sample extract on page 278 of the Student's Book. Elicit reasons why this talk is unsuccessful for the intended audience. Features that combine to make this sample talk inappropriate include:

➤ use of slang or vogue words and expressions: 'Mental', 'like', 'man'
➤ non-standard grammar: 'They don't know nothing about stuff happening to us every day'; 'They ain't…'; 'We was…'
➤ no real consideration of the audience: this may be appropriate for the speaker's peers, but not for parents
➤ mostly opinion; only one fact!

Q3 can be done in pairs, taking the factors listed above into account, and with the person listening to the speech deciding whether the incorrect features have been successfully corrected or not.

Extra support: Model the reworking of the speech extract:

➤ *'Thing is, nobody likes rules' might become 'The fact is that few people our age will admit to liking rules, even if they know they are necessary.'*

The speaker wants the audience on his/her side, so this is less dogmatic and forceful, but still acknowledges young people's natural resistance to authority.

Chapter 11: Approaching speaking and listening

BUILD THE SKILLS

Pairs should read the passage in the Student's Book. It is important that they recognise Sara's tone as appropriate for her audience.

Q4 can then be done in pairs or groups of four, with feedback to the whole group. Emphasise to students that they must both identify Sara's use of bulleted features and explain how these make her talk appropriate to her audience. Allow 15 minutes.

DEVELOP THE SKILLS

For **Q5**, give pairs 5–10 minutes to identify the failings in the way Majid speaks. Then agree, line by line, how to improve each feature listed in **Q5**.

> **Extra support:** Offer a guide to improving Majid's conversation:
>
> ➤ Majid: 'Boring traffic jams.' This is an incomplete sentence, which adds nothing valuable to his first sentence. Majid simply voices his anger. He shows no awareness of the teacher's attempts to elicit useful information, which might help to turn this into a genuine discussion.

For **Q6**, students can engage in the analysis, either singly or in pairs for those with less confidence. Remind students that they are assessing the suitability of the extract for a class similar to theirs. Again, it will be useful to read the sample opening aloud. Possible response for **a)** include:

➤ It sounds up-to-date ('nowadays').
➤ It draws in the listener by using 'you'.
➤ It makes Greece sound appealing by using words such as 'secluded' and 'unforgettable'.
➤ It paints a picture, encouraging the listener to imagine being there.

Possible responses for **b)** include:

➤ She acknowledges that the listener may have different preferences ('if you don't want').
➤ She considers the attractions and gives a vivid example.

APPLY THE SKILLS

Q7 is probably best set as homework. Students will need some time to assimilate what they have learned in the lesson. Stress that, despite the guidance offered in the Student's Book, content is only one factor to consider when selecting the appropriate speaking style. A follow-up lesson can be allocated to give students the chance to peer-assess their work.

TAKING IT FURTHER	More able students will select appropriate vocabulary and varied sentence forms. Their vocabulary should be clearly right for the subject: for example, assuredly employing specialist terms in informative contexts or, in emotive contexts, using terms that elicit the response desired from the teacher. Similarly, with sentence forms, there will be fluent crafting: in precision of expression in informative presentations and in subtle implications in persuasive ones.
	You could ask students to prepare either a presentation giving advice to students taking parents on a school tour, or a talk they might give to a group of parents at the start of a school tour.

Chapter 11: Approaching speaking and listening

11.2 Choosing and researching a presentation topic

Resources:
- Student's Book: 11.2, pp. 282–285
- PowerPoint slides 11.2a–f

Assessment objectives:

SL2 Present facts, ideas and opinions in a cohesive order which sustains the audience's interest

EXPLORE THE SKILLS

Read through the opening section on page 282 of the Student's Book. Point out that a student's first consideration is: what do I want my audience to take away from my presentation? Ask students to suggest possible purposes, such as informing or arguing.

Sum up by reinforcing that they need to link the topic to the listener's experience. The subject matter may be very personal (for example, the birth of a sibling) or about a more obscure topic (for example, the hammered dulcimer). The student may be enthusiastic about the subject, but the audience may not be. The audience may even be hostile to a view being expressed. Suggest that students consider who will be assessing them, and what their interests might be.

Before students answer **Q1**, use **PPT 11.2a–f** to run through possible areas (and levels) of research, to put them in a better position to decide which they could talk about successfully.

Extra support: List sources for research purposes: libraries, websites (caution that not all are reliable), news agencies (such as newspapers, television and radio), specialist magazines, other people.

Extra challenge: Offer some less age-related topics; these may encourage students to be more thorough, or to look deeper into a subject that interests them. Examples might include the following:

➢ Argue that some sports stars are overpaid.

➢ Persuade people that they should relax more.

➢ Inform people of the greatest threats to our way of life.

BUILD THE SKILLS

Regarding level of difficulty, point out that a mainly factual presentation may seem more straightforward than one involving persuasion. However, to engage the audience successfully is not particularly easy – no one wants to listen to a list!

Allow five minutes for students to explore angles for **Q2** in small groups and to make individual mind-maps or spider diagrams. Then hold a five-minute feedback session.

Extra support: All three topics lend themselves to 'for or against' debate:

➢ TV companies have to pay big salaries to attract big-name presenters, but should they encourage less well-known ones?

➢ Exam pressure may be helpful, a necessary evil, or simply damaging.

➢ Zoos may be seen as animal prisons or centres for conservation and education.

Allow another five minutes for students to complete **Q3** in pairs. Then hold a five-minute feedback session.

Extra challenge: Ask students to assess and compare the effect of each of the two responses in the Student's Book on the audience. Is the selection of material effective?

Chapter 11: Approaching speaking and listening

Point out that Response 1 mostly gives information, while Response 2 mentions almost nothing about the trip, but immediately begins to discuss wider issues. Here is a good example of how, usually, a lower-level response will *present* a topic competently, to interest the audience, whereas a more successful response will *develop* a topic, to make the best impact on the audience.

DEVELOP THE SKILLS

Spend a few minutes discussing 'relevant' content. Obviously, this refers to important details, which are clearly connected to the main topic; but sometimes a detail may not appear relevant immediately: it may, for example, offer a light moment in a serious topic. For example, mentioning that Lucy was probably still chewing her breakfast is a humorous and effective touch.

Tell students that an audience may be deeply involved in the presentation, but will still need moments to assimilate or reflect. Including some less vital details (such as Lucy's breakfast) will give the audience the necessary listening space, enhancing their overall appreciation.

Q4 should be tackled in small groups or pairs. One option would be for the groups to list facts, and then to feed back to the class. You could then allocate one of the talk topics (tourist destination and so on) to each group. They would then select facts, and finally the groups would feed back to the class.

Q5 could be done in pairs after reading the Muhammad Ali extract. Take feedback, eliciting the following points from students:

- There are seven facts.
- They are used to demonstrate how Ali quickly established himself as a top-class boxer.
- The student's main point is that Ali is the greatest boxer, but that he is also known for his political stances.
- Apart from the factual record, she says he was handsome and includes his own quotation of himself. Here is an example of a detail that, at first, could seem trivial – even irrelevant – but it suggests why he was 'loved' (for his character) as well as being regarded as a great boxer.

Run through the bullets at the end of this section in the Student's Book to summarise the strengths of the Muhammad Ali extract.

APPLY THE SKILLS

While **Q6** is intended as an individual task, it could also be done in pairs to encourage self- and peer-assessment. Remind students of the conclusions on the topics suggested earlier: competent students *present* topics, showing good factual knowledge and mostly suiting material to their audience; more successful students *select and shape* their material to manipulate audience response.

Remind students to research more material than they think they will need. They may need to do some quick 'editing' as they speak, or someone in the audience may also be knowledgeable on the topic and require detailed answers to questions not covered by the presentation.

Students could continue to work alone for **Q7**, but pair feedback would be helpful.

TAKING IT FURTHER	Students could create a scrapbook on an issue or subject on which they might give a presentation, and find information to appeal to different audiences. Alternatively, they could consider possible aspects of their subject, and how they might interest different audiences. For example, for Muhammad Ali, they might research the mindset that made him successful, his background, his importance as a black icon, his persona, his private life and so on.

Chapter 11: Approaching speaking and listening

11.3 Structuring your presentation

Resources:
- Student's Book: 11.3, pp. 286–287
- PowerPoint slides 11.3a–i

Assessment objectives:

SL2 Present facts, ideas and opinions in a cohesive order which sustains the audience's interest

EXPLORE THE SKILLS

Emphasise to students the importance of an effective structure. This aspect alone can significantly improve a presentation: it gives the speaker an air of confidence and authority; it gives the audience confidence that this is a presentation with direction, which is worth listening to. In this respect, the opening and ending are very important.

Begin by focusing on the introduction to **Q1** on page 286 of the Student's Book. One of the most difficult concepts for students to grasp is 'logical order'. Often, they can recognise it, but there is no formula to produce it: each presentation has its own logic.

One way to test the concept is to explain that a logical order is one where no other arrangement of the details would sound better in that presentation, by that speaker. Recommend that students use this test whenever deciding on an order for a presentation. They should also be able to explain the progression from each section of their presentation to the next.

As the details of each presentation on a school subject will vary, **PPT 11.3a–d** offer a short example of how 'logical order' might be interpreted.

For **Q2**, suggest to students that they produce too many, rather than too few, details. When everyone has found all possible details, given the time and sources available, an informed decision can be made on the overall structure of the presentation. Students can then select and order the material to best effect. It is always better to have to leave something out than have to search for more information.

BUILD THE SKILLS

It may be constructive to show **PPT 11.3e–f** before answering **Q3**. Then students can move on to trying the three specific techniques referred to in the bullet points.

Mention to students that these techniques are best used sparingly and with tact. The tone of the presentation relies as much on choice of language as any other factor: for example, any flippant use of humour may prove inappropriate in a presentation on a serious subject, such as a disease which is potentially upsetting to some of the audience. On the other hand, in 'your favourite school subject' humour may well be appropriate, perhaps allowing the student to make some pertinent points that might otherwise land them in trouble!

Extra support: Work through **PPT 11.3e–f** systematically. These offer three suggestions for how the presentation might begin and the effect of each one.

Extra challenge: Ask students to pick a rather obscure topic for a presentation and think of a way to establish a link in their opening between the subject and the listeners' experience, in order to engage the audience. For example, they might choose 'medieval sports'. The student may have enthusiasm for field sports. They then research the background to, perhaps, archery and discover that this, like many modern field sports, has its origin in the need for military training in the Middle Ages. This provides the opening link.

Chapter 11: Approaching speaking and listening

DEVELOP THE SKILLS

Run through the text about choice of endings and show **PPT 11.3g–h**, before students tackle **Q4** individually. They could then read each other's conclusions in pairs before tackling **Q5** individually.

They could continue to work in pairs, or combine in small groups, to read aloud and compare the effectiveness of their two conclusions.

In **Q6**, numbering the sentences will help students get to grips with the task. They should recognise that this is essentially a list. Suggestions for improvement include:

- a simple reordering: for example, 6, 2, 4, 5, 3, 1, 7 (this is provided on **PPT 11.3i**)
- sentence 3 could clearly give more specific details on the books and equipment available
- sentence 2 might read: 'I've not been paid by any member of staff to say this, but our Maths staff have to be the best!'

APPLY THE SKILLS

Allow students at least 15–20 minutes to complete **Q7** individually. Their main focus should be on creating an effective beginning and ending, but clearly these must suit the overall structure of the presentation.

You could arrange a follow-up session to hear some, or all, of these; or perhaps have students present to each other in groups of five. Each student can then be peer-assessed by the others in the group for the effectiveness of their overall structure, and their openings and conclusions.

TAKING IT FURTHER	In groups, students could choose possible presentation topics, such as their favourite school subject, and devise possible examples of rhetorical questions, humour, and powerful facts (as listed under 'Build the skills') that they could use in openings for each topic.

Chapter 11: Approaching speaking and listening

11.4 Engaging your audience

Resources:
- Student's Book: 11.4, pp. 288–289
- PowerPoint slides 11.4a–h

Assessment objectives:

SL1 Articulate experience and express what is thought, felt and imagined

SL2 Present facts, ideas and opinions in a cohesive order which sustains the audience's interest

SL3 Communicate clearly and purposefully using fluent language

EXPLORE THE SKILLS

Introduce the idea that the use of imagery, rhetorical devices and humour can enliven even a factual informative presentation. These devices should not be overused, however, and each must always suit the overall tone of the presentation. There is no formula; students need to develop good judgement when using these techniques.

As a warm-up on imagery, ask half the class to provide examples of similes and the other half to provide examples of metaphors on the subject of 'Getting up to go to school'. Spend two or three minutes sampling them and ask students to comment on their effectiveness or suitability.

Example similes:

> 'Getting up for school is like heaving myself out of a swamp/opening a present.'

Example metaphors:

> 'I'm a bear coming out of hibernation/a happy skylark greeting the day.'
> 'The alarm clock catapults me out of bed.'

Extra support: Remind students of the difference between similes and metaphors, using **PPT 11.4a**.

For **Q1** and **Q2**, allow students to work in pairs for 5-10 minutes. Hold a short feedback session. If necessary, guide them to the following examples from the sample response on page 288. These illustrate how good use of technical devices encourages listeners to develop ideas for themselves, thus becoming more involved in the presentation.

> Imagery – there are two prominent examples:
> - simile: 'like a god' – in Caliban's eyes, Prospero, with his magic, often whimsically disposes benefits or punishments. Ferdinand refers to the music that Prospero invokes, as waiting 'upon some god o' the isle'.
> - metaphor: 'serpent' – the serpent has an obvious connection with the snake in the Garden of Eden. Even the island may be regarded as a kind of Eden, insofar as it features two innocents: Miranda and Ferdinand.

> Alliteration – 'He holds himself': the effort of exhaling the 'h' consecutively helps stress the words, suggesting Caliban's hatred of Prospero's authority.

> Repetition:
> - 'He demands and he demands': the rhythm on the first syllables is slightly awkward, emphasising the burden Caliban feels himself to be under.
> - 'As if…': this occurs four times, but the student skilfully avoids overuse. The first use sets up the idea of Prospero's attitude: the next three demolish it.

> Minor sentence – 'Always craving more': following the repetition of 'He demands', this reinforces how Prospero is never satisfied. By omitting the subject of the sentence, the student has made Caliban put the focus on the perpetual craving.

Chapter 11: Approaching speaking and listening

PPT 11.4b shows an alternative extract, which also makes good use of the same technical devices.

> **Extra challenge:** Ask students to work out how the imagery examples on **PPT 11.4c–d** create their effects:
> - visual – creating an image through choice of detail
> - aural – use of alliteration and onomatopoeia in 't', 'g', 'cr', 'br', 'ck' and 'ar' suggesting sounds
> - kinaesthetic – assonance and alliteration in 'slipped' and 'shifted', the rhythm of the sentence suggesting the movement.

BUILD THE SKILLS

Before students start **Q3**, spend two minutes on the effectiveness of 'triples' – repetition in threes, as with the 'as if' from the Caliban response on page 288 of the Student's Book. For example, 'Despite having hideous blisters on his feet, Albert insisted on running again, and again, and again.' The second 'and again' suggests that Albert is determined; the third might imply that Albert is very courageous – or that the speaker thinks he is an idiot who will never learn!

Add that the speaker can modify the effect of the repetition by the way it is spoken. In the above example, the speaker might pause before the last repeat, and deliver the words as a kind of sigh. Invite some students to offer different interpretations.

This should prepare students for improving the extract in **Q3**.

DEVELOP THE SKILLS

For **Q4**, explain to students that there are three main reasons for adding rhetorical questions (**PPT 11.4e** gives an example of each):

- to engage the audience, quickly
- to encourage the audience to consider the speaker's viewpoint for themselves
- to sound less dogmatic, as though the speaker is exploring the topic in the company of the audience.

Students can add their own rhetorical questions to the sample response.

For **Q5**, emphasise that the use of humour is risky, because not everyone shares the same sense of humour. Irony, for example, can be cutting and so be inappropriate for some audiences. As a short extension, explore the examples in **PPT 11.4f–g**, which illustrate that care must be taken with irony.

Exaggeration can be presented to students as an aspect of humour, since this is often the effect. Again, show that care must be taken by working through **PPT 11.4h**.

APPLY THE SKILLS

Once students have written their presentation openings in **Q6**, allow time to hear a selection of these. Students will benefit from practising their delivery and judging the effect on their audience, while listeners will benefit from assessing the others' results.

> **Extra support:** Allow students time to discuss possible jobs in pairs before they begin to write.
>
> **Extra challenge:** Students could write and deliver the whole presentation.

TAKING IT FURTHER	Students could choose another literary character (perhaps a Shakespeare character) and write a presentation like the one in the Student's Book in the voice of Caliban, using at least one simile, one metaphor and one rhetorical question.

Chapter 11: Approaching speaking and listening

11.5 Developing a role

Resources:
- Student's Book: 11.5, pp. 290–291
- Worksheet 11.5a–b
- PowerPoint slides 11.5a–c

Assessment objectives:

SL1 Articulate experience and express what is thought, felt and imagined

SL3 Communicate clearly and purposefully using fluent language

EXPLORE THE SKILLS

In Topic 11.4, reference was made to the fact that presentations do not always need to be given formally. Encourage students to include a role-play element, as this opens up a range of alternative methods of presentation. For example, they could speak in role as a character in a novel or play, comment on the present in role as a time traveller from the past or future, or speak as a real-life historical figure reflecting on their achievements and their mistakes.

Encourage students to discuss why some characters or historical figures would be more interesting to play than others – especially where there is some controversy about the character's actions or motivation. This could link to work in English Literature. For example, a student could role-play Lady Macbeth as she waits for Macbeth to return from killing Duncan, considering her motives. Is she self-seeking, or does she simply want the best for her husband and feel that he needs a push from her to give him the courage to pursue his own ambitions?

Extra support: Use **Worksheet 11.5a** to help students to develop their ideas about possible role-play subjects. You have the option of adapting the sheet to include figures or characters that your class will know about. In addition, students could research given subjects, or fill in their own choices.

Point out that gathering information as suggested in the bullet list on page 290 of the Student's Book will provide a sound foundation for creating a convincing character. With this in mind, in **Q1** caution students about creating clichéd, superficial characters. On the other hand, they should avoid creating too much background material with insufficient focus. **PPT 11.5a–c** offer some additional prompts for creating the background to the roles in Q1. Allow five minutes for this.

When students have chosen and introduced their character to their groups for **Q2**, hold a brief plenary and ask each trio who created the most believable set of character details. Encourage them to identify what it was that made it successful – for example, particular details or a combination of details. Invite students to question those who have presented a character.

BUILD THE SKILLS

Introduce **Q3** by explaining to students that the purpose of a monologue is to convey the character's thoughts and, often, feelings to the audience. In some circumstances – film for example – a voice-over can be employed, but it is usually more dramatic, and in role-play more realistic, for a character to speak the monologue. Emphasise that students are not meant to be engaging in argument, but presenting monologues that give what will probably be opposite views.

Chapter 11: Approaching speaking and listening

Extra support: Show students a YouTube video clip of Neil Armstrong's moon landing, and the website for the homelessness charity Shelter. You could also suggest helpful words and phrases that might be used by those speaking for or against space exploration, such as:

➢ inspirational, human endeavour, 'one small step for man, one giant leap for mankind', natural curiosity

➢ expenditure, exorbitant, colossal, astronomical sums, priorities, vulnerable, humanity, social responsibility.

Use **Worksheet 11.5b** to help students to develop their ideas and vocabulary.

DEVELOP THE SKILLS

For **Q4**, ask pairs to read the role improvisation text aloud, preferably at least twice, so that they can hear the effect of the language.

Pairs should conclude that:

➢ the phrase 'only rarely in my life' emphasises how special this moment was; 'crossed the finish line' creates a mental image of the moment; this is a fluent and eloquent complex sentence

➢ 'absolute agony' is a powerful phrase; the repetition in 'long, long way' is simple but effective

➢ the speaker conveys both her personal feelings and those of the crowd.

For **Q5**, point out that the way students deliver lines can affect the impact of the performance. More effective continuations will maintain the sense of the speaker's admiration and emotional involvement, but may move the speech on rather than just providing more of the same. For example, a new paragraph could switch to the runner's training, and the experts' expectations at the start of the race, or perhaps to a point earlier when he was a long way behind the leading runner.

Note that we do not find out whether Alexandro actually won, or was simply heroic in finishing despite problems.

Extra challenge: Ask students to write a paragraph that could be used before the one given, perhaps giving details of how tough the race was, and so on.

APPLY THE SKILLS

If practical, set practising for **Q6** as homework and have students perform in groups in a follow-up lesson.

TAKING IT FURTHER	Students should create complex roles that suggest implicit aspects of the character. They will do this by adopting the most appropriate speaking style, using a range from highly formal, correct standard English to informal, possibly ungrammatical or dialectal forms; and will also use appropriate facial expressions and body movements to support their meaning.
	Students could workshop their role-plays in groups, critiquing each other and focusing especially on refining how they might imply character – as it would probably seem unnatural for someone to speak at length about their own character. Lady Macbeth could, for example, imply her own ambition by speaking enviously of what men can do in the world that women cannot do. She could imply that she is a driven character by pacing up and down and speaking in a tense, urgent manner.

Chapter 11: Approaching speaking and listening

| 11.6 | **Preparing for conversation** |

Resources:
- Student's Book: 11.6, pp. 292–293
- PowerPoint slide 11.6

Assessment objectives:

SL2 Present facts, ideas and opinions in a cohesive order which sustains the audience's interest

SL5 Listen and respond appropriately in conversation

EXPLORE THE SKILLS

Make it clear to students that their conversation will be with you (or another teacher if this is the case), and will follow on from their presentation. Their preparation should involve knowing about their subject beyond what they have had time for in their presentation, and anticipating what sort of questions they might be asked. They should also understand that questions or comments will be designed to draw them out and enable them to do their best, rather than to trip them up or exhaustively test their knowledge.

For **Q1**, students could work in pairs and make a list of possible individuals they could speak about, then make notes individually on the one they choose and what questions might be asked. Use **PPT 11.6** to help them develop ideas. They could also be asked to justify their choice, either within the group or to the class.

Extra support: Help the whole class by sharing their ideas on what constitutes a 'great' individual. For example, could a pop star or footballer be considered as great as someone who has helped to change the world for the better, such as Nelson Mandela? Could a general who has built an empire but not necessarily advanced humanitarian causes be 'great'?

Extra challenge: Encourage some students to look beyond obvious historical figures and consider lesser figures, such as a relative.

BUILD THE SKILLS

For **Q2**, help students to approach the question: 'My life outside school and what makes it interesting' by considering what interests them, and what another person might find interesting about their life. One option would be to pair students who do not normally work together and who would therefore not know much about each other, in order to encourage curiosity. For example, students might take where they live for granted and perhaps be bored by it, but another student might be interested to know what it is like.

If students are already working in pairs, decide whether you want them to continue in the same pair for **Q3** or switch. When they have had time to make their lists, take feedback from at least some of the class.

For **Q4**, read out the two responses to the class, or get students to read them aloud. You could encourage one or two initial ideas from them as a class, then allow them to discuss in pairs, before feeding back to the class.

Possible comments on the responses are:

➢ Response 1 makes the important point that most of us will be old one day, and that we would be kinder to the elderly if we realised that. However, it does this in a rather bland and simple way. There is no advantage in saying, 'I have a friend who suggests…'. It would be more effective to say, 'I think that…'. There is nothing in this response to engage the listener's imagination.

➢ Response 2 acknowledges the difficulty, suggesting from the start that this is a tricky, and therefore interesting, question. It specifies Age Concern, uses the image of 'a magic wand', and introduces a personal anecdote effectively.

Chapter 11: Approaching speaking and listening

DEVELOP THE SKILLS

Q5 introduces the idea of using the teacher's comments and questions in the conversation to develop a point, showing good listening skills and the ability to acknowledge the possible truth in another viewpoint. In pairs, students should practise accepting some validity in what their partner says, not simply agreeing with it or dismissing it wholesale.

> **Extra support:** Help students to consider other possible benefits of online resources, such as their relatively low cost.
>
> **Extra challenge:** Get students to try the exercise on a different presentation, for example, putting forward the idea that schools should only teach subjects that are of direct practical use to all students, and should therefore abandon subjects such as history, drama or art.

Possible alternatives to the student response in the Student's Book are:

➢ 'Certainly, online resources have the advantage that students can work on them at their own speed, but equally they may be distracted and start looking at other sites.'

➢ 'Online resources can be helpful, but their ability to diagnose a student's needs is very limited.'

APPLY THE SKILLS

For **Q6**, begin by discussing the statement with the class. Try to get views on both sides. If necessary, ask challenging questions, such as: 'Wouldn't everyone prefer a free handout to having to work? Why work if you don't need to?'.

Get at least some pairs of willing students to act out their teacher–student conversations for the class.

> **Extra support:** Give a list of phrases that help to signal acknowledgement:
>
> ➢ 'Certainly'
>
> ➢ 'That's a valid point, but...'
>
> ➢ 'I see what you mean...'.

TAKING IT FURTHER	More able students will have material that is thoroughly researched. They will also have developed the material beyond what might seem the anticipated limits of a conversation, in order to be ready to initiate/anticipate the development of that discussion, if necessary, possibly by the use of answers that invite further consideration of the topic. To encourage this type of planning, students could use mind-mapping, spidergrams and discussion to explore further possible topics related to those they have considered. For example: ➢ Hobbies: What makes a good hobby? What purpose does a hobby serve? ➢ Saturday jobs: How might a part-time job benefit a student? ➢ Helping the elderly: What level of responsibility do we have towards others – such as friends, family members, members of our community, others in our society?

Chapter 11: Approaching speaking and listening

11.7 Responding to talk, seeing implications and paraphrasing

Resources:
- Student's Book: 11.7, pp. 294–295
- PowerPoint slides 11.7a–g

Assessment objectives:

SL5   Listen and respond appropriately in conversation

EXPLORE THE SKILLS

Begin by pointing out to students that this lesson is about listening, and that there is more to it than just concentrating on someone's voice. The lesson addresses listening skills as being vital in everyday life and in work situations, but especially with a view to doing well in the teacher-student conversation part of the assessment.

Extra challenge: Ask students to suggest how listening skills might be useful for the following:
- police officer
- nurse
- chat show presenter
- teacher
- gardener (they need to listen to clients' instructions).

The lesson begins with the script of a student discussion, but the learning from it applies equally to the assessment. Draw students' attention to the 'Checklist for success' on page 295 of the Student's Book. Make sure that they understand the idea of paraphrase (you could remind them that this is also important in summary questions).

Students should tackle **Q1** in pairs. Then show them **PPT 11.7a–d**, discussing the first three, which look at the contributions of the other students in the discussion as well as Lucy's, before finishing with the summary contained on the fourth slide, 'Poor listening skills'.

BUILD THE SKILLS

Ask students what they understand by the word 'imply'. Point out the difference between 'imply' and 'infer': we can *imply* (suggest or hint at) a meaning in what we say, and we can *infer* (deduce) what someone else means. Ask one or two students to say, 'I love your new dress. It's so… different' in a way that they think conveys what its implied meaning might be. If necessary, draw out the idea that this could imply that the speaker thinks the dress is ridiculous, and that it is 'different' from anything anyone with any taste would wear.

For **Q2**, get two students to read aloud the student-teacher conversation. Discuss it with the class, drawing out the following inferences:

- Geography could be useful for someone going abroad.
- Dan is showing his ignorance by not even knowing what country he went to – or even if Mallorca is a country (it is part of Spain).
- The student and his family might have had a better holiday if they had, in effect, done some geography – by researching the climate and customs of their holiday destination.

Chapter 11: Approaching speaking and listening

DEVELOP THE SKILLS

Ask another pair of students to read out the next student–teacher conversation extract. Ask how Sonia, in her one line, shows a better response than Dan did. (She paraphrases what the teacher says.)

> **Extra support:** Explain that paraphrasing shows that you have received the meaning of what someone is saying, not just heard the words, and that it works especially well if a speaker is expressing opinions or feelings. Give students a further example, such as:
>
> *Teacher: I think homework could provide students who find it hard to concentrate on work in class to focus on a task without distraction.*
>
> *Student: So you think students who work better alone benefit from being set homework?*

Divide the class into groups to discuss space exploration for **Q3**. Discuss with them what 'preparing a conversation' might involve. Draw out that they should consider their own views on the subject, and how to justify them, but also anticipate arguments for the other side. If they are undecided, they should weigh up the opposing views.

There are two possible ways to arrange this activity:

➢ Let the groups, divided into 'for' and 'against' space exploration, have their discussion, then make notes on the points made by the 'opposition' to their own views, and finally summarise the opposite viewpoint.

➢ Get the groups to work in two pairs: one having the conversation, and the other noting main points on each side, and then summarising.

You may find it helpful to show students **PPT 11.7e**, especially if you are following the second option above.

> **Extra support:** Give students some starter ideas on both sides of the argument:
>
> ➢ **For:** Human beings have a basic urge to explore, and even for the great mass of people not going into space, this urge is partly satisfied by seeing others doing so, and finding out more about the universe.
>
> ➢ **Against:** There is poverty throughout many parts of the world, even in some countries that spend large amounts of money on a space programme. It would be better to use money to relieve suffering on earth than on exploring other planets.

APPLY THE SKILLS

The Student's Book suggests groups of three for **Q4**, but you could vary this. Keep to the same groupings used for **Q3** if you think this worked well. Encourage students to think about the subject before launching into their discussion. You could have a short preliminary discussion as a class, especially around the question of what constitutes wasting time. For example, it could be argued that nothing that people enjoy is a waste of time. You could quote the popular anglers' saying: 'Half of my time I spend fishing; the rest I just waste.'

> **Extra challenge:** Show the class **PPT 11.7f** and read it out to them. Then turn it off and tell students to summarise it. Use **PPT 11.7g** to help them assess how well they did. For even more challenge, read out the text of **PPT 11.7f** without showing it. You could show it briefly once students have made their notes, before showing **PPT 11.7g**.

TAKING IT FURTHER	Students could listen to presentations and/or discussions and then attempt to paraphrase them or produce written summaries. It may also be instructive to play a version of Chinese whispers. Students should work in pairs and speak for a minute, making three main points in an argument about which they feel strongly. They should then swap partners and attempt to pass on the arguments. The listener should then feed them back to the original speaker, who comments on how accurate the new version is.

Chapter 11: Approaching speaking and listening

11.8 Developing and supporting ideas with confidence

Resources:
- Student's Book: 11.8, pp. 296–297
- PowerPoint slides 11.8a–c

Assessment objectives:

SL3 Communicate clearly and purposefully using fluent language

SL5 Listen and respond appropriately in conversation

EXPLORE THE SKILLS

Explain what the topic title means: developing relates to anticipating counter-arguments and considering how to deal with them, and seeing how an argument connects to other issues. Supporting materials might include key facts, statistics, quotations, examples and anecdotes.

Q1 could be tackled as a class activity, with you collecting ideas and noting them on the board. Alternatively, get students to discuss the topic in pairs, then take feedback.

Extra support: Show **PPT 11.8a** as an example of possible arguments on both sides.

Draw out ideas such as:

Against a ban:

- Competitive sport raises people's standards and expectations and is therefore inspiring, especially to the young.
- At the professional level, it contributes hugely to the economy.
- It provides entertainment, which helps people to relax.
- People can work out aggression, being harmlessly competitive by supporting a team.
- A ban would be unenforceable.

For a ban:

- Competitive sport discriminates against those who have no sporting skills, especially in schools.
- At the professional level, it gives people unrealistic expectations, encouraging them to think that they might as well just watch a sport on TV rather than get exercise themselves.
- It would be better if people competed in socially useful activities rather than pointless sports.
- It would be better to encourage cooperation rather than competition in our society.
- Competitive sport simply wastes time that could be used more productively.

For **Q2**, point out that the activity focuses on a teacher–student conversation about professional competitive sport. Students could tackle it in pairs, then take class feedback. Draw out the following:

- Abi combines a personal viewpoint ('obscene amounts') with exact figures for one example that supports her view, which she gives clearly and fluently. She does not say, *There's one player – Gomez or something – who earn … what was it… anyway, loads of money, and he's just been offered, like, another million or something to move to… somewhere else.*
- She partly accepts the teacher's point about players being an inspiration, but has a knowledgeable counter-argument, with sums that back it up.
- She shows that she has thought about the alternatives to people following professional sport – being personally engaged in it.

Q3 looks at the types of questions a teacher might ask in the conversation, so that students can learn to understand their nuances. Read through the sample questions. Ask how students might take their cue from

Chapter 11: Approaching speaking and listening

the question and respond effectively. For example, *Pythagoras' Theorem enabled practical measurements used in building.* Students should then work in pairs to identify how the teacher uses questions in the **Q2** conversation extract. Take feedback, drawing out:

➢ *What kind of money do top players earn?* This checks the student's knowledge of their subject, as well as offering an opportunity to develop the conversation.

➢ *…aren't these players an inspiration to others?* This challenges the student by citing a popular argument, with an implied invitation to argue against it.

➢ *But what's wrong with just watching on TV?* This gives her an opportunity to develop her argument.

After pairs have discussed **Q4**, take feedback. They could suggest:

➢ *What about the benefits to the national economy?*

➢ *Would it help if players' earnings were regulated and kept to sensible figures?*

➢ *Isn't it just a fact of life that when people are very good at something they quite reasonably expect to get paid a lot – like pop stars, for example?*

BUILD THE SKILLS

Q5 could be tackled by pairs or small groups. Use **PPT 11.8b–c** to give possible answers.

> **Extra challenge:** Students could further develop the points or counter-arguments in the PowerPoint slides.

DEVELOP THE SKILLS

Students could work in pairs for **Q6**, but need to write answers individually.

> **Extra support:** Ask volunteers to rephrase the teacher questions to make their meaning clearer:
>
> a) Shouldn't education focus on practical lessons that are relevant to the world of work, like maths, not on subjects like history?
>
> b) As cars kill people, shouldn't we make them illegal?
>
> c) Shouldn't we all be able to communicate with people from other countries in their own language?
>
> **Extra challenge:** Suggest the following starter ideas:
>
> a) Education should be to improve quality of life, not just earning power.
>
> b) Modern human life depends on mobility.
>
> c) Foreign languages are irrelevant to people who do not plan to work abroad.

APPLY THE SKILLS

Students should work on **Q7** in pairs, but could join into groups of four to practise the presentations and conversations, with those students not immediately participating acting as observers and giving feedback. After students have completed this activity, they should peer-assess using the 'Checklist for success'.

> **Extra support:** Tell students to begin by considering how they will interpret 'travel'. For example, they might argue that nowadays we barely need to leave our homes because of the internet and social media.

TAKING IT FURTHER	Students could make notes on how to develop, challenge or support the following viewpoints: ➢ Classical music is better than pop. ➢ There should be fewer food programmes on TV. ➢ Sport should be optional in schools. ➢ Good manners matter.

Chapter 11: Approaching speaking and listening

11.9 Practice tasks and sample responses

Resources:
- Student's Book: 11.9, pp. 298–303
- Worksheets 11.9a–c
- PowerPoint slides 11.9a–b

Assessment objectives:
SL1 Articulate experience and express what is thought, felt and imagined
SL2 Present facts, ideas and opinions in a cohesive order which sustains the audience's interest
SL3 Communicate clearly and purposefully using fluent language
SL4 Use register appropriate to context
SL5 Listen and respond appropriately in conversation

YOUR TASK

Extracts from the scripts of sample presentations and conversations have been included to give students an opportunity to practise their assessed speaking and listening. They could also provide students with ideas for their own presentations.

Display **PPT 11.9a–b** and remind students of the key skills tested for each part of this assessment – the presentation and the conversation.

EXPLORING RESPONSES

The Student's Book offers two annotated sample responses each for the presentation and the conversation designed to represent sound achievement (Response 1) and excellent achievement (Response 2). Depending on the ability range of your class, you may want to work with the actual marking criteria, which are available on the Cambridge website. These responses have been reproduced without annotations on **Worksheets 11.9a–c**, so students could work to add their own annotations before completing **Q1–4** and looking at the commentaries and feedback provided in the Student's Book.

Having worked with the sample responses, identifying areas for improvement and seeing what each response has done well, students should annotate their own response with similar comments, or – if appropriate – redraft them in light of what they have learned from the process. Some suggested answers follow.

Q1
- overly casual expression: 'some of the drivers were crazy'
- repetition: 'my'; 'it was'
- simple sentences that would be better turned into a single complex one: 'My favourite was Nero. He followed me everywhere.' (My favourite, Nero, followed me everywhere.)
- use of humour: 'Also, I don't grunt as much as my brother does!'

Q2
- a short sentence as the dramatic climax to a paragraph: 'And my grandmother has Alzheimer's.'
- simple sentences used as dramatic examples: 'Then she wasn't sure what day it was.'
- sophisticated vocabulary: 'degenerative disease'
- dialogue used to show the tragic reality: 'Do I have meals on wheels tomorrow?'

Q3
- challenging and encouraging a response: 'The governments do send money to help, don't they?'
- developing an idea: 'but I suppose they give as much as they can'

Q4

...**Where it is a different game**. [1] People can say what they like about players being over-paid and behaving like huge babies – which we all know they do – but the excitement generated is amazing. I took my mother to a match and she goes regularly now. I still cannot believe it, but she is **swept away** [2] by the drama of it all. There are many things wrong with football finance and there is corruption too, **but that cannot really detract from** [3] **all that it represents to hundreds of millions of people around the world...** [4]

[1] student finishes teacher's sentence, to support own idea

[2] uses a cliché, but still emotive language

[3] excellent use of formal standard English

[4] concludes with intelligent summary of his thoughts

12.1 An introduction to Practice Paper 1

Resources:
- Student's Book: 12.1, pp. 306–312
- Worksheets 12.1a–f
- PowerPoint slides 12.1a–w

Assessment objectives:
R1 Demonstrate understanding of explicit meanings
R2 Demonstrate understanding of implicit meanings and attitudes
R3 Analyse, evaluate and develop facts, ideas and opinions, using appropriate support from the text
R4 Demonstrate understanding of how writers achieve effects and influence readers
R5 Select and use information for specific purposes
W1 Articulate experience and express what is thought, felt and imagined
W2 Organise and structure ideas and opinions for deliberate effect
W3 Use a range of vocabulary and sentence structures appropriate to context
W4 Use register appropriate to context
W5 Make accurate use of spelling, punctuation and grammar

If you wish to use this paper as a summative assessment, then no preparation is required. Allow students two hours to complete it under exam conditions and then move to Step 9. However, if you prefer to use the paper as a 'walk through' of an examination-type experience with guidance and preparation, then follow steps 1–8 below.

Step 1

Ask students to read 'An introduction to Practice Paper 1' on page 306 of the Student's Book. Read the section 'Which skills should I be using?' out loud. Ensure that students understand the terms 'explicit meaning', 'implicit meaning', 'summary', 'extended response' and 'writer's effects'.

Hand out **Worksheet 12.1a**, which contains all the questions. Working in pairs, students should use four colours to highlight the questions to show which type of reading skill each one is addressing. Use **PPT 12.1a–h** to show correct highlighting and explanations.

Extra support: Suggest that students look for key words such as 'explain, using your own words' (for explicit or implicit meaning questions), 'feelings' (for an implicit meaning question) and 'language' (for writers' effect questions).

Extra challenge: Invite students to create their own additional questions of each type, based on Text C.

Step 2

Explain that knowing the time allowed for an exam is useful as a guide to ensure that they complete the whole paper and do not spend too much time on one question at the expense of others. It also gives the correct importance to high-tariff questions. **PPT 12.1i** gives a guide for working out timings. Ask students to return to **Worksheet 12.1a** and annotate it to show how many minutes they should allow for each question.

Step 3

Ask students to annotate the practice exam-style paper with the advice recommended in the 'Tips for success' on page 306. This is a quick consolidation task of marking up questions to indicate how/where to manage time carefully, where to explain/where to use own words and so on.

Chapter 12: Practice papers and guidance

Then remind students about picking out key words in the questions and give them five minutes to do this. Use **PPT 12.1j–p** to identify the key words in each question.

Step 4

Next, explain that you are going to go through the paper, one question at a time, and model for students how to prepare for each one, and what skills and techniques to use. Allow students two minutes to read Text A in the Student's Book. Discuss the various strategies that they might use to tackle words that they are not familiar with. Allow a further three minutes' reading time.

> **Extra support:** Give students time to review the reading techniques covered in Chapter 1.

Step 5

Students should then complete **Question 1 parts a)–e)**. They could do this in one session, using all 20 minutes available, or you could split the session into five, using timings indicated by the mark allocations. Encourage students to take note of the key words that they have already highlighted and also to look at the space available for each answer and the number of marks, before they write.

Step 6

Next, introduce the concept of Summary writing. Give students five minutes to read Text B. Again, you could build a break into this in order to support readers finding the vocabulary difficult. Remind students of the difference between main ideas, details and opinions before they start to make notes. Then allow 20 minutes working time.

Step 7

Introduce the concept of writing about language and writers' effects. Allow 13 minutes for **Question 2 parts a)–c)**. Before students complete part **d)**, you may wish to remind them about the meaning of the word 'powerful'. You could also display **PPT 12.1q**, the writing scaffold explained in Topic 7.4 of the Student's Book, and ask them to copy and use this for help. Give students a further 20 minutes for this part of the question.

Step 8

Finally, introduce Text C and allow five minutes reading time before asking students to create a notes grid using **Worksheet 12.1b**. Allow 10 minutes for this activity. Next, remind students of the conventions of a script, then allow 20 minutes for writing.

Step 9

Once students have completed the practice exam-style paper, encourage them to engage with the success criteria and to assess their own work.

a) Give students **Worksheet 12.1c** and ask them to work through the tasks, which are based on two sample responses to Question 1(f). Feed back using **PPT 12.1r–w**. Then ask them to mark their own answer.

b) A similar activity could be completed using **Worksheet 12.1d**, which contains two sample responses to **Question 2(d)**.

c) **Worksheet 12.1e** provides an example of a sample extended response with opportunities for students to annotate in order to guide their evaluation. It is worth discussing the way that the sample does not follow the three bullets in a straightforward structure, yet manages to cover each of them. They could then peer assess a partner's work.

Step 11

Once students' responses have been reliably marked, hand out **Worksheet 12.1f** and ask students to conduct a self-review, looking at their own strengths and weaknesses and identifying targets for improvement.

Chapter 12: Practice papers and guidance

12.2 An introduction to Practice Paper 2

Resources:
- Student's Book: 12.2, pp. 313–316
- Worksheets 12.2a–g
- PowerPoint slides 12.2a–s

Assessment objectives:
R1 Demonstrate understanding of explicit meanings
R2 Demonstrate understanding of implicit meanings and attitudes
R3 Analyse, evaluate and develop facts, ideas and opinions, using appropriate support from the text
R4 Demonstrate understanding of how writers achieve effects and influence readers
R5 Select and use information for specific purposes
W1 Articulate experience and express what is thought, felt and imagined
W2 Organise and structure ideas and opinions for deliberate effect
W3 Use a range of vocabulary and sentence structures appropriate to context
W4 Use register appropriate to context
W5 Make accurate use of spelling, punctuation and grammar

If you wish to use this paper as a summative assessment, then no preparation is required. Allow students two hours to complete it under exam conditions and then move to Step 6. However, if you prefer to use the paper as a 'walk through' of an examination-type experience with guidance and preparation, then follow steps 1–6 below.

Step 1

Ask students to read 'An Introduction to Practice Paper 2' on page 313 of the Student's Book. Read the section 'Which skills should I be using?' out loud. Ensure that students understand the terms 'directed writing', 'analyse', 'evaluate', 'argue', 'narrative writing' and 'descriptive writing'.

Step 2

Read Question 1 out loud and ask students to annotate the question on **Worksheet 12.2a** so that they are clear what they need to write about, who they are writing as and to, what the purpose of their writing is and which form they are writing in. Make sure that students understand the conventions of writing a letter.

Extra support: Suggest that students revisit Topic 3.6 of the Student's Book to review the conventions of a letter.

Step 3

Allow students five minutes to read Text A in the Student's Book. Discuss the various strategies that they might use to tackle words that they are not familiar with, then allow a further five minutes' reading time.

Step 4

Hand out **Worksheet 12.2b**, and ask students to complete the activities on it, evaluating sample responses to Question 1. Students should then complete Question 1 themselves, taking 50 minutes. You may wish to suggest that they create a grid with three columns to support note-making and planning:
- points made in Text A
- agree or disagree
- evidence or counter-argument and evidence.

© HarperCollins *Publishers* Ltd 2018

Chapter 12: Practice papers and guidance

Allow 20 minutes for this task, then instruct students to begin writing their letters. After 25 minutes, suggest that students proofread their work for five minutes, as vocabulary, register and technical accuracy are important in this task.

Step 5

Move on to Section B. Make sure that students remember what 'composition' is. Allow them 10 minutes to brainstorm ideas for at least two of the four possible tasks using **Worksheets 12.2c–d** before they select one. You may wish them to plan all four, or limit them to two to save time. The worksheets allow students to select possible features of their compositions. Emphasise that the most successful compositions are often those where the student writes from personal experience.

Students should then use their completed grids to decide which task they wish to write the full response for.

Allow 40 minutes writing time. After this, suggest that students proofread their work for 10 minutes, as vocabulary and technical accuracy are important in this task.

Step 6

Once students have completed the practice exam-style paper, there are a number of activities to encourage them to engage with the success criteria and to assess their own work.

a) Give students **Worksheet 12.2e** and ask them to rate the two sample responses using the descriptors provided. You can allow them to choose either sample to assess, or ask them to focus on the genre of composition that they chose in the practice exam-style paper. Give feedback using **PPT 12.2a–i**.

Then ask them to answer the same questions about their own compositions.

b) An annotation activity could be completed using **Worksheet 12.2f**. Students could annotate the two responses, which will encourage them to engage with success criteria, as directed. Give feedback using **PPT 12.2j–s**.

Step 7

Once students' responses have been reliably marked, hand out **Worksheet 12.2g** and ask students to conduct a self-review, looking at their own strengths and weaknesses and identifying targets for improvement.

Chapter 1: Key reading skills

Worksheet 1.2: Scanning a text

Student's Book Q3 Using the extract from *Q & A* by Vikas Swarup, complete the table below to explore how the writer suggests that the house is unpleasant.

Words read	Is this about a house?	Are the words unpleasant?	Other thoughts
'I live in a corner of [the city]'	no, about an area		corner sounds like a trap – not nice
'in a'	yes, 'in' suggests we are going to get a description of a house next		
'cramped'		yes, means too small for comfort	
'hundred-square-foot'	yes, about its size		I am used to a bigger room so I would not like this
'shack'	another word for a house	this word means not well made or temporary, so yes	
'which has (a) no natural light'			
'or (b) ventilation'			
'with a corrugated metal sheet serving as a roof over my head'			
'It vibrates violently'			
'whenever a train passes overhead'			
'There is no running water'			
'and no sanitation'			

© HarperCollins *Publishers* Ltd 2018

Chapter 1: Key reading skills

Worksheet 1.4 Selecting information to synthesise

Student's Book Q2 Underline and number all the different phrases that show the problems of extreme weather conditions. The first example has been done for you.

> Extreme winds, such as those found in hurricanes, tornadoes, and some thunderstorms can <u>overturn caravans</u> (1), tear off roofs and topple trees, causing extreme distress to many people and financial hardship to whole communities. Some of the strongest tornadoes can demolish houses completely, leaving people homeless and vulnerable to disease and criminal harm. People may be knocked down or struck by debris and many places may lose electricity. Flooding and storm surges can destroy buildings and roads, contaminate water supplies, halt other essential services and drown people. Large hail stones can damage cars and roofs, and destroy crops, but rarely kill people. Heat waves can lead to drought, which causes crop loss as well as health issues and death from dehydration.

Student's Book Q3 Now reread the extract and put the phrases that you have numbered under headings. Write your headings in the boxes provided; you don't have to use all the boxes. Decide whether each phrase needs a new heading or if can be placed under an existing heading. The first heading and example have been done for you.

Destruction of property		
1		

174 © HarperCollins *Publishers* Ltd 2018

Chapter 1: Key reading skills

Worksheet 1.5a: Exploring explicit meaning (1)

Student's Book **Q2** Using a dictionary, fill in the table below to explore the explicit meaning of the writer's words and their effect on the reader.

Word	Precise meaning	How this affects the reader	What the writer wanted to achieve
infinite	having no limits or measurable extent	makes clear how vast her imagination is	understanding of the girl's character
stuffed	very full	large number of objects in house made clear; makes it feel cramped	understanding of the girl's home environment
yellowed			
dusty			
artificial			
museum-like			
calm			
wrapped			
separated			

© HarperCollins *Publishers* Ltd 2018

175

Worksheet 1.5b: Exploring explicit meaning (2)

Chapter 1: Key reading skills

Student's Book Q2 Using a dictionary, fill in the table below to explore the explicit meaning of the writer's words and their effect on the reader.

Word	Precise meaning	How this affects the reader	What the writer wanted to achieve
infinite	having no limits or measurable extent	makes clear how vast her imagination is	understanding of the girl's character
stuffed	very full	large number of objects in house made clear; makes it feel cramped	understanding of the girl's home environment
wild			
loud			
messy			
unbiddable			
scalped			
attenuated			
insectile			
brassy			
adorned			

Worksheet 1.6a: How does Dickens create character?

Student's Book **Q4** Using the extract from *Great Expectations*, fill in the table below to explore how Dickens establishes the two characters.

Pip: What is said/done / How others react / Words used to describe him	Effect: What it tells us about him	Effect: What it suggests about his relationships

Magwitch: What is said/done / How others react / Words used to describe him	Effect: What it tells us about him	Effect: What it suggests about his relationships

Worksheet 1.6b: Analysing effects through implicit meanings

Chapter 1: Key reading skills

Student's Book Taking it further Read the next section of *Great Expectations* below and answer the questions about implied character that follow.

'Now lookee here!' said the man. 'Where's your mother?'

'There, sir!' said I.

He started, made a short run, and stopped and looked over his shoulder.

'There, sir!' I timidly explained. 'Also Georgiana. That's my mother.'

'Oh!' said he, coming back. 'And is that your father alonger your mother?'

'Yes, sir,' said I; 'him too; late of this parish.'

'Ha!' he muttered then, considering. 'Who d'ye live with,—supposin' you're kindly let to live, which I han't made up my mind about?'

'My sister, sir,—Mrs Joe Gargery,—wife of Joe Gargery, the blacksmith, sir.'

'Blacksmith, eh?' said he. And looked down at his leg.

After darkly looking at his leg and me several times, he came closer to my tombstone, took me by both arms, and tilted me back as far as he could hold me; so that his eyes looked most powerfully down into mine, and mine looked most helplessly up into his.

'Now lookee here,' he said, 'the question being whether you're to be let to live. You know what a file is?'

'Yes, sir.'

'And you know what wittles is?'

'Yes, sir.'

After each question he tilted me over a little more, so as to give me a greater sense of helplessness and danger.

'You get me a file.' He tilted me again. 'And you get me wittles.' He tilted me again. 'You bring 'em both to me.' He tilted me again. 'Or I'll have your heart and liver out.' He tilted me again.

I was dreadfully frightened, and so giddy that I clung to him with both hands, and said, 'If you would kindly please to let me keep upright, sir, perhaps I shouldn't be sick, and perhaps I could attend more.'

---

1 What action implies that the convict is afraid?

....

2 What does the word 'considering' imply is going through his mind?

....

3 What is implied by 'And looked down at his leg'?

....

4 What explanation implies that the narrator is an adult telling a story of his childhood?

....

5 What does the narrator's language in his final speech imply about his upbringing?

....

Chapter 1: Key reading skills

Worksheet 1.7a: Changing atmosphere

Task Change the 'happy' atmosphere of this piece of writing – first to 'miserable', then to 'frightening' – by altering the words and phrases that have been underlined.

Happy

I looked up at the <u>shining sun</u> in the sky and, feeling <u>happiness</u> deep in my heart, <u>laughed</u> out loud. The trees <u>swayed gently</u>, <u>birds sang</u> from the branches, and I felt <u>a warm glow</u> envelop me. I began to <u>walk lazily</u> through the forest, <u>smiling</u> at the <u>beauty</u> that surrounded me. <u>Pausing</u> at the bank of a stream, I <u>gazed</u> at the <u>glistening</u> waters before <u>jumping lightly</u> to the other side. I found myself in a field of <u>bluebells</u> and a <u>soft aroma drifted to</u> my nose. As my mind filled with <u>peace</u>, I <u>reclined on</u> the ground and <u>drifted into sleep</u>.

Miserable

I looked up at the _____ in the sky and, feeling _____ deep in my heart, _____ out loud. The trees _____ , _____ from the branches, and I felt _____ envelop me. I began to _____ through the forest, _____ at the _____ that surrounded me. _____ at the bank of a stream, I _____ at the _____ waters before _____ to the other side. I found myself in a field of _____ and a _____ _____ my nose. As my mind filled with _____ , I _____ the ground and _____ .

Frightening

I looked up at the _____ in the sky and, feeling _____ deep in my heart, _____ out loud. The trees _____ , _____ from the branches, and I felt _____ envelop me. I began to _____ through the forest, _____ at the _____ that surrounded me. _____ at the bank of a stream, I _____ at the _____ waters before _____ to the other side. I found myself in a field of _____ and a _____ _____ my nose. As my mind filled with _____ , I _____ the ground and _____ .

© HarperCollins *Publishers* Ltd 2018

Chapter 1: Key reading skills

Worksheet 1.7b: Analysing how writers create atmosphere

Student's Book Q6 Complete the tick chart to show the different elements used to create the mood.
Add five more words or phrases used to create the mood in the extract from *Set in Stone*.

Student's Book Q7 In the final column, write words or phrases of your own that would make the approach to the house exciting and optimistic.

Words or phrases	Time of year	Time of day	Weather	Land-scape	Object	Action	Sound	Exciting words or phrases
darkness		✓						
branches								
mossy earth								
trickle of water								
faint mist								
wrought-iron gates								
a loud grating squeal								

180 © HarperCollins *Publishers* Ltd 2018

Chapter 1: Key reading skills

Worksheet 1.8a Exploring emotive language (1)

Student's Book **Q6** Fill in the chart to explore emotive language and its effects.

Word/phrase	Effect on reader	Reason why the writer wants that effect
partially devoured	We think of the shocking sight of the remains, and the savage power and appetite of the creatures.	He wants us to be disgusted and to fear for Mr Fison.
coiled copiously		

© HarperCollins *Publishers* Ltd 2018

Worksheet 1.8b: Exploring emotive language (2)

Chapter 1: Key reading skills

Student's Book Q6 Fill in the chart to explore emotive language and its effects.

Word/phrase	Effect on the reader	Reason why the writer wants that effect
partially devoured	We think of the shocking sight of the remains, and the savage power and appetite of the creatures.	He wants us to be disgusted and to fear for Mr Fison.
coiled copiously		
glistening texture		
tentacle-surrounded mouth		
curious excrescence		
evil interest		
preying upon human flesh		
slowly uncoiling		
creeping		
soft purring		
pouring		

Worksheet 1.9a: Exploring sensory connotations

Student's Book **Q1** Fill in the chart to explore sensory connotations and their effect.

Word/phrase →	Explicit meaning →	Sensory connotations →	Effect
All around me was darkness.	no light, cannot see	fear, menace blindness	character feels scared place is frightening something bad is going to happen
a wailing shriek			
I could smell the coolness of the mossy earth			

Student's Book **Q2** Fill in the table to highlight the different words and phrases used to stimulate the senses in the beach description.

See	Hear	Touch	Taste	Smell
Slush-grey and ice-white gulls toddlers wrestle	scream	sticky	salt spray lingers	candyfloss wafts

Worksheet 1.9b: The effects of sensory language

Chapter 1: Key reading skills

Student's Book Q4 Fill in the table to explore different word types and their sensory effects.

Word/phrase	Noun	Adjective	Verb	Adverb	Effect
Slush-grey		✓			Precise colour, makes us picture dirty snow. This does not sound positive and adds to the feeling of unease or unhappiness.

Worksheet 1.9c: Writing about the effects of sensory language

Student's Book Taking it further

In this passage from Emily Brontë's *Wuthering Heights*, the narrator, Catherine Linton, almost falls out with Linton Heathcliff.

Add words/phrases to the table to explore different word types and their sensory effects.

> One time, however, we were near quarrelling. He said the pleasantest manner of spending a hot July day was lying from morning till evening on a bank of heath in the middle of the moors, with the bees humming dreamily about among the bloom, and the larks singing high up overhead, and the blue sky and bright sun shining steadily and cloudlessly. That was his most perfect idea of heaven's happiness: mine was rocking in a rustling green tree, with a west wind blowing, and bright white clouds flitting rapidly above; and not only larks, but throstles [thrushes] and blackbirds, and linnets, and cuckoos pouring out music on every side, and the moors seen at a distance, broken into cool dusky dells; but close by great swells of long grass undulating in waves to the breeze; and woods and sounding water, and the whole world awake and wild with joy. He wanted all to lie in an ecstasy of peace; I wanted all to sparkle and dance in a glorious jubilee. I said his heaven would be only half alive; and he said mine would be drunk: I said I should fall asleep in his; and he said he could not breathe in mine, and began to grow very snappish. At last, we agreed to try both, as soon as the right weather came; and then we kissed each other and were friends.

Word/phrase	Which sense appealed to?	Effect
'hot July day'		

Chapter 1: Key reading skills

Worksheet 1.12 Form and purpose

Student's Book Q1 Complete the table below to answer the question 'How would you expect form to influence content in the following texts?'. Explain your reasoning.

Form	Likely influence on content
an article in a free in-flight magazine	
a celebrity autobiography	
a newspaper review of a currently running play	

Student's Book Q2 Tick the purposes that you think would apply to each of the forms below. You can tick more than one purpose for each form.

Form	Inform	Advise	Persuade	Entertain
a news report				
a holiday brochure				
an accident prevention leaflet				

Worksheet 1.13: Deducing audience

Student's Book **Q1** Rank the factors in the table below according to how far they determine how you could be identified as part of a target audience. Give your reasoning.

For example, you might have a specialist hobby and read magazines on the subject.

Factor	How you rank it (1–7)	Comments on your ranking
where you live		
how old you are		
how much you have to spend		
your gender		
your level of education		
your specialist interests or pastimes		
your existing knowledge of a subject		

Worksheet 2.1 — Identifying word classes

Task Draw lines to match the word class on the left to the correct description on the right.

Word class	Description
verb	a word that links two words, phrases or clauses together (for example, *and*, *because*, *although*, *but*)
conjugate	a word that indicates a relationship between people or things, usually in space or time (for example, *before*, *on*, *to*, *by*, *under*)
tense	a word that expresses an action (*go*) or a state (*feel*, *like*)
adverb	a word that replaces a noun, to avoid repetition
preposition	a word that modifies or intensifies a verb or adjective
determiner	the form a verb takes to show the time of an action
pronoun and possessive pronoun	to change the form of a verb, usually giving it a different ending
conjunction	a word that specifies a noun (for example, ***a*** film, ***this*** cup, ***my*** cat)

Worksheet 2.3 — Using modal verbs

can	could	be able to
may	might	
shall	should	
must	have to	
will	would	

1   Choose one of the modal verbs above and create a sentence you might use or hear today.

....

....

2   In small groups, complete the dialogue below with suitable modal verbs.

'Hi Sadiq, _____ you come to the picnic tomorrow?' said Rav.

'Yes, but I _____ need to go shopping first,' replied Sadiq,

'because we _____ need enough food for everyone.'

'Of course, I _____ buy some.'

Chapter 2: Key technical skills

Worksheet 2.4a Getting commas right

Commas are used:

1 to **separate items in a list**.

   The colours in a rainbow are red, orange, yellow, green, blue, indigo and violet.

   There is no comma between the last two items as there is an *and*.

2 to **separate parts of a sentence**. If you are writing a complex sentence, then a comma separates the main clause (second clause in the example) from the subordinate clause (first clause in the example).

   Despite the fact that the rain had stopped, the man continued to hold an umbrella above his head.

   Notice that there is a subject and a verb in both clauses and that one can stand alone and one cannot. Where the two clauses meet is the place for a comma!

   When deciding whether to use a comma, ask yourself the following questions:

   - Are there two or more clauses?
   - Which clause can stand alone?

   Insert a comma before or after the main clause.

3 to **add more information**.

   'I'm not standing for this!' yelled the manager, aggressively pointing at the whole team.

   Here we learn more about the manager, but it is not a clause.

---

1 List all the members of your family:

   There is ....

   ....

   ....

2 Put commas in the correct places in these sentences.

   a) The queue to the football stadium snaked through the town which meant that the traffic was at a standstill.

   b) Having waited until the lights had changed Anya cycled straight across the junction.

3 Use a comma to add more detail about the speakers to the following conversation.

   'I do believe that we have met before,' said the man ....

   'Do you play cricket?' said the second man ....

   'Yes, for the local team, but only when I can,' replied the first man ....

   'Ah, that will be it. I was here last month. You thrashed us,' replied the second man. ....

   ....

Worksheet 2.4b: Getting apostrophes right

> **Apostrophes** are used:
>
> 1 to **show possession with a noun**, for example:
>
>   *Bella's basket; the girl's football; Miko's flute; the box's lid; the women's cell phones.*
>
>   (Do not use apostrophes in straight plural forms of nouns, for example:
>   *I bought some apples and mangoes.*)
>
> 2 to **shorten words in contracted forms**, for example:
>
>   *can't* instead of *cannot*
>
>   *don't* instead of *do not*.
>
> When you are writing these shortened forms, check where the letters are that you have missed out and mark the spot with an apostrophe: *shouldn't*. If you cannot see how the word has been shrunk, don't use an apostrophe.

1. Look at the examples of apostrophes to show possession above. Think of five more.

   ....

   ....

   ....

   ....

   ....

2. Shorten the following:

   would not = ...

   could not = ...

   will not = ...

   it is = ...

   there is = ...

   she has = ...

   we have = ...

3. Write down three more examples of apostrophes being used for contraction.

   .... = ...

   .... = ...

   .... = ...

Worksheet 2.4c: Colons, semi-colons, brackets and dashes

Remember that often:
- a **colon** signals to the reader: *and I'm going to tell you why*
- a **semi-colon** signals to the reader: *and I'm going to tell you a little bit more about that*
- **brackets** signal to the reader: *don't forget that*
- a **dash** signals to the reader: *know what I mean?*

Task 1 Choose a character: politician, comedian, charity worker or TV presenter. Decide on the type of punctuation you think would convey their role and personality. For example:

I am a politician and I am going to tell you exactly why I believe I am right so I will be using the colon.

Next choose an issue of importance to your character – global warming, rights for young people, improved transport systems or the rise of celebrities.

- My chosen character: (for example, *Nelson Mandela*) ....
- Punctuation to suit this character: (for example, *dash*) ....
- My chosen issue/topic: (for example, *reconciliation*) ....

Write a short speech using punctuation to help to convey your meanings. Begin:

Today, I would like to talk about moving forward – there is no time for us to stand still. There is no passion to be found playing small – in settling for a life that is less than the one you are capable of living.

Worksheet 2.5: Understanding speech punctuation

Chapter 2: Key technical skills

Rules for speech punctuation.

1. Put speech marks around the actual words spoken, including any punctuation – this might be a comma, an exclamation mark, a question mark or a full stop.
2. Use a new line for each new speaker. When the speech is not a question or exclamation, put a comma before the closing speech mark.
3. If the speaker comes first in a sentence, add a comma afterwards and then the speech inside speech marks. Begin speech with a capital letter and end with a full stop.
4. You can place the speaker mid-sentence if you wish. If the sentence of speech continues on, do not give the first word of the speech a capital letter.
5. If someone speaks more than one sentence but the speaker is mentioned in between, use a full stop and then a capital letter to start the next part of the speech.

---

1 Rewrite the text below using the five rules for punctuating speech. The text in bold is correctly punctuated. You could also add clearer descriptions of who is speaking.

> *I ran up the corridor towards the exam room. Out of breath, I turned the handle and burst in. 'You're late!' hissed my teacher. But I was just... You're late she said again. Sit down he whispered. Sorry. I was given the exam paper. The clock said 10:07. I had been seven minutes late.*
>
> *One hour and fifty-two minutes later pens down was thundered across the room. I left as soon as I could. I didn't want twenty questions about where I had been from everyone. But it was unavoidable. What happened to you she said. Nothing I said back. But you were so late. I didn't think they would let you take the examination. Neither did I said someone.*

....

....

....

....

....

....

....

....

....

....

2 Continue the dialogue, using correct speech punctuation.

....

....

....

Worksheet 2.7 Using connectives

Student's Book Q3 Add appropriate connectives to the following email written by a check-in assistant to her boss, who was ill and away from the airport for the day.

.... (time) *was incredibly busy at the airport.*

.... (cause/effect) *there were long queues up to my desk. Apparently, the traffic in the city was terrible.*

.... (development) *there was a student demonstration, which closed the main road.*

.... (contrast) *most passengers made it on time,*

.... (contrast) *one family, poor things, had a nasty shock when they handed me their tickets. They'd got the wrong day!*

Worksheet 2.8: Proofreading an article

Task Choose one of these articles and proofread it. You need to correct mistakes in spelling, punctuation and grammar.

Fire in Portugal turns UK sky red

Forest fires in portugal cuase 'miracle sun set' over Grate Britain.

Sky watcher all over the UK were astounded by the rare sihtg of beautifull orange-red skys. The Met office receives many enquires last nigt inquiring what had happened. A spokesman sad "we we're at frits surprided by the number off calls we had. But we would lik to reassure the public that the is nothing to worry about. He went on to explan that the atmosferic disturbance was as a result of thr recent firs in Portugal.

US airport brought to a standstill

Houston airport shuts by tornado.

Travellers in Euston airport last night wear dissapointed to discover that all flights where canceled because off a string of Tornados that hit the city on tuesday.

Mr Gomez of Dallas, texas, told hour reported last night how he had been, "trapped in his car for ate hours unable two get home."

Air traffic controll said that the situation was now stable and flights we're expected to resume to day.

Brazil nut shortage sparks granola crisis

shoppers go 'nuts' for granola as stores run out.

A recent short age of brazil nuts caused by last years bad whether, as lead to shops across Europe and North America running low on breakfast serial.

Dr De Silva off Brazil's institute of food explained that the shortage were likely too last into next year. He said. "the pour weather last Febury will mean at lease eighteen months of lowe harvests." Shoppers may well have to wait until then to enjoy there favorite breakfast treat

---

Is the Antarctic ice cap shrinking?

Polar base set to be abanded by melting ice cap.

Another season of higher than usal tempratures ha meant that a international polar research baes maybe left deserted if it cannot be relocated before the icesheet it sits on melts.

Proffessor Quereshi, an renowned expert in wild life conservation poined out that the is a disaster for see life two. "all though it is a shame for the scientists working on the base he said, "it is devastatin for the seals and pengwins."

Worksheet 2.9: Levels of formality

Task Work in groups of three or four. Draft a line of speech for each character below. Focus on the nouns and verbs that might give the listener a clue as to who they are.

Try not to slip into stereotypical choices!

Who is the most formal? What might they say?

Dentist: ....

Judge: ....

Head teacher: ....

Banker: ....

Politician: ....

Who is the least formal? What might they say?

Carpenter: ....

Bus driver: ....

Student: ....

Writer: ....

Engineer: ....

Mother: ....

Worksheet 2.10: Voice and role

Task You can tell a lot about people from what they say and how they say it. Work in groups of four to read the statements from four people below. Who are they? What is their role? How do you know?

Once you have shared your ideas, match the statement to the role. Make sure that you can explain your choice, referring to the language used for each one.

> Of course we were very proud to see our lad up on stage. To think it was only two years ago that he left home and started his career. We took so many photos!

actor Sunil

Why have I chosen this role?
....
....
....
....

> I felt so nervous. Of course, we'd rehearsed for weeks but nothing prepares you for curtain up. Waiting in the wings felt like an eternity. I didn't think it went that well, to tell the truth.

theatre reviewer

Why have I chosen this role?
....
....
....
....

> Sunil Vaswani's landmark performance in the central role was a revelation. He combined a certain vulnerability and power at the same time and spoke Shakespeare's verse with clarity and control.

interviewer

Why have I chosen this role?
....
....
....
....

> So, Sunil, this is your first major stage role and it looks like you nailed it, according to the reviews. Does this mean you'll be looking for parts in films soon?

Sunil's mum

Why have I chosen this role?
....
....
....
....

Worksheet 3.1a: Identifying word classes

Chapter 3: Key writing forms

Technique	Example from Jolie's speech	Example from your partner's speech
Sets out the context for speech.		
Uses personal pronouns to connect with the audience directly.		
Provides reasons for speech.		
Uses personal anecdote to engage interest.		
Uses vivid descriptive images to build picture.		
Develops and provides further detail on the speech's purpose.		
Uses repetition to punch home message.		
Uses pattern of three to create rhetorical impact.		
Uses repetition to stress a point.		

Worksheet 3.1b: Identifying techniques and effects

Task Use this worksheet to discuss parts of the speech with your group. Your teacher will allocate a section of the speech for you to focus on. You can underline, highlight or annotate significant words and sentences.

We're here today to talk about millions of desperate families – families so cut-off from civilization that they don't even know that a day like this exists on their behalf. Millions. And numbers can illuminate but they can also obscure. So I am here today to say that refugees are not numbers.

They're not even just refugees. They are mothers and daughters and fathers and sons – they are farmers, teachers, doctors, engineers, they are individuals all. And most of all they are survivors – each one with a remarkable story that tells of resilience in the face of great loss. They are the most impressive people I have ever met and they are also some of the world's most vulnerable. Stripped of home and country, refugees are buffeted from every ill wind that blows across this planet.

I remember meeting a pregnant […] woman in a completely abandoned camp. […] She couldn't travel when everyone else was relocated because she was too late in her pregnancy. She was alone with her two children and another woman. There was nothing for miles around the camp – not a single tree, no other people in sight. So when they asked me to come in for tea I said I didn't feel it necessary. But […] they take pride in how they treat their guests so they insisted and they guided me into a small dirt house with no roof to keep out the scorching heat, and they dusted off the two old mats that they ate, slept and prayed on. And we sat and we talked and they were just the loveliest women. And then with a few twigs and a single tin cup of water, they made the last of their tea and insisted on me to enjoy it.

Since before the parable of the Widow's Mite it has been known that those who have the least will give the most. Most refugee families will offer you the only food they have and pretend they're not hungry. And the generosity of the poor applies not only to refugees. We should never forget that more than 80% of refugees are hosted and have been for years and years in the poorest developing countries.

Worksheet 3.2: Identifying roles in an interview

Student's Book Q1 Read the interview about Siberian tigers. Annotate the dialogue with notes about the different roles of each speaker, and how this is represented in the way they speak. Use the statements on the PowerPoint slide and any ideas of your own.

Reporter: I'm here to talk to Dr Sandra Cappello, a consultant for animal charity Save Our Species.

Expert: Good evening.

Reporter: So, Dr Cappello – with just under 500 tigers still in the wild, it seems like conservation efforts have failed, haven't they?

Expert: Well, it's true that numbers have dwindled. There were once many more tigers in China, Mongolia and Korea. Places such as the Eastern Himalayas were ideal for them but it's a fragile landscape.

Reporter: (interrupts) You haven't answered my question. Have efforts failed? I have been reporting for years on this issue and it's just not improving.

Expert: There are so many problems – we can't do everything. Many, many organisations are committed to protecting different tiger species, but it's a monumental task.

Reporter: So, what would you say is the biggest threat to them?

Expert: It's difficult to single one out – but loss of habitat is clearly a huge issue. Once hunting grounds have disappeared, it can take literally hundreds of years to recover them.

Reporter: Right – I get it. No trees, no tigers.

Expert: It's not quite as simple as that, but broadly speaking that is the situation.

Reporter: Thank you, Dr Cappello. That's all we have time for.

Worksheet 3.3: Understanding content, structure and style

Student's Book Q2 Read the diary extract and make notes on the content, structure and style of the writing.

Monday, 11 March

What a day it's been! I overslept and missed the school bus and then, when I finally arrived, I found out the whole class was on a science trip and they had already left. I felt such a fool. I had to sit on my own outside the head teacher's office all day. It was so boring!

I'm back home now, sitting in my room. I haven't told Mum or Dad I missed the trip. If I do, they'll go mad. Dad's home. I'd better pretend I'm asleep.

Content: This is what the writing is about – what subjects has the writer chosen to include? Why do you think they are important to the writer? Why do they make the diary interesting to read?

Structure: This is about *how* the information has been organised – have incidents been grouped together for any reason? Have they been described in chronological order or do very important incidents come first? What information about the writer do we get from the sequence of events in the diary?

Style: This is about the choice of words, sentences and paragraphs the writer has made. Are the choices linked to who they are and where they live or what they do, or are they linked to what effect the writer wants to have on the reader?

Fill in the gaps below.

The diary is about a day when a student _____ and misses a school trip

because of a series of unfortunate incidents. They _____ .

Then, they miss the _____ .

Then they need to _____ . Finally, they are too

_____ to tell their _____ because they

think they will _____ .

Worksheet 3.5: Writing a feature article

Chapter 3: Key writing forms

Student's Book Q6 Highlight the ideas and facts from these two articles that you will use in your own feature article.

Mountain Goat Kills Hiker
by Alex Robinson

ROBERT BOARDMAN, 63, was hiking with his wife and friend in Olympic National Park on Monday when he was attacked and killed by a mountain goat. The trio was hiking up a popular switchback trail and decided to stop for lunch when the goat approached them and started acting aggressively.

Boardman tried to scare the goat off, but instead of running away, it charged him goring him badly in the leg. More hikers came to try to help Boardman, but the goat stood over the man's body and wouldn't let any other hikers come to his aid.

An hour after the attack, rescuers finally arrived at the scene but Boardman died from his injuries. Park officials eventually shot and killed the goat.

Apparently, that specific goat had shown aggressive tendencies in the past. 'It has shown aggressive behaviour, however, nothing led us to believe it was appropriate to take the next level of removal,' park spokeswoman Barb Maynes told the Associated Press. 'This is highly unusual. There's no record of anything similar in this park. It's a tragedy. We are taking it extremely seriously and doing our best to learn as much as we can.'

The goat is being examined by scientists to see if it had any diseases that could have caused it to act so aggressively.

From www.outdoorlife.com

FIRST, CATCH YOUR FERAL KITTEN. THEN CALL IN THE EXPERTS.

My neighbourhood is inundated with feral cats, scraggy wild things that cadge food from animal lovers in winter and cadge baby blackbirds and robins from their nests each spring. Typically, I've moaned about this without taking any responsibility – until last week, when I became so exasperated, I set a humane trap.

I bought a wire cage to see if I could catch a squirrel or rat to show my animal-mad daughter, Esme. Luckily she was at school when the door slammed on an adorable kitten. Clueless about what I should actually do, for the first time in my life I called the RSPCA. Rather like the first time I needed a hospital and was astounded by the brilliance of the doctors and nurses, the RSPCA was amazing.

The charity knew all about my street's cat problem and had caught 20 feral cats so far. I was asked to take "21" to meet an RSPCA officer at a nearby vet, where the kitten was checked (cats are assessed and adults scanned for microchips to ensure they are not pets) and pronounced a feral tomcat.

Because 21 is only eight weeks old, he will be found a home as a pet. Adults are neutered and released wherever they came from, which my neighbourhood blackbirds won't welcome, but feral cats have hard lives and only survive for a couple of years.

The RSPCA has now lent me a better trap so I can join other neighbours in helping feral cats and other wildlife, at no expense to the taxpayer. Bravo for the big (cat) society. One problem remains: Esme is tearfully begging to keep the next catch.

From 'First catch your feral kitten' by Patrick Barkham, *The Guardian*

Chapter 3: Key writing forms

Worksheet 3.6a: Identifying levels of formality in letters

Student's Book **Q1** Use the table below to note down the features you identify in the two letters.

Informal letter	Formal letter
Content – what is the letter about? Why has it been written?	Content – what is the letter about? Why has it been written?
Structure – how has the information been organised?	Structure – how has the information been organised?
Style – how would you describe the language used and the 'voice' of the writer?	Style – how would you describe the language used and the 'voice' of the writer?

Now summarise the features of the letters.

The two letters are similar in the way that they both ....

....

....

However, the two letters are different because...

....

....

....

© HarperCollins *Publishers* Ltd 2018

Chapter 3: Key writing forms

Worksheet 3.6b: Identifying the styles used in letters

Student's Book **Q2** Use the table below to make notes about the different styles you can identify in the two letters.

Informal	Formal
What kind of vocabulary is used?	What kind of vocabulary is used?
Are there abbreviations?	Are there abbreviations?
What do you notice about the sentences?	What do you notice about the sentences?
Is punctuation used?	Is punctuation used?
How does the email open/close?	How does the letter open/close?

204 © HarperCollins *Publishers* Ltd 2018

Worksheet 4.2 Ordering paragraphs

Student's Book **Q3** Cut out the four boxes and see whether the article makes sense if the paragraphs are placed in a different order.

These specialised words go back many, many years. In fact, back in the 16th century, Shakespeare wrote a speech in his play *The Taming of the Shrew* in which the main character, Petruchio, talked about how he was going to tame his wife as if she were a hawk!

Falconry is a centuries-old activity, and it is still revered today. It is the act of hunting animals in their natural habitat through the use of a trained bird of prey.

Nowadays, falconry is used for more pleasant purposes. People hire displays for fairs, exhibitions and even weddings. But, don't forget the ancient skills or training that go into it as you watch such a display this summer.

The process of training hawks is highly skilled. It begins with 'manning' – that is, getting the hawk used to your presence. Once the hawk trusts you and will feed calmly on your gloved first, training can begin. The hawk now has to learn to come to you for food. First, it needs to be attached to a line – called a 'creance' – and placed on a post or an assistant's hand. Then, you hold a piece of meat in your gloved first so the hawk can see it. To start with, it will probably only come for a very short distance, but after a few days you can increase the distance to about 50–100 metres. When the hawk comes this far without hesitation, you are ready to let it fly freely. Then, using a 'lure' (a line with meat at the end) you can train it to follow or come to you.

Worksheet 4.3: Improving persuasive speech

Chapter 4: Writing for purpose

Task How could the following speech be improved? Make a list of the problems that you see, then consider how to improve them before redrafting below.

> *Fingerprint identification is a good idea because it improves safety on our phones and our tablets. It is a good idea because it makes thieves not want to steal our things because they would not be able to use them. It is a good thing because people won't have to remember loads of different codes and passwords.*

Problems:

1 Adjective 'good' is used three times in three sentences.

2 Connective 'because' is used three times.

3 No emotional input to persuade the reader of a need to change.

4 ....

5 ....

Solutions:

1 The phrase 'a good idea' could be replaced with 'worthwhile' or 'effective'; 'is a good idea' could be replaced by 'makes sense'. The final sentence could begin with 'It has the added advantage that…'.

2 The second sentence could link more closely to the first: 'Thieves will not want to steal our things if they will not be able to use them'. See above for third sentence, or use 'since'.

3 Emotive language could make a reader feel that the improvement would enhance their lifestyle: 'Fingerprint identification could make your life easier by taking the password screen off your phone, meaning easy access to talk to your friends or make those essential purchases'.

4 ....

....

5 ....

....

Now redraft the paragraph:

....

....

....

....

....

....

....

Worksheet 4.4: Structuring persuasion

Task Cut up the three pieces of information and decide which is the best order. Read the information aloud and experiment with making an effective delivery.

Parents and older siblings do not set a good example for the children as they guzzle plastic bottles full of coloured, fizzy drinks on the way to and back from school every day.

The sales of fizzy drinks in the shops around this school have risen to a ten-year, all-time high.

Local dentist reports alarming figures for children's dental treatment; a 75% increase in cavities and an 80% rise in extractions for children. Alarm bells are ringing.

Chapter 4: Writing for purpose

Worksheet 4.5 Adding personal experience to an argument

Student's Book Q4 Use this table to develop ideas for adding personal experience to an argument. Complete each unfinished sentence and add at least one new one, to contribute to an argument in favour of cycling to work.

A	To be honest, I used to find it quite frightening riding in heavy traffic to get to work, but…
B	It would normally take me about half an hour to drive to work in town, much of that time being spent sitting in traffic. Now…
C	I find cycling to work quite a liberating experience. No more driving around trying to find a parking space. Now I just…
D	I did have a friend who got knocked off her bike, but…
E	I know people worry about traffic fumes, but for me, this is far outweighed by…

Chapter 4: Writing for purpose

Worksheet 4.6a: Using connectives to develop a viewpoint

Task Read the paragraph below, then follow the three steps in the table to practise expressing different viewpoints using connectives.

> Do bins need emptying every week? Controversially, my local council does not think so. We are left with overflowing bins spoiling our streets every two weeks as we wait, desperately, for collection day.

Step 1	Change the conjunctive adverb 'controversially' to one of the following: *stingily, thankfully, strangely, unfortunately, fortunately*	Do bins need emptying every week? ...., my local council does not think so. We are left with overflowing bins spoiling our streets every fortnight as we wait, desperately, for collection day.
Step 2	Change the adverb 'desperately' to one of the following: *patiently, calmly, bravely, resolutely*	Do bins need emptying every week? ...., my local council do not think so. We are left with overflowing bins spoiling our streets every fortnight as we wait, ..., for collection day.
Step 3	Change the conjunction 'as' to one of the following: *and, but, while, because*	Do bins need emptying every week? ...., my local council do not think so. We are left with overflowing bins spoiling our streets every fortnight .... we wait, ..., for collection day.

What is the effect of using these different conjunctions and conjunctive adverbs?

Write a sentence of your own to finish the paragraph, summing up the viewpoint developed above.

....

....

....

....

....

Worksheet 4.6b: Developing an argument

Chapter 4: Writing for purpose

Student's Book **Q10** Use the table below to track the progress of the debate in the article about fracking, to show how the different ideas are presented.

Sentence	Conjunction or conjunctive adverb	Effect (To contrast? To show an outcome?)
Hailed as… colourful.	or	presents the positive and negative sides
It enables us... price of energy.		
Nevertheless... generation.		
Dirty coal… climate change.		
However,… fuel.		
Its emissions… global warming.		

Worksheet 4.8a: Planning discursive writing

Student's Book **Q2** Use the table below to organise the information about chocolate in the Student's Book into 'pros' and 'cons'. Try to put points that might counter-balance each other in opposite columns.

Pros	Cons
100 g dark chocolate per day could reduce the risk of a heart attack or stroke by 21%. (*British Medical Journal* research)	Typical ingredients in a chocolate bar: butter, sugar, cream or milk, lots of calories that can make you put on weight.

© HarperCollins *Publishers* Ltd 2018

Chapter 4: Writing for purpose

Worksheet 4.8b — Structuring content

Student's Book Q3 The following sentences are of three types:
- topic sentences
- supporting information
- writer's viewpoint.

Cut them up and read them out to arrange them in piles for each type. Then try to connect them together to form four full paragraphs.

Chocolate can be good for your health in a range of ways.

Caffeine can help make you more alert.

If eaten to excess, chocolate can damage your teeth.

It cannot be denied that chocolate contains calories.

Caffeine does have good qualities as well as bad, doctors agree.

---

100 g dark chocolate per day could reduce the risk of a heart attack or stroke by 21%. (*British Medical Journal* research)

One student said, 'I bought a large bar of chocolate recently and finished it all in one go, and I felt really guilty, especially when the dentist told me a week later that I needed two fillings.'

Typical ingredients in a chocolate bar: butter, sugar, cream or milk, lots of calories that can make you put on weight.

I am going to feel less guilty about my morning cup of coffee now.

There are plans I'm sure to make low calorie chocolate, if it hasn't been done already.

The message is clear, don't eat to excess, but don't deny yourself either.

I am looking forward to managing my risk of heart attack or stroke with 100 g of dark chocolate.

Worksheet 4.9: Semantic fields

Student's Book **Q9** Extend the semantic fields by adding **nouns** to each column.

Storm	Forest	Creatures	River
thunder	tendrils	red ants	muddy banks
raindrops	roots	python	
disappearing sun	canopy	tree frog	
darkness, gloom	leaves		
oppression			

Now create a 'semantic field table' of **verbs** you could use in relation to each feature.

Storm	Forest	Creatures	River
			swirl
			flow

Worksheet 4.10: Creating character

Student's Book Q4 Fill in the table below to develop your own ideas about each character, building on those given in the Student's Book. You could consider:

- their backstory (their past, which might influence what they are like)
- their ambitions or motivation
- strengths and/or weaknesses
- typical behaviour or speech.

Character	Your ideas
Jake	
Michelle	
Priya	
Marco	
Your new character	

Worksheet 5.1: Skimming, scanning and locating information

Student's Book **Q7** Read the text about the Kirirom national park again. Use your skimming and scanning skills, and your understanding of facts, opinions and information related to a specific theme, to answer the following questions.

> ### Kirirom National Park
>
> All that remains of the king's palace is the fireplace. Twenty feet tall, it was built in the 1940s by the king and his **acolytes**. It stands on a flattened mountain top. The view is of Cambodia's only high-altitude pine forest, in Kirirom national park – two hours' drive southwest of Phnom Penh. The scenery is almost alpine, the skinny pines saluting the sun, the air aromatic and fresh. [During a period of unrest] the palace [was smashed] along with 150 surrounding villas that once made up the king's "Happy Mountain" resort. Some buildings are intact – more deserted than ruined.
>
> Today, Kirirom is popular among locals but often overlooked by foreign visitors. Away from the hot chaos of the capital, there are peaceful treks, mountain biking and dips in waterfalls. A stay at Kirirom Mountain Lodge (doubles from US$35; from $60 on weekend), a converted 1940s villa near Oamrei Phong village in the centre of the park, Moroccan chef Bouchaib serves flatbread, honey-dripped and dotted with raisins. Guests can eat while surveying the green expanse of cardamom forests below.
>
> From 'Undiscovered South-East Asia' by Nathan Thomson, *The Guardian*

a) Give two facts about the king's palace, according to the text.

....

....

b) Give two examples of things that you can do in Kirirom national park, according to the text.

....

....

c) Give two features of the natural landscape in Kirirom national park, according to the text.

....

....

Chapter 5: Comprehension

Worksheet 5.2: Literal and implied meanings

Student's Book **Q4** Complete the following table using the quotations from the box below. For each statement, choose one piece of evidence that has literal meaning and one that implies meaning. Two boxes have been completed for you.

Statement about the text	Quotation with literal meaning	Quotation with implied meaning
The weather is hot.	'the sun was blazing'	
The beach is busy.		'searching for a spot'
The children are happy.		
The writer feels that tourists have ruined the beach.		

~~'the sun was blazing'~~
~~'searching for a spot'~~
'children were happily playing games'
'people were queuing for glasses of iced water'

'tourism had spoiled the peace and the beauty'
'smiling faces brightened the scene'
'this place was once paradise'

Student's Book **Q5** Look at your list of quotations with implied meanings. Underline the specific words in those quotations that suggest meaning then note down below what they suggest.

....
....
....
....
....
....
....
....

Worksheet 5.3a (1) Practice questions: comprehension questions

Student's Book Q1–5 Read the text below and answer the questions that follow.

Kratié town and its surrounds

Few tourists stray into Cambodia's "wild east" where, beyond Kampong Cham, the main roads are dirt tracks or just poorly surfaced. Yet this sparsely populated region offers a quintessential slice of Cambodian rural life largely unaffected by the world beyond.

Kratié is a little market town 216 miles north-east of Phnom Penh. A spattering of tourist-friendly cafes and hotels has sprung up near the central market place or facing the Mekong river. An evening stroll is the ideal time to absorb the spectacle of sunset. It's like watching a giant blood orange fall from a tree in slow motion. As the sun dips behind the treeline it turns the sky a dazzling vermilion, tinting purple the French colonial villas, traditional wooden stilt houses and Wat Roka Kandal – a beautiful temple that dates back to the 19th century.

The nearby river island of Koh Trong boasts the alluring possibility of seeing Cantor's giant soft-shell turtles in the wild. After a short ferry ride from an unsheltered wharf, the Preah Soramarith Quay (preceded by a long, hot wait), visitors enter a bucolic world of fruit plantations and rice paddies still tilled by Cambodia's iconic white cows, the humped zebu.

The local community office advertises rural homestays organised by NGOs, bicycle hire and ox cart tours. The 8.5-mile perimeter route takes you right around the island's edge. It's unchallenging and climaxes with the sight of a floating Vietnamese village buoyed-up just off the south-west tip of the island. The Vietnamese are a recognised ethnic minority in Cambodia and this community lives offshore, though they've established a Vietnamese-style temple on the island. An unexpected treat after a hard day's pedalling is Rajabori Villa Resort in the north-east of the island, where it's possible to cool off in the pool for just $5 (doubles from $65 a night).

The route north out of Kratié is so breathtakingly scenic one almost forgives the dismal quality of the roads. It's a necessarily bumpy tuk-tuk ride in order to take in Kratié's rare ecological treasures. In Phnom Sambor, 22 miles north of Kratié, visitors are guaranteed a sight of the soft-shell turtles. In the hallowed grounds of the Pagoda of One Hundred Columns, a small breeding centre aims to return the turtles to the river.

Closer to Kratié the fishing village of Kampie offers boat trips to view Kratié's other aquatic marvel, the Irrawaddy dolphins. Though locals have long revered the dolphins, believing them to be half human, half fish, their numbers have diminished in recent years due to electric rods and explosives used for fishing. Don't expect any flipper-style antics, these retiring creatures only surface to breathe.

From 'Undiscovered South-East Asia' by Thomas Bird, *The Guardian*

Worksheet 5.3a (2): Practice questions: comprehension questions

1. Give **two** facts about Kratié according to the second paragraph.

   ....

   ....

2. Using your own words, explain what the text means by:

   a) 'climaxes with the sight' (paragraph 4)

   ....

   b) 'breathtakingly scenic' (paragraph 5)

   ....

3. Reread paragraph 3. Give **two** reasons why people might visit the island of Koh Trong.

   ....

   ....

4. Reread paragraphs 2 and 6.

   a) Identify **two** things that tourists can enjoy in the town of Kratié.

   ....

   b) Explain some of the different attitudes displayed towards dolphins.

   ....

   ....

   ....

5. Using your own words, explain why some people may find visiting Kratié and its surroundings too challenging.

   ....

   ....

   ....

   ....

   ....

   ....

Worksheet 5.3b

Sample responses: comprehension questions

Chapter 5: Comprehension

Student's Book **Q6**   For each exam-style question, identify one thing in the sample responses that could be improved.

1 Give **two** facts about Kratié according to the second paragraph.

> - The Wat Roka Kandal is a beautiful 19th-century temple.
> - Kratié is in the east of Cambodia.

2 Using your own words, explain what the text means by:
   a) 'climaxes with the sight' (paragraph 4)
   b) 'breathtakingly scenic' (paragraph 5)

> a) The village you see is really impressive.
> b) The scenery is nice.

3 Reread paragraph 3. Give **two** reasons why people might visit the island of Koh Trong.

> - The chance to see giant soft-shell turtles in their natural habitat.
> - The ferry ride is short.

4 Reread paragraphs 2 and 6.
   a) Identify **two** things that tourists can enjoy in the town of Kratié.
   b) Explain some of the different attitudes displayed towards dolphins.

> a) Go shopping in the market and watch a giant blood orange fall from a tree.
> b) The writer is really impressed by the dolphins. The locals kill the dolphins with explosives because they think they are half-human, half-fish. They like the dolphins because they can make money by taking tourists to see them.

5 Using your own words, explain why some people may find visiting Kratié and its surroundings too challenging.

> People might find visiting Kratie too challenging because it is dirty and the roads are poorly surfaced. This makes any journeys really bumpy. It's also really hot and sometimes there is nowhere to take shelter. The temples sound boring and it would be really tiring having to cycle everywhere.

Chapter 6: Summary writing

Worksheet 6.2 — Locating, selecting, ordering and summarising

Task Read through this extract from a travel brochure about Tokyo. Then summarise, in 50–75 words, the different things a tourist can do when visiting Tokyo.

Remember to:
- skim the passage, looking out for information on what a tourist can do
- scan it to select key phrases
- underline these, then number them in a logical order
- write your summary, putting the information into your own words.

While lustrous skyscrapers, flashing neon and a wave of people burst frenetically across the streets of Tokyo, its extensive parks and gardens recline in tranquil beauty. This is a land of wonder, where natural and manufactured beauties merge in harmony as ancient and modern collide. We only use hotels on the Yamanote loop railway line, which makes it easy for you to embark on a city tour – for which we can provide comprehensive and insightful pre-departure notes.

Get up early for the amazing Tsukiji fish market and enjoy a sushi breakfast. Then take a stroll through the huge Ueno Park to the impressive National Museum or the Imperial Gardens, gazing across at the moated palace. Explore historic Asakusa with its temples and traditional handicrafts before plunging into the grandiose shopping and entertainment districts of Shinjuku, Shibuya and Ginza. There is so much to see and do (and buy), that you will want to spend plenty of time delving into Tokyo.

The city is also a good base for exploring some of Japan's best sights, the most famous being the conical perfection of Mount Fuji. Capped with snow and swathed in cloud, she looks down to Hakone with its sculpture park, volcanic hot springs and scenic Lake Ashi. Buddhist temples speckle the seaside town of Kamakura, once the country's capital, and there are pleasant walks around the area, whilst in Nikko you can see splendidly carved temples and shrines. The historical side of the country is fascinating and it is really worth visiting these reminders of its past. A peaceful boat trip to the Izu Islands, which reach down into the Pacific, reveals images of forgotten Japan; with beaches, hot springs and hidden shrines, these pretty isles are rarely visited by westerners.

Visiting Tokyo will be an experience you will cherish forever.

Chapter 6: Summary writing

Worksheet 6.3 Summarising key points

Student's Book **Q4** Using your own words as much as possible, rewrite each sentence below as a concise summary. Try to use no more than ten words for each one.

1	My mum's sister really liked working her way through as many books, magazines, newspapers and text books as she could possibly get her hands on.
2	The shop my dad runs sells pens, paper, ink cartridges, etc., and it is always full of people who just love shopping there.
3	At the end of the working week, when it's got dark and the stars are coming out, I like to just sit back, have a long, cool drink and watch some of the nonsense that is on the television.
4	My dad's father is really old – nearly 80 years old – but he still likes going out all the time and meeting his friends, his family and the people that he used to work with.
5	The world faces a range of environmental problems, probably the foremost of which is global warming, caused almost certainly by human influences like traffic and industrial pollution – especially from fossil fuels.
6	There are so many different ways to spend a day in London, including, of course, the numerous art galleries, like the Tate National – which was the original Tate Gallery and has all the J. M. W. Turner paintings, the Tate Modern (not for conservative tastes!), or world-class museums such as the British Museum and the Victoria and Albert.

© HarperCollins *Publishers* Ltd 2018

Worksheet 6.4: Sample question

Chapter 6: Summary writing

Task According to the text, what plans are there for reintroducing the lynx, and what are the arguments in favour of this?

You must use continuous writing (not notes) and your own words as far as possible.

Your summary should not be more than 150 words.

Lynx could return to Britain this year after absence of 1,300 years

After an absence of 1,300 years, the lynx could be back in UK forests by the end of 2017. The Lynx UK Trust has announced it will apply for a trial reintroduction for six lynx into the Kielder forest, Northumberland, following a two-year consultation process with local stakeholders.

The secretive cat can grow to 1.5m in length and feeds almost exclusively by ambushing deer. Attacks on humans are unknown, but it was hunted to extinction for its fur in the UK. The Kielder forest was chosen by the trust from five possible sites, due to its abundance of deer, large forest area and the absence of major roads.

Sheep farmers and some locals are opposed to the reintroduction, but Dr Paul O'Donoghue, chief scientific advisor to the Lynx UK Trust and expert adviser to the International Union for the Conservation of Nature (IUCN) believes there are good reasons for reintroducing the predator.

'Lynx belong here as much as hedgehogs, badgers, robins, blackbirds – they are an intrinsic part of the UK environment,' he told the Guardian. 'There is a moral obligation. We killed every single last one of them for the fur trade, that's a wrong we have to right.'

Rural communities would also benefit from eco-tourism, O'Donoghue said: 'They will generate tens of millions of pounds for struggling rural UK economies. Lynx have already been reintroduced in the Harz mountains in Germany. They have branded the whole area the 'kingdom of the lynx'. Now it is a thriving ecotourism destination and we thought we could do exactly the same for Kielder,' he said.

Lynx would also boost the natural environment, said O'Donoghue, by reducing the overgrazing of forests by deer, allowing other wildlife to flourish. 'We have a massive overpopulation of roe deer in the UK,' he said. 'We are one of the most biodiversity poor countries in the world. We need the lynx, more than the lynx needs us.' [...]

If lynx are reintroduced, it would be very difficult for eco-tourists to see the mainly nocturnal animals, O'Donoghue said: 'Lynx are very secretive and elusive, but that's completely irrelevant. It's a chance to walk in a forest where lynx live, a chance to see a lynx track, to see a lynx scratching post. And if you did see a lynx in the wild, it would be the wildlife encounter of a lifetime.'

From 'Lynx could return to Britain' by Damian Carrington, *The Guardian*

Worksheet 7.1: Using synonyms

Chapter 7: Analysing language

Task Working with a partner, come up with as many different synonyms as you can for the following verbs.

eat	look	make	move	think

Choose two words from each column and use them in a short paragraph. Check each word's specific meaning in a dictionary to ensure that you are using them precisely.

....

....

....

....

....

....

....

Worksheet 7.3a — Sensory and emotive language

Chapter 7: Analysing language

Student's Book Read through the text and answer the questions that follow.
Q1–Q3

> At first, we walked along the beach, hoping to circle the coast, but the sand soon turned to jagged rocks, which turned to impassable cliffs and gorges. Then we tried the other end, wasting precious time while the sun rose in the sky, and found the same barrier. We were left with no choice but to try inland. The pass between the peaks was the obvious goal so we slung our bin-liners over our shoulders and picked our way into the jungle.
>
> The first two or three hundred metres from the shore were the hardest. The spaces between the palm trees were covered in a strange rambling bush with tiny leaves that sliced like razors, and the only way past them was to push through. But as we got further inland and the ground began to rise, the palms became less common than another kind of tree—trees like rusted, ivy-choked space rockets, with ten-foot roots that fanned from the trunk like stabilizer fins. With less sunlight coming through the canopy, the vegetation on the forest floor thinned out. Occasionally we were stopped by a dense spray of bamboo, but a short search would find an animal track or a path cleared by a fallen branch.
>
> After Zeph's description of the jungle, with Jurassic plants and strangely coloured birds, I was vaguely disappointed by the reality. In many ways I felt like I was walking through an English forest, I'd just shrunk to a tenth of my normal size. But there were some things that felt suitably exotic. Several times we saw tiny brown monkeys scurrying up the trees, Tarzan-style **lianas** hung above us like stalactites—and there was the water: it dripped on our necks, flattened our hair, stuck our T-shirts to our chests. There was so much of it that our half-empty canteens stopped being a worry. Standing under a branch and giving it a shake provided a couple of good gulps, as well as a quick shower. The irony of having kept my clothes dry over the swim, only to have them soaked when we turned inland, didn't escape me.
>
> From *The Beach* by Alex Garland
>
> **Glossary**
>
> **liana:** a long, woody vine (often used by monkeys to swing from tree to tree)

1. The writer has created a detailed sensory picture for the reader. How has he achieved this?
   a) Which nouns has the writer chosen for their precise literal meaning?
   b) Select adjectives and adverbs that help to create a sensory picture.

2. The writer has also conveyed the narrator's different thoughts and feelings. How have these been presented?
   a) Which verbs show that the narrator found the exploration of the island difficult?
   b) Which adjectives add to the impression that the narrator found the journey difficult?

3. Reread the first paragraph. Look at the list of paired words below. Considering what the words tell you about the narrator's feelings or experiences, decide which is the most powerful word in each pair.
   a) try   picked
   b) barrier   inland
   c) sky   precious
   d) goal   pass

Chapter 7: Analysing language

Worksheet 7.3b — Powerful phrases

Student's Book **Q6** Reread the second paragraph of the extract on page 164, then complete the table below. Choose powerful phrases, apply subject terminology and consider what the phrase suggests about the narrator's feelings or experiences. Some examples have been given.

Chosen phrase	Subject terminology	Effect
'strange rambling bush'	noun phrase	This shows the vegetation is unusual which makes the narrator's journey more interesting and could suggest something is wrong.
	simile	
		This shows that the journey was physically difficult but that the narrator was determined to continue.
'dense spray of bamboo'		

© HarperCollins *Publishers* Ltd 2018

Chapter 7: Analysing language

Worksheet 7.4 Exploring analysis

Student's Book **Q2** When writing about a text, it is important to focus on specific details, give clear and precise explanations and try to make use of subject terminology.

Annotate the following two examples of analysis. Look for:

- a clear point
- a relevant quotation
- analysis of specific language
- development of analysis
- terminology
- concise explanations.

Decide which example is the best and why.

Which aspects of the less successful example need improvement?

Example 1

> In the second sentence, the writer uses the verb phrase 'wasting precious time' to convey the narrator's feelings when exploring the island. The verb 'wasting' suggests that he is getting frustrated by their inability to get across the island. The adjective 'precious' adds to this frustration by creating a mood of urgency: the narrator feels the hours of the day are quickly passing and they are running out of time. These examples of word choice clearly show his feelings.

Example 2

> The writer uses the words 'wasting precious time' when they are exploring the island and failing to find a way to get further inland. Despite wanting to explore, the narrator feels that the day is being 'wasted' and this word is a powerful way to show how he feels. The word 'precious' is also powerful as it describes the hours of the day. The text said the sun had already 'rose in the sky' which means that they are running out of time because they are spending so long trying to find a passable route around the island.

Worksheet 7.5a (1) Practice questions

Student's Book
Q1–4

Read this extract from Alex Garland's novel, *The Beach*. Answer the questions that follow.

After a long journey, the narrator has finally arrived at his hotel.

The first thing I did after shutting the door behind me was to go to the bathroom mirror and examine my face. I hadn't seen my reflection for a couple of days and wanted to check things were OK.

It was a bit of a shock. Being around lots of tanned skin I'd somehow assumed I was also tanned, but the ghost in the mirror corrected me. My whiteness was accentuated by my stubble, which, like my hair, is jet black. UV deprivation aside, I was in bad need of a shower. My T-shirt had the salty stiffness of material that has been sweated in, sun-dried, then sweated in again. I decided to head straight to the beach for a swim. I could kill two birds with one stone — soak up a few rays and get clean.

Chaweng was a travel-brochure photo. Hammocks slung in the shade of curving palm trees, sand too bright to look at, jet-skis tracing white patterns like jet-planes in a clear sky. I ran down to the surf, partly because the sand was so hot and partly because I always run into the sea. When the water began to drag on my legs I jumped up, and the momentum somersaulted me forwards. I landed on my back and sank to the bottom, exhaling. On the seabed I let myself rest, head tilted slightly forward to keep the air trapped in my nose, and listened to the soft clicks and rushes of underwater noise.

I'd been splashing around in the water for fifteen minutes or so when Étienne came down to join me. He also ran across the sand and somersaulted into the sea, but then leapt up with a yelp.

'What's up?' I called.

Étienne shook his head, pushing backwards through the water away from where he'd landed. 'This! This animal! This... fish!'

I began wading towards him. 'What fish?'

'I do not know the English — Aaah! Aaah! There are more! Aaah! Stinging!'

'Oh,' I said as I reached him. 'Jellyfish! Great!'

I was pleased to see the pale shapes, floating in the water like drops of silvery oil. I loved their straightforward weirdness, the strange area they occupied between plant and animal life.

From *The Beach* by Alex Garland

Chapter 7: Analysing language

Worksheet 7.5a (2) Practice questions

1. Identify a word or phrase from the text which suggests the same idea as the words underlined:

    a) The narrator <u>carefully inspects</u> his face in the bathroom mirror.

    ....

    b) The narrator's dark hair <u>emphasised</u> the paleness of his skin.

    ....

    c) When Etienne is stung by a jellyfish he <u>jumps from the water and cries out in pain</u>.

    ....

    d) Because the white sand reflected the light, it was <u>almost blinding</u>.

    ....

2. Using your own words, explain what the writer means by each of the words underlined:

    > I was <u>pleased</u> to see the pale shapes, floating in the water like drops of <u>silvery</u> oil. I loved their straightforward <u>weirdness</u>, the strange area they occupied between plant and animal life.

    ....

    ....

    ....

    ....

    ....

    ....

3. Explain how the phrases underlined are used by the writer to suggest the narrator's responses to the jellyfish. Use your own words in your explanation.

    > I was <u>pleased to see</u> the pale shapes, floating in the water <u>like drops of silvery oil</u>. I <u>loved their straightforward weirdness</u>, the strange area they occupied between plant and animal life.

    ....

    ....

    ....

    ....

    ....

    ....

    ....

Worksheet 7.5a (3) Practice questions

4. Reread paragraphs 2 and 3, describing the narrator's feelings about himself and the beach. Select four powerful words or phrases from each paragraph. Your choices should include imagery. Explain how each word or phrase is used effectively in the context. Write 200–300 words.

Chapter 7: Analysing language

Worksheet 7.5b Sample responses

Student's Book **Q5–8**

1. Identify a word or phrase from the text which suggests the same idea as the words underlined:
   a) The narrator <u>carefully inspects</u> his face in the bathroom mirror.
   b) The narrator's dark hair <u>emphasised</u> the paleness of his skin.
   c) When Etienne is stung by a jellyfish he <u>jumps from the water and cries out in pain</u>.
   d) Because the white sand reflected the light, it was <u>almost blinding</u>.

   > a) check
   > b) shock
   > c) 'Aaah! Stinging!'
   > d) the sand was so hot

2. Using your own words, explain what the writer means by each of the words underlined:

   I was <u>pleased</u> to see the pale shapes, floating in the water like drops of <u>silvery</u> oil. I loved their straightforward <u>weirdness</u>, the strange area they occupied between plant and animal life.

   > pleased – unlike Etienne, he isn't scared
   > silvery – shining like silver
   > weirdness – behaving like a freak

3. Explain how the phrases underlined are used by the writer to suggest the narrator's responses to the jellyfish. Use your own words in your explanation.

   I was <u>pleased to see</u> the pale shapes, floating in the water <u>like drops of silvery oil</u>. I <u>loved their straightforward weirdness</u>, the strange area they occupied between plant and animal life.

   > pleased to see – the narrator had seen the jellyfish before and wanted to see them again.
   > like drops of silvery oil – the jellyfish were silver and oily looking
   > I loved their straightforward weirdness – the narrator is fascinated by the jellyfish.

4. Reread paragraphs 2 and 3, describing the narrator's feelings about himself and the beach. Select four powerful words or phrases from each paragraph. Your choices should include imagery. Explain how each word or phrase is used effectively in the context. Write 200–300 words.

   > The word 'shock' is a powerful way to describe what the narrator feels when he looks in the mirror because he was expected to look more tanned. The word 'sweated' is also powerful because it shows how hot it was. The phrase 'soak up a few rays' describes how he wants to go sunbathing.
   >
   > The palm tree is described as 'curving'. This is good because it sounds quite peaceful and graceful which matches the atmosphere on the beach. This is similar to the phrase 'the soft clicks and rushes' which is a powerful way to describe what he hears underwater. The word 'clicks' makes it sound unusual which is suitable because he's underwater and the word 'rushes' links to the movement of the sea over him. However, because he says 'soft' this makes it seem really gentle and relaxing because he's enjoying himself.

Chapter 8: Extended response to reading and directed writing

Worksheet 8.1 Form, Purpose, Audience and Tone (F-PAT)

Student's Book **Q1** Annotate this task using the F-PAT acronym as a starting point:
- Form
- Purpose
- Audience
- Tone

You are Alfredo, again. You have been researching information about starting a new business selling soft drinks and snacks. You have just negotiated a really good price from a wholesale supplier and now you need to persuade your uncle, a local businessman, to invest in the start-up costs. Describe how you are going to market your products to the three different audiences at a football game:

- the Suns
- the Shades
- the Balcony people

Write an email to your uncle, starting with:

'Dear Uncle José,

I am writing to propose that you join me in a new business venture...'

Write about 250 to 350 words.

Up to 15 marks are available for the content of your answer, and up to 10 marks for the quality of your writing.

Worksheet 8.6: Three steps to synthesis

Chapter 8: Extended response to reading and directed writing

Student's Book **Q2**   Work through the three steps, filling in the blanks.

1 Combine

This step could mean using a compound sentence. Use a connective, such as *and, but, so,* or *because* to link two points. For example:

The family took over the whole playground + Their little boy was dropping litter all over the grass.
= The family took over the whole playground and their little boy dropped litter on the grass.

Remember **Q2**: *Extinction is going to be a problem because of climate change but we do not need to accept it.*

Which two sentences were combined to make the one above?

....

....

....

2 Summarise

This step means reducing a text to its most important points by combining ideas. So:

The family took over the whole playground and their little boy dropped litter on the grass.
= The playground was dominated by one very messy family.

Remember **Q2**: *Climate change will make extinction a problem but we can change it.*

Which words have been removed?

....

3 Create

This step requires the making of a new point from the summarised parts:

Some families have no sense of appropriate use of space.

Remember **Q2**: *We don't have to put up with the removal of species.*

Worksheet 8.7 Structuring a paragraph

Student's Book **Q2** Cut the table into strips, then work as a group of four to restructure the paragraph. There are two identical sets of sentences on this page.

It can turn people into strong supporters of conservation.

Yet, I disagree because if that child is given a false view of nature, then that is not healthy.

They need to know the reality about…

The writer also asserts that children's first experience with magnificent animals such as pandas can create a life-long interest in nature.

It can turn people into strong supporters of conservation.

Yet, I disagree because if that child is given a false view of nature, then that is not healthy.

They need to know the reality about…

The writer also asserts that children's first experience with magnificent animals such as pandas can create a life-long interest in nature.

Chapter 8: Extended response to reading and directed writing

Worksheet 8.8a — Practice question: extended responses to reading

Student's Book **Q1** Read the following task, then write a response of 250–350 words.

> Imagine that you are Richard Branson and you have been asked to speak about extreme sports at a local college. Make sure that you include:
>
> - what happened that day
> - what Branson learned about himself
> - what he would say to students who are facing problems or in adversity.
>
> Base your report on what you have read in the text, but be careful to use your own words.
>
> **Begin:** 'I am delighted to have been invited here to share my experience with you…'.

Worksheet 8.8b
Sample responses: extended responses to reading

Chapter 8: Extended response to reading and directed writing

Student's Book **Q1**

Response 1

> I am delighted to have been invited here today to share my experience with you. The experience I had was very exciting but very dangerous and I almost died.
>
> What happened was that I was attempting a record-breaking balloon flight but my balloon ran out of fuel. I was over the sea and it was foggy – I knew I was going to crash eventually. At first, I didn't know what to do as my mind felt all fuzzy. I wrote letters to my children and wife as I thought it was the end. Finally, I came up with a plan to survive. I let all the fuel out of the balloon and used it as a giant parachute, then just before it hit the sea I jumped out. I was wearing a life-jacket and the sea was icy but I was alive!
>
> I learned a lot about myself. One thing I learned was that my dyslexia made things difficult for me: I could not distinguish between right and left and this meant I didn't know how to open the parachute. But I was clever too because I realised there was another way to survive. I worked out I could use the balloon as a parachute to survive – and that is what I did. I also kept calm and realised that panicking doesn't solve anything.
>
> So, if you are facing problems or things that frighten you, then I would say that you can definitely overcome them. There are lots of things you can do: for example, dyslexia didn't hold me back. You can use your intelligence and keep calm and work out answers to your problems. That is what I did and it saved my life. Thank you for listening to me.

Response 2

> I am delighted to have been invited here today to share my experience with you. What happened had a profound impact on me, and taught me incredibly valuable lessons.
>
> In essence, I was attempting a record-breaking balloon flight but had got into terrible difficulty over a freezing cold sea and was running out of fuel. Can you imagine that? Faced with probable death, I wrote 'goodbye' notes for my family; I couldn't think clearly and all the options seemed to lead to my inevitable destruction, but finally I cleared my mind and worked out a way to get through it. Using the balloon as a parachute, I plunged into the sea but without harming myself. I survived!
>
> The experience taught me that I could work out solutions to problems through cool thinking: that panicking doesn't help. Equally important, it told me that I loved life and that I would do anything to survive and see my family. It showed me that even though I had problems such as dyslexia I could overcome them through lateral thinking.
>
> This, then, is my message to you. Whether the challenges you face are big or small, don't fixate on your weaknesses. You are more capable than you think! Keep a cool head and consider all the options – somewhere inside you is the answer you seek.

Chapter 8: Extended response to reading and directed writing

Worksheet 8.9a: Practice questions and sample responses: directed writing

Student's Book **Q1** Read the task and the passage that follows it. Then write your response to the task in 250–350 words.

> Write a speech to be given to students at your school about the effects of global tourism.
>
> In your speech, you should:
>
> - evaluate the views given in the text about the effects of tourism
> - give your own views, based on what you have read, about tourism to beautiful or historical places, and how it should be dealt with.
>
> Base your speech on what you have read in the text, but be careful to use your own words. Address both of the bullet points.
>
> **Begin your speech:** 'Thank you for giving me the opportunity to talk about this important issue…'

Chapter 8: Extended response to reading and directed writing

Worksheet 8.9b (1) Sample responses: directed response to reading

Student's Book **Q1**

Response 1

> Thank you for giving me the opportunity to talk about this important issue. I can see that tourism is on the increase and it needs to be looked at.
>
> It is really clear that lots more people are now travelling around the world. So, this means lots of delays at airports, plus more people going to beauty spots and famous places. Like Venice where there are these monstrous cruise ships which must be very ugly to look at.
>
> But it isn't just famous places but also places like Skye in Britain which are being spoiled by traffic jams. It is awful when a place like this is ruined because of visitors.
>
> Also, there are places like Dubrovnik where you can't even walk in the centre because there are too many people.
>
> But people want to travel, and I want to travel when I'm older. It's so much cheaper now and hotels are much better. Plus tourism makes a lot of money for cities and countries so that mustn't stop. Lots of people work in tourism, about 1 in 11 people.
>
> So we all need to think hard before we take a holiday to some lovely place like Venice or Thailand. Because the traffic and the number of people will make it a bit unreal, not like it's supposed to be. Perhaps we won't enjoy it as much as staying at home, because we must not forget that there is a lot to do and see in our own country. Thank you.

Worksheet 8.9b (2) Sample responses: directed response to reading

Response 2

Thank you for giving me the opportunity to talk about this important issue. The gift of being able to travel the world is one I'm sure we all look forward to as we get older, but we need to question its effect.

The fact is that global tourism has seen a huge increase and this has had a profound effect on the world's most popular destinations. Venice, for example, sees 28 million visitors a year, many arriving on ugly cruise ships. I ask you – is this the best backdrop for such an ancient city? The sheer weight of traffic is also a major problem, with roads like the ones to the pretty Isle of Skye getting clogged up, and so too is the fact that people are unable to walk through the centre of popular cities due to the staggering number of visitors.

What does this mean for us as young people? It is difficult because on the one hand I don't want to visit places that are so overwhelmed, you cannot even see the sights, but I do want to expand my horizons. I also recognize that such tourism has benefits too: there is a good chance, for example, that one in every eleven of us in this room will end up with a job in tourism. And every government is pleased with the money tourism brings in.

Ultimately, I think the issue of what sort of travel we want is important. Will staying in a dull modern hotel and taking a few snaps on your phone as you battle the hordes really satisfy you? When we leave school, we have a choice – to blindly follow the crowd or do something different. As young people, we can blaze a trail for how we want travel to look in the coming years. For my part, I'm going to begin by getting to know my own country first – on foot or bicycle. I hope you do too.

Chapter 9: Composition

Worksheet 9.1 Identifying key details in a task

Student's Book **Q4** Highlight and annotate the key words in the task that you have chosen from the first two. Then do the same for the third task.

Describe an occasion when two people meet for the first time.

'Although it was almost midnight, I heard the sound of footsteps approaching our house. I opened the door…'. Use these two sentences to start a story.

Describe a scene in which a customer complains to a shop manager about an item he/she has bought.

© HarperCollins *Publishers* Ltd 2018

Chapter 9: Composition

Worksheet 9.3: Looking at structure and detail

Read the two descriptions and consider the effects of structure and detail.

Description A

> She was taller than I expected her to be. She had these long limbs – graceful, not gangly. Her arms were bare and freckled from the late August sunshine. I wondered absently whether she'd used sun cream; I couldn't smell it. Her hands were practical: short nails, no jewellery, no nail varnish. I knew that her fingerprints left no traceable print from the files I'd read about her earlier.

Description B

> She had fingerprints that left no trace – I knew this from her ample file I'd read earlier. Practical hands: no nail varnish, no rings, nothing that would slow her down. Her arms were long and limber, used to climbing and fighting. She was taller than I thought she would be. She surprised me.

Which description do you prefer? Why?

....

....

....

How does the focus change in Description B?

....

....

....

How has the writer added description to interest the reader?

....

....

....

Write one more sentence to continue your preferred description.

....

....

....

Chapter 9: Composition

Worksheet 9.4 Using imagery

Extra challenge Fill in the table with suitable words to complete the image in the first column. Then identify whether it is simile, metaphor or personification in the second. Finally, comment on its effect in the third column.

Example	Technique	What is the effect?
a) The sand, which was every shade of gold, was like a blanket beneath the people's		
b) The clouds were wandering		
c) The lighthouse stood .... and proud.		
d) The grey .... by the water's edge were like sleeping seals.		
e) The beach is silent. It breathes a slow sigh of .... and rests before it is awoken again tomorrow.		
f) The sea was a ferocious		
g) The sand was as fine and as smooth as		

© HarperCollins *Publishers* Ltd 2018

Chapter 9: Composition

Worksheet 9.5a — Creating an interesting narrative

Student's Book **Q1**

Who is approaching?	A stranger in the house? Another member or members of the family?
Who are 'you'?	Are you a teenager in a house like your own? Or are you someone else, older, an adult?
Why has the person come to the house?	To meet someone? To reveal a secret? To steal something?
What will happen next?	An argument? A chase? A mysterious event?
What might have happened earlier?	Other visitors? Someone watching the house for weeks?

Worksheet 9.5b: Narrative structure

Student's Book **Q12**

Grab the reader's attention – hook	
Develop the plot – add detail and events	
Add a complication – twist in plot	
Climax – cliff-hanger moment	
Ending – return to equilibrium	

Worksheet 9.7 (1) Sample responses

Chapter 9: Composition

Student's Book **Q1 and Q4**

Descriptive writing
Response 1

> The secret place I enter is through a tall hedge. There is a door with a large handle and when I pull it, the door opens slowly. Through the door, the garden opens up and I can see, feel, hear and smell so many things.
>
> The first thing to attack my senses is the smelliness of the flowers. It is almost overpowering and hits me in a great wave. I am not sure I like it all that much, but the discovery of the garden is so amazing that I control myself and continue walking. It's just so amazing.
>
> Now I see old trees bending down over me with curved branches like old men's arms which seek to grab me. I push them to one side and find I am standing on a stone bridge over a sparkling stream. There are lots of fishes to see.
>
> All around the garden is the tall hedge, like a box, and inside there are lots more hedges creating a maze-like effect. I feel like I am inside a game and don't know where to turn. Now I am not sure of the way out so I go back the way I came over the little bridge and past the old man trees. But I cannot find the door.
>
> I look up above and the sky is a brilliant blue. Birds from the garden, ones I don't recognise – they don't look very nice or friendly – well, they swoop down and peck close to me. I think they are some sort of seabird, which seems strange because we are not near the sea. The grass by the path is like a green blanket, soft and inviting, so I sit down while I consider what to do next.
>
> Now the smell of the flowers is really getting to me. They are so sickly and suffocating. It is surely time for me to leave so I go to have another look for the door, which will let me escape. This time, miraculously, it is there.
>
> I feel like *Alice in Wonderland* waking up but I haven't been asleep so this is not a dream. I will come back to this garden again if it is still here.

Worksheet 9.7 (2) Sample responses

Descriptive writing
Response 2

At the top of my parents' dull, grey apartment block is a set of iron stairs that lead onto the roof – or so I thought. The metal sign warns, 'No entry – danger,' so I can't tell you what gets into me that afternoon when I decided to climb them.

Forcing open the heavy trap door, I stepped into another world. For there, facing me was the most lush, luxuriant garden I have ever seen. An arch, twisted round with the delicate fingers of fragrant pink roses confronted me, and beyond was a matted walkway, sprinkled with sand, like golden paper.

As I took my first tentative steps, the tinkling sound of tiny fountains at either side rose up, like a thousand mini-orchestras tuning up. They glimmered as water spouted from sculptures. Below, the sound of the brutal city streets continued. Cars snarling like wild cats. People chattering like monkeys. I am at peace. Away from it all.

Yet there was more. Off the main pathway were further routes. I explored each in turn, each revealing a new delight. Down one, a hammock swung between bamboo trees, as if its owner had just disappeared. Down another, were rows of tiny flowers I didn't recognise, which seemed newly planted. I had no idea what was watering them but despite the intense tropical heat they were thriving.

How could I have missed this place? Who created it? Whoever it was must have realised that we all need an escape from the speed of everyday life. This was a real oasis, not a mirage. It felt like mine, as if I was the first explorer.

My dreams were broken by a melody interfering near my side. I glanced down at the pathway railing. On it, a row of tiny bluebirds, six or seven, I can't recall exactly, sat like a little choir, chirping out their song – just for me! I reached down and one hopped onto my hand and tilted its head as if checking me out. Then, in a flash of blue it was gone and so were the others. Perhaps they'd heard something.

I suddenly felt like an intruder. Time to leave. Will I tell my parents? I felt like I wanted to keep the place to myself, like a dream which you think you will ruin if you reveal it.

I closed the door behind me. Immediately it was as if the garden had never existed. Below I could hear the sounds of couples arguing in their apartments, pots bubbling in kitchens, televisions blaring out.

I was back in the real world.

Chapter 9: Composition

Worksheet 9.7 (3) Sample responses

Narrative writing
Response 1

I was on the stairs in the middle of the night when I heard the phone call. It was a very hot night and I couldn't sleep and needed a drink. I was coming down the stairs, rubbing my eyes, when I saw my father by the phone. He was speaking quietly and he had his back to me so he couldn't see me. The hall is long and narrow so there was no way he could spot me.

'He mustn't find out. Have you got that?' my father whispered.

I could not tell if he was worried or angry, but I began to ask all sorts of questions to myself. Who was 'he'? I was the only boy in the house, so it must be me. My father and mother had been acting quite secretively, it was true. They seemed to be whispering to each other all the time.

'I realise this is the best time to phone, but be careful. Don't call again. I'll call you,' my father said.

Be careful about what? Was my dad involved in something bad? Had he got into debt? But why hide it from me?

The next day, I watched my parents carefully. But they didn't give anything away. I even followed my dad to the train station one morning before going to school, but nothing strange happened.

In any case, my mind began to think about other things. It was my birthday at the weekend. That was when it all made sense! Of course, my dad had been talking to someone about my present! He wanted to keep it secret from me. But why speak to someone in the middle of the night? That was still weird.

The day came. I opened my presents which were what I'd asked for – like a new bike but no real surprises. Then my dad said he needed to pop out to get something – and could I help him? I said yes of course.

Suddenly, we seemed to be going to the airport. What was going on?

Our car pulled up at the short stay parking. I saw someone walking towards us. No. It couldn't be! It was! It was my older sister who had emigrated to America five years ago. She had come back just for my birthday. So that was why my dad was talking in the middle of the night.

'Hello, little brother!' she said, hugging me.

Worksheet 9.7 (4) Sample responses

Narrative writing
Response 2

I heard my older brother Fabrice's hushed tones as I walked past his room. The door was slightly open, a shard of light slicing the air, and I could see him, in his tracksuit, sitting on the edge of his bed, speaking on his mobile

'No way, man. I can't do it! You got me?'

Fabrice sounded anxious, upset. What was going on?

Suddenly it went quiet. The call was over. I heard footsteps padding over the floorboards coming towards me. I froze. My brother opened the door wide.

'What you doing? Listening, huh?' he said, angrily. He pushed me up against the wall, his eyes sparks of fire.

'No – well – I heard something, but I didn't understand,' I replied. 'I mean…', I didn't have time to finish.

'Keep it that way!' He slammed the door.

That weekend we were at a big athletics meeting at Wood Park. My brother was a brilliant runner and he was the favourite for the 100-metre race. It was mid-afternoon, the sun baking the sandy track. He was prowling about beside it, like a caged cheetah, his muscles rippling in his back. In his own world. But then, just before the race began, the cheetah seemed to melt away. I saw him talking to a gang of older boys. One of them – a thin, pale boy with a ring in his nose – grabbed him by his white vest. The boy poked a finger into Fabrice's chest. What about those muscles, Fabrice, I asked in my head? You don't have to take this!

But next I knew, Fabrice was coming towards me. He had tears running down his face, but walked straight past.

Something got into me. Maybe a little bit of that cheetah spirit. I needed to know what was going on. So, I followed them. Hid out of view while they gathered behind the old pavilion, smothered in graffiti, smears of white and red. Tears, they looked like. I heard it all.

Soon I was back in the grassy arena, and tracked my brother down. He was tying up his running shoes – left shoe first, always the same routine.

'I know what is happening,' I told him. 'You mustn't lose the race. It's not right!' I added, as forcefully as I dared. He didn't look up, just paused and then moved on to the other shoe, meticulously folding the perfect white laces over each other.

He stood up, stared for a moment into the distance, at nothing it seemed…

Before I knew it, the race had begun. At first my brother was a long way behind. But that was his usual style. His strength would batter through in the last 30 metres. But he'd left it late. Too late, surely? He was going to lose because of that gang, because someone wanted to fix the race for a bit of cash. But no… I was wrong. Suddenly he was surging through! It was like he was in his own corridor of air, swift as the cheetah, swifter maybe. He dipped on the line. He'd won! He'd won!

Soon a man in a business suit was giving him a long red sash with a shiny medal on it. When the man had shaken Fabrice's hand, I went over.

As I approached I saw the gang of boys walking over too. They did not look happy at all.

'What are you going to do?' I asked.

Fabrice put his arm around my shoulders.

'Guess we'll just have to face the music together, won't we?' he said, gripping me tightly.

Worksheet 10.1a Comparing styles

Chapter 10: Approaching written coursework

Task Prepare a comparison of the style and content of 'The Thought Tree' and 'The Worst School Bus Ever'.

The easiest way to compare two texts is by using connectives to indicate similarity or difference between two quotations. For example:

- to indicate similarity: *similarly, likewise, also*
- to indicate difference: *however, in contrast, conversely*.

You could follow this structure to make a comparison:

1 Make a point about the first text that you have noticed.
2 Use a quotation to show where you got this idea.
3 Add a connective to show similarity or difference.
4 Make a point about the second text.
5 Explain how/why it is similar or different.

Here is an example comparison between the two texts:

> The descriptive opening of 'The Thought Tree' creates a calming mood, with thoughtful description of the tree – 'huge, curving branches'. In contrast, 'The Worst Bus Ever' begins in an informal and chatty way – 'Let's be honest'. This makes 'The Worst School Bus Ever' seem more direct and upbeat at first.

Now write your own comparison of the two texts.

Chapter 10: Approaching written coursework

Worksheet 10.1b Developing impressions of writers

Student's Book **Q2** Complete the table below to show what impression you get of the writer of 'The Thought Tree' and where that impression comes from.

My impression of the writer	Where I get this impression from

Now complete the table for 'The Worst School Bus Ever'.

My impression of the writer	Where I get this impression from

With a partner, compare the impressions you get of the two writers. How are they similar or different? Make some notes below. Be prepared to explain your ideas to the class.

....

....

....

....

....

© HarperCollins *Publishers* Ltd 2018

Chapter 10: Approaching written coursework

Worksheet 10.1c: Developing ideas about a childhood memory

Student's Book Q6 You are now going to think about a childhood memory that you could write about. Use the organiser below to develop your ideas for this piece of writing.

What could your title be?	What ideas would you focus on?

What details could you include?

How could you sustain or develop the account?

What impression of yourself would you like to give the reader?

Chapter 10: Approaching written coursework

Worksheet 10.2 Writing to discuss, argue and/or persuade

Student's Book **Q1** Use the space below to create a mind-map of ideas for topics or issues that interest you. You could consider:
- personal or local issues (things that affect the way you live) – for example, pocket money, traffic issues in your neighbourhood, thoughts about your career or future
- wider issues or ideas (for example, your thoughts about nature, wildlife, the older generation, gender issues, cultural ideas).

my ideas

Student's Book **Q2** When you have thought of as many ideas as you can, circle one or two that you would choose as a focus for your piece of writing. Think about how you would:
- find articles or other forms of writing about them
- research information (facts, statistics and other ideas) on the same topic.

Where could you find other articles or information on the topic?	How could you conduct research to find further information, facts and statistics?

© HarperCollins *Publishers* Ltd 2018

251

Chapter 10: Approaching written coursework

Worksheet 10.3 Planning a response to a task

Student's Book **Q4** Use the organiser below to develop a plan for your task. Remember:
- Begin with an appropriate introduction that fits the type of text and audience.
- Use clear paragraphs to explore each point (use the boxes below to help you do this, adding more on the back if needed).
- End with a concluding sentence that expresses your point of view.

Introduction		
Point 1: Explain	Point 1: Explore	Point 1: Express
Point 2: Explain	Point 2: Explore	Point 2: Express
Point 3: Explain	Point 3: Explore	Point 3: Express
Point 4: Explain	Point 4: Explore	Point 4: Express
Conclusion		

Chapter 10: Approaching written coursework

Worksheet 10.4 Features of descriptive writing

Student's Book **Q2** Use the table below to develop your understanding of descriptive writing skills.

- Read the skills in the left-hand column. Discuss with a partner what you think the skill means, and how you would achieve this in your writing.
- Add an explanation of the skills to the middle column.
- When you have read the texts, add any examples of the skills being used to the right-hand column.

Descriptive writing skill	What does it mean? How would I achieve this?	Examples from extracts
Create a convincing, well-defined picture (offering depth and detail to the description).	*Focus on the details that create an effect to bring the image to life. Imagine the little things I would notice if I was there.*	*a soft light wind swayed the heavy folds of the patterned curtains* • *In Praise of Gardens*
Provide a variety of focuses, for example, using 'camera-style' techniques – zooming in on detail or widening out to more distant 'shots'.		
Create a vivid or powerful atmosphere, mood or setting.		
Use well-chosen imagery, sensory language and sentence variety to bring the description to life.		
Have a clear structure: this could be chronological, or to do with a change of mood, setting, use of contrast or a shifting perspective.		
Include details that 'show' rather than 'tell' the reader about the scene or a character's feelings.		
Where appropriate, use material that arises from personal experience (although you can adapt and add to it as necessary).		

© HarperCollins *Publishers* Ltd 2018

Chapter 10: Approaching written coursework

Worksheet 10.5a: Identifying forms, structures and uses of language

Student's Book **Q7** Use the table below to analyse examples A–D:
- What form has been used (for example, poem, diary entry)?
- How is the extract structured (for example, chronologically)?
- How would you describe the language (for example, chatty, upbeat, reflective)?

Form	Structure	Language	Ideas I could use

Chapter 10: Approaching written coursework

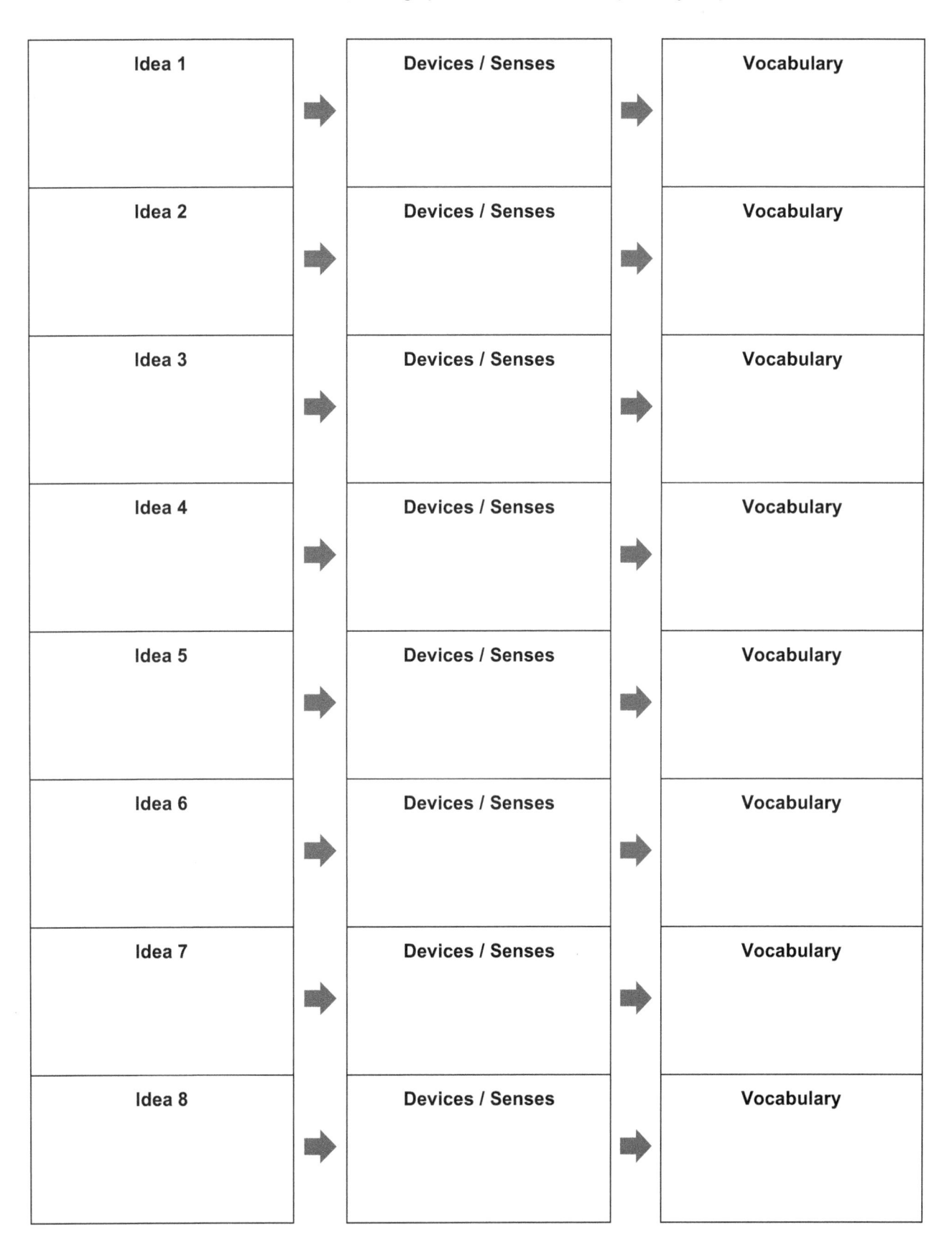

Worksheet 10.5b — Planning a descriptive task

Student's Book Q9 Use the space below to develop a detailed plan for your descriptive writing. Aim for eight fully developed ideas. Consider the devices and key vocabulary you will use in each section, adding specific ideas and examples to your plan.

Idea	Devices / Senses	Vocabulary
Idea 1		
Idea 2		
Idea 3		
Idea 4		
Idea 5		
Idea 6		
Idea 7		
Idea 8		

© HarperCollins *Publishers* Ltd 2018

Worksheet 10.6: Planning a narrative

1. Write one sentence to describe your storyline.

   ....

   ....

2. Now think about what will happen in the five-part structure of your story.

3. List your narrative choices, thinking about the following categories.

Form	Narrative voice	Style/mood

4. Add any further details (for example, descriptive techniques, direct speech).

5. Use the checklist to assess your plan. Be prepared to adapt things if necessary.

Does my story…	Yes	No
Have a limited number of characters?		
Include a problem or difficulty?		
Have a simple plot that readers can follow?		
Have one main location or setting?		
Include an effective beginning or ending?		

Worksheet 10.7 Developing narrative writing

Chapter 10: Approaching written coursework

Student's Book Q2 Read 'The snake and Antonia', then note down five things you learn about the character in the left-hand column of the table below. Swap with a partner, challenging them to find evidence to support your points, while you find evidence to support theirs. Write the evidence on your partner's sheet, then swap back and compare your ideas.

What I learned about the character	Evidence to support this

Student's Book Q2 Use these prompts to help you think about how effective the extract is. Select particularly effective parts of the text, think about which 'should' statement or piece of advice from John Braine it meets, then comment on the effects on the reader.

Which parts of the text did you find particularly effective? Add quotations here.	Why? Which 'should' statement/piece of advice does this meet?	How does this affect you as a reader? Why is it useful?

© HarperCollins *Publishers* Ltd 2018

Chapter 10: Approaching written coursework

Worksheet 10.8a — Exploring and redrafting structure

Check the overall structure of your text:

- What does the first sentence suggest? How will it affect the reader? Should it stay at the beginning or be moved?
- What follows this? Does it add anything? Is it logical? Would anything work better if it was earlier or later in the text?
- What does the last sentence suggest? How will it affect the reader? Should it stay at the end or should it be moved.

Read these examples. They are different versions of the extract in the Student's Book. With a partner, discuss the above points and make notes in the boxes provide.

Version A

> This is the place my dreams and hopes began. There, under the huge, curving branches of the willow, I would lie with my back against the knotty trunk, staring up at the clouds which flickered through the leaves, forming and reforming themselves in greys and whites.

	My ideas
First sentence	
Middle section	
Last sentence	

Version B

> There, under the huge, curving branches of the willow, I would lie with my back against the knotty trunk. This is the place my dreams and hopes began. I would stare up at the clouds which flickered through the leaves, forming and reforming themselves in greys and whites.

	My ideas
First sentence	
Middle section	
Last sentence	

What would happen if you…
- changed one or more full-stops to exclamation marks
- used a semi-colon?

Worksheet 10.8b: Drafting and improving your work

To practise the process of drafting and improving, study the extract from a narrative task below then complete the tasks that follow.

> **This student has been asked to write a narrative piece with the title 'The Crash'.**
> **The extract begins part-way into the story.**
>
> In the car, the couple squabbled. The cold was soon biting at their fingertips, forcing clenched fists and folded arms. Heaters on full blast fought with the cold. The radio lightened the mood with annual Christmas classics, which invited Jenny to compete with The Pogues in 'Fairytale of New York'.
>
> Jenny, who had now stoped singing had her full focus on the road ahead. The snow, which now covered the land, left little to distingish where the road lay. Snaking roads demanded strict atention and, as Jenny slowed to take the approaching bend, the car became unresponsive, the ice was in control now. The car was veering towards the embankment.
>
> 'Steve, I can't do anything!' shouted Jenny.
>
> Steve snatched the steering wheel but his attemts to redirect the car were fruitless. The car spun out of control. The back wheels clipping a boulder which signified the road ending. Hurtling down the embankment, they were projected towards the windscreen. Glass showered the couple, as the inverted car slid screeching grinding and crunching before coming to rest against a large tree. While the lanes returned to perfect silence and the snow kept falling.

1 In pairs, follow the three-step proofreading process. Annotate the extract with your thoughts on the following:
   - Is it logical? Does it create impact in the right places? Are you able to follow the story? Do any ideas need shifting around?
   - Check for technical accuracy. Use the strategies the class has developed to check for errors in spelling, punctuation and grammar.
   - Identify problem phrases or sentences. Try to work out what doesn't work and think about how it can be changed.

2 Now that you have annotated the extract with ideas for the above, think about how else the story could be improved. Write down some ideas about: sentence structure, vocabulary and descriptive devices. Specifically, you could write about the following:
   - Why are the couple squabbling?
   - How else could the weather be described in paragraph one, other than 'cold?'
   - In paragraph two, the writer refers to 'the snow'. Could a metaphor be used instead?
   - What else could the writer do to suggest Jenny's feeling of panic as she loses control?
   - How could the sense of tension and drama be increased in the final lines of the story?
   - Overall, are there any places we are 'told' where we could be 'shown?'

Chapter 10: Approaching written coursework

Worksheet 10.9a (1) Coursework-style task and responses: Assignment 1

1. Identify the key requirements of the question below.

> You have read an article about a topical issue. Write a response to the article giving your views on the issue and arguing your case.
> (In this case, the article explores the revival in the sales of printed books).

Underline/highlight the key parts of the question and annotate them with ideas about what they require you to do.

2. Annotate the response below with your ideas about how well the student has performed. In pairs, identify three things this student could have done to improve their response.

> Dear Sir,
>
> I read the article about print and ebooks in your paper. The writer states how 'the book revival is gathering pace' and how sales of ebooks are going down. This makes it sound like this is a good thing as 'revival' means coming back to life. But I think this makes it sound like ebooks are really bad, and I don't agree.
>
> The writer also mentions someone who says, 'consumers, young and old, appear to have established a new appreciation for this traditional format.' But I am not one of them. I do not wish to go back in time to old books as they do not fit in with my lifestyle. Who wants to lug a great big old mass of paper with them? Not me.
>
> Another point that the writer makes is that people are sick of looking at screens all the time. They need a 'respite' which makes reading ebooks sound like an illness! However, I do not feel ill when I read an ebook. Lots of ebook electronic devices have screens that do not affect your eyes as much as the usual ones, so I don't agree there.
>
> The writer says it is 'to do with the tangible nature of books, their designs and their feel. It is the physical book that evokes a memory,' This is rubbish – I don't agree.

Worksheet 10.9a (2): Coursework-style task and responses: Assignment 1

3 Rewrite the final paragraph of the response, so that it works more persuasively.

....
....
....
....
....
....
....
....

4 Now consider the sample response below. Is this better or worse than Response 1? Why? Work with a partner to compare the two responses.

> I am delighted to be able to talk to you all about one of my favourite things – books! Now, you might not think this is a big issue – everyone loves a good book! – but you'd be wrong. You see, for the last few years people like you have been choosing to read ebooks rather than the paper ones. There was a real danger that printed books would die out – but, thankfully, it seems this is not the case.
>
> The reason I am talking to you is that I read an article recently which said that for the first time for many years, ebook sales were going down. Print books were having a 'revival'. This sounds like they are coming back to life, and that's wonderful news. Can you imagine a world without brightly coloured covers and paper you can flick through? Boring, dull and deadly.
>
> The article also stated that we all spend too long staring at screens, 'day and night' and we need a break. I agree – I get fed up of staring at my phone or my tablet; the light from the screen really hurts my eyes. Research has shown that people who have work roles involving substantial screen time are more likely to suffer sleep problems, headaches and similar issues. It seems clear that staring at that rectangular white space can't be good for you.
>
> Another important point from the article which I want to share with you is that experts believe people like the 'traditional format' of books. I think this is a good point. Tradition is very important, isn't it?

Worksheet 10.9b (1)
Coursework-style task and responses: Assignment 2

Chapter 10: Approaching written coursework

> You have just spent your first night in a new town or city.
> Describe your surroundings and feelings as you awake.

1. Read the example response to this task given below. Identify three specific things that could be improved in this response. Use the 'Excellent progress' points on page 276 to help you.

> From the top floor of the hotel I saw a tangled network of dusty streets and sand-coloured buildings topped with red or brown roofs. I heard a symphony of sounds, like the clatter of cattle and the distant horns of cars and trucks which weaved between the crowded inhabitants. There were cyclists and motorbikes too, dodging in and out of the crowds, stopping, then going again. No one waited for the traffic lights, although all took notice of the police officer in white gloves waving people past. From the dawn onwards it seemed this place is a hub of noise and activity.
>
> Later I went back to my apartment as the evening faded and the baking sun slowly slid down over the edge of the city. But nothing stopped and the city never slept. Just new people appeared. New cars and workers going to night-time work. Everything seemed jumbled up like whoever built the city just threw all the buildings up in the air and let them fall on the ground as if playing a game.
>
> I was really nervous about my new job but decided I needed to welcome my new life.

Compare your comments to the annotations in the Student's Book. Using these, and working with a partner, write three pieces of advice to the student on the sticky notes you have been given. Be prepared to explain your ideas to the class!

Worksheet 10.9b (2): Coursework-style task and responses: Assignment 2

Now think about Response 2 below. Think about the progress indicators for Assignment 2 and the writing skills on the board. Is this an improvement on Response 1? Discuss your ideas with a partner and annotate the sample response with your thoughts.

The City is an Ocean

I wake to the sight of a huge, silver eel. It is the highway which curls around the coral buildings, suffocating the little roads and paths, like tiny minnows. It growls and snarls and swallows onrushing vehicles and throws them out again, forever hungry and never satisfied.

In offices, I can see sharks patrol the corridors in business suits, their jagged words cutting down their enemies. Smaller fish – little frightened crabs – scuttle into rooms to avoid their bosses and cower behind doors or under desks, afraid they'll be netted. The shark's narrow eyes settle on a useless bloater, a slow-moving salesman who failed to hide. He's not been selling much so the shark snaps him up and sends him home, never to return.

Above the city, I look up and see the sky is another ocean. It is serene, still and deep blue. It reminds all fish of other peaceful worlds, where no nets come and food is free.

Back on the streets below, my eyes pick out married couples and friends who cling to each other like sea-urchins, wrapping their fronds and spines around each other's bodies. They sway along the pavement in the breeze, fearful of being swept up by the tide of time. It's only six hours till work begins again.

Slowly as I settle to my new surroundings, the waves sleep and the eel settles too. It eats but now more slowly. Half-watching, waiting, ready for the rush of the new day.

Now compare your ideas to the feedback given in the Student's Book. Use these ideas to write an email to this student, giving them advice on how to improve their work.

Worksheet 10.9c (1): Coursework-style task and responses: Assignment 3

> Write a narrative piece in which the following words appear:
> 'I knew we didn't have long'.

Read the example response to this task below. Think about your class's ideas about how to move from 'sound' progress to 'excellent' progress and look back at the progress indicators. Which category do you think this student reaches? Why? Annotate the extract with your ideas and be prepared to give feedback to the class.

Stranded by the sea

So we were stuck and it was all Carla's fault.

'I didn't want to come to this stupid cave in the first place,' I said.

Carla didn't say anything. We both felt so cold and I could see the water levels creeping up. We huddled on a ledge but it was very narrow and we weren't sure if it would be high enough.

Then something stirred in the surface of the water.

'What's that?' Carla screamed.

'I don't know.' I replied.

There was another movement, and then a sort of hand reached up for our ledge. It looked like a young woman's hand as it has slim long fingers. Then slowly the rest of the person emerged from the grey-looking water. It was a beautiful lady with long, flowing hair, like a doll.

I had no idea how she got there, because the water was so cold no one would survive for long. The huge waves were now crashing into the cave's entrance and I knew we didn't have long.

'Come,' the woman said, holding out her hand.

'I'm not jumping into that!' Carla stated.

'If you do not follow me, you will die, it is your choice.' Said the woman. Then she added. 'I know a tunnel under water, but you must trust me, you need to hold your breath for a few seconds.'

I took one look at Carla and jumped. Then the water hit me like a slap in the face from an ice-block. Then I was underwater and to my shock I saw what the woman looked like. She had a tail of a fish which was shimmering green and blue. Perhaps the cold water was blinding me and I couldn't see properly that would explain it.

Next I heard Carla splosh into the water too.

Worksheet 10.9c (2): Coursework-style task and responses: Assignment 3

Now read the second response to the task below. How does this compare to the progress indicators? How does it compare to Response 1? Make notes and then study the feedback given in the Student's Book. What else could we add to help this student improve?

The shrinking land

I knew we didn't have long. Now the sand had shrunk to a tiny area of about two metres square around me. The cold easterly wind howled and in the dark I could no longer see my fellow fishermen.

They say that when your life is under threat your past flashes before your eyes. In my case, all I could remember was my wife's face that morning when I left.

'You don't have to go out on the sands. Everyone says it's dangerous,' she told me.

We were standing in our one-room hut; the baby was crying, and the electricity meter had run out. The radiator was cold as stone, and I could feel the icy winter draught sliding through the gap under the door.

'I do,' I told her. 'We have no money.'

She was right of course and perhaps now I wouldn't see her again. I thought of my fellow fishermen and women and wondered if they knew the sands and tides better than me. Perhaps they were safe at home now with their families.

I looked for a light or any sign of life. Where was the beach? There was no moon or stars to guide me, but I had to move or I'd be dead. I plunged waist up into the swirling water, hooked around me like some ghastly grey snake, and headed in a straight line.

But the water rose even further. Now it was at my chest! There was nothing for it: I just dropped my baskets of fish – the fish that paid my paltry wages – so that I could swim. I felt utterly miserable. Even if I survived I would lose my job. I didn't like the gang boss, the smug man in the expensive coat who'd picked me out of the line of men looking for work, but I needed this. Yet if I came back with no catch they would get rid of me. Discard me like an unwanted bit of useless seaweed.

I imagined my wife and baby. My son with his sharp, blue eyes – like the little pebbles on the beach. I had to make it for them.

Suddenly I saw a light! A hazy oval shimmering and dipping up and down. It pulled me like a magnet towards it, and finally I felt hope – surely I could survive now? We would see in the next few horrible minutes.

Worksheet 11.5a: Ideas for role-plays

Chapter 11: Approaching speaking and listening

Task Complete the table to develop your ideas on how you might portray the characters and historical figures listed. There is room for you to add some of your own.

Character/figure	What is controversial?	Style of speech, gesture	What they might say
Lady Macbeth	Self-seeking or 'a good wife'?	tense, urgent	'He's too loyal for his own good!'
Shakespeare			
Muhammad Ali			
Henry VIII			

Chapter 11: Approaching speaking and listening

Worksheet 11.5b — Role-play vocabulary

Student's Book **Q3** Include the words and phrases below in sentences that you might speak when role-playing someone either for or against spending money on space exploration. One has been done for you.

Word/phrase	Sentence
inspirational/inspire	We cannot all take part in space exploration, but we can all be inspired by its achievements in our daily lives.
endeavour	
natural curiosity	
awe-inspiring	
research	
mysteries	
expenditure	
colossal	
astronomical sums	
priorities/prioritise	
vulnerable/vulnerability	
humanity	
responsibility/responsible	
justify	

Worksheet 11.9a — Sample individual talk

My week in Italy

My holiday was with my brother, my mother and father. We decided to do something different this year, so we flew to Rome. Then we rented a car and drove down to the bay of Naples. That was quite an experience, because some of the drivers were crazy. When my mother was driving, my father kept covering up his eyes but in fact she was much safer than him.

When we arrived at the accommodation, it was great. It was miles from anywhere on a hillside in a converted farm. The people who ran it had a family of cats who seemed to fight with each other all the time but never bit us. They lay next to us when we were next to the pool and they were waiting outside the door every morning. My favourite was Nero. He followed me everywhere. They said that he adopted someone every week, from the people renting the property. I wonder if he liked me because I get up much earlier than my brother so there was more time to play. Also, I don't grunt as much as my brother does!

We went off to see things some days, like Pompeii and Herculaneum. Both of those towns were buried when Vesuvius exploded back in Roman times and you can see just what life was like back then. They had central heating and wall paintings and you can walk in the buildings themselves. It's very hot though, so you have to take water with you, to stop dehydration…

Alzheimer's disease

I imagine most of you will have some idea of what Alzheimer's disease is: it progressively takes away the memory, so that sufferers lose touch with reality more and more, until they eventually can't even recognise their wife, their husband, or their children. They jumble the past and present. Until there is no past or present for them. They can't even recognise night or day. And my grandmother has Alzheimer's.

We noticed it starting when her memory suddenly got worse. She struggled to cook our special meal on Friday night, which had always been her treat for us at the end of the week. Then she wasn't sure what day it was. She didn't know what she had done earlier in the day. People's names were forgotten even more easily than they had been before. She needed – help.

We actually thought that we needed help too, but as time goes on, you discover that the early stages were nothing. It is a degenerative disease, which can only get worse. She takes tablets and somehow manages to still live alone, but now it is as if she is in a different kind of world altogether. Conversations are always the same:

'What day is it?'

'Wednesday.'

'Do I have meals on wheels tomorrow?'

'Yes, they'll be here.'

'Do I have to pay for them?'

'No, they are all paid for.'

'What day is it?'

'Wednesday.'

'Do I have meals on wheels tomorrow…'

Worksheet 11.9b: Sample conversation (1)

Fundraising

Teacher: That was all very impressive, Noor. Tell me: did you reach your target for the funds you hoped to raise?

Noor: Yes, I did. In fact, I collected more than I was expecting, because people were so generous. And they were worried about the people who were suffering, obviously.

Teacher: Yes, we all were. So, do you think it's right that we should have to try to raise money like this?

Noor: We try to give money to the people who need it so badly.

Teacher: Of course – but might it not be better if all the money needed came straight from governments? After all, you raised a good deal, but they could give so much more, because they have so much more, haven't they?

Noor: I suppose so. The governments do send money to help, don't they?

Teacher: Yes, indeed. But do you think it's enough?

Noor: I haven't really ever thought about that – but I suppose they give as much as they can, just like everybody else, because they have other things they need to spend money on too. I know what you mean, though. It would be good if they gave some more.

Teacher: Do you think rich countries give enough in foreign aid generally?

Noor: It would always be better if they gave some more, especially when there has been a volcano or an earthquake or floods. People living in villages can't help themselves if they have no homes and no jobs and they've lost everything. I think governments should give more.

Worksheet 11.9c — Sample conversation (2)

The World Cup

Teacher: World Cups make a lot of money. Isn't it true, though, that the host countries make relatively little? Doesn't the organisation, FIFA, make an absolute fortune?

Shane: I'm afraid you're right. They even demand that they are not taxed on the profits they make, so they can just walk away with the proceeds. Countries like Brazil, who hosted the competition in 2014, got publicity and built new stadiums, but that was all: it's so bad that the people who had to build the grounds were only paid a fraction of what they deserved every day. It's shocking.

Teacher: Yet you still think the World Cup is wonderful?

Shane: Yes. You have to split the football and the excitement away from the corruption behind it…

Teacher: Can you do that? Should we do that?

Shane: I see what you are saying – but if you love football, what's the alternative?

Teacher: Watch tennis?

Shane: Well… you could only watch your favourites on television most of the time, not live; and, frankly, tennis doesn't have the passion. At football, you can sing and shout and even be tribal again if you want. It's a release from the problems of the world, just for 90 minutes each week. Unfortunately, tennis doesn't offer you that. Have you ever been to a live football match?

Teacher: No, though we all see it on television...

Shane: People can say what they like about players being over-paid and behaving like huge babies – which we all know they do – but the excitement generated is amazing. I took my mother to a match and she goes regularly now. I still cannot believe it, but she is swept away by the drama of it all. There are many things wrong with football finance and there is corruption too, but that cannot really detract from all that it represents to hundreds of millions of people around the world…

Chapter 12: Practice papers and guidance

Worksheet 12.1a (1) Practice Paper 1: Reading

Question 1

(a) Give two reasons why the cave was an unpleasant place to be according to the text. [2]

(b) Why was it so important to get out of the quicksand in paragraph 1? [1]

(c) Why do you think Brady described himself as 'frantically' wading after the snake when he sees it in paragraph 4? [2]

(d) Reread paragraph 5 ('After a brief… bit me').

   (i) Explain, using your own words, what the writer means by the words in italics in the following phrases:

- the python popped out of the crack in *a blur of coils* (lines 31–2) [2]
- The snake's head was *horrifyingly all over the place* (line 38) [2]
- *popping in and out* of the fecal soup (line 39) [2]

   (ii) Give two reasons why catching the python was a dangerous activity. [2]

(e) Explain why the snake wound was particularly painful for Brady. [2]

[Total: 15]

(f) According to Text B, what changes in wildlife-themed TV shows has the writer experienced since their childhood?

You must use **continuous writing** (not note form) and **use your own words** as far as possible.

Your summary should not be more than 150 words.

Up to 10 marks are available for the content of your answer and up to 5 marks for the quality of your writing.

Question 2

(a) **Identify a word or phrase from the text** which suggests the same idea as the words underlined:

   (i) Gerald <u>likes</u> the appearance and contents of Theodore's study. [1]
   (ii) Gerald believes that the collection of books contains a <u>good range</u> of fiction, non-fiction, fact and fantasy. [1]
   (iii) Theodore is quite <u>formal and distant</u> towards Gerald despite knowing him well. [1]
   (iv) Gerald is <u>fascinated</u> and wants to know about everything. [1]

(b) **Using your own words,** explain what the writer means by each of the <u>words underlined</u>:

> Sitting there, neat and correct in his tweed suit, Theodore would chew his toast slowly and <u>methodically</u>, his beard bristling, his eyes kindling with <u>enthusiasm</u> at each new subject that swam into our conversation. To me his knowledge seemed <u>inexhaustible</u>. He was a rich vein of information and I mined him assiduously.

   (i) methodically [1]
   (ii) enthusiasm [1]
   (iii) inexhaustible [1]

(c) **Using your own words** explain how the <u>phrases underlined</u> are used by the writer to suggest what Theodore is like. [3]

> Sitting there, neat and correct in his tweed suit, Theodore would <u>chew his toast slowly and methodically,</u> his beard bristling, his <u>eyes kindling with enthusiasm</u> at each new subject that swam into our conversation. To me his <u>knowledge seemed inexhaustible</u>. He was a rich vein of information and I mined him assiduously.

Worksheet 12.1a (2) Practice Paper 1: Reading

(d) Reread the description of:

- Theodore's laboratory in paragraph 1 beginning 'Theodore would welcome me…'
- Gerald's feelings about Theodore in paragraph 12, beginning 'Sitting there, neat and correct…'

Select **four** powerful words or phrases from **each** paragraph. Your choices should include imagery. Explain how each word or phrase selected is used effectively in the context.

Write about 200–300 words.

Up to 15 marks are available for the content of your answer.

Question 3

You are Gerald Durrell. Many years after the events described in this extract, you are asked to give a speech to a group of interested parents about the importance of introducing children to the natural world. The interviewer asks you three questions:

- What do you remember seeing and feeling on your visits with Theodore?
- What do you remember about Theo, his behavior and the way he treated you?
- Why do you think that this kind of experience is valuable?

Write the words of the interview.

Base your interview on what you have read in Text C, but be careful to use your own words. Address each of the three bullet points.

Begin your interview with the first question.

Write about 250–350 words.

Up to 15 marks are available for the content of your answer, and up to 10 marks for the quality of your writing.

Worksheet 12.1b: Extended writing notes

Step 8

Use the grid below to make notes on Text C.

	Point	Detail	Inference
What you saw and felt at Theo's	1. 2. 3. 4.		
What Theo was like and how he treated you	1. 2. 3. 4.		
Why you think this kind of experience is valuable	1. 2. 3. 4.		

Worksheet 12.1c — Evaluating sample responses: Question 1

Step 9

Read the sample responses to **Question 1(f)**. Using three different colours, highlight where the writer has used a main idea, details and opinions.

Response A

There are so many animal documentaries on nowadays; too many if you ask me! They are much better entertainment though as they tell stories like the one he says about where a meerkat was ill and could have died. He also says that the presenters are more high profile than they used to be. I think Brady Barr is more of the star of his shows than the animals he finds – well apart from the python that bit him. I'm glad modern presenters aren't dull – voiced and whispered to the camera though – it's fun to see them doing stupid things like putting their hand in something's mouth. Overall, I prefer modern programmes

---

Response B

Modern TV shows about wildlife are superior in every way to the old-fashioned ones. Firstly, there are more of them, they cover more of the globe and more beasts than before. We also get to see the creatures in their own habitat which is much better for them. The presenters are very engaging and actively involved in the shows, which can be a distraction. The shows themselves make us more involved as they look at the challenges faced by these amazing creatures rather than just showing us them.

Which answer is better? Why?

....

....

....

....

Circle any places where you can think of a synonym to replace a word or phrase that has been copied from the text.

Worksheet 12.1d (1): Evaluating sample responses: Question 2

Step 9

Read the sample responses to **Question 2(d)**. Identify the following elements using different colours, then discuss the questions that follow.

- point
- evidence
- literal meanings
- associations
- language devices
- effect

Response A

Theodore's laboratory is full of items, without a space to spare. Durrell writes that it is 'lined' with tall bookshelves, suggesting that every surface is covered, like a skin. This creates a positive sense of womb like cosiness which helps us to realise how comfortable and safe he felt there as a child.

Everything in the laboratory is described as having life and vigour. Durrell personifies the books, saying that they 'rubbed shoulders' suggesting that they are packed closely together. However, the idea given by the personification suggests a positive, companionable atmosphere not one of aggression or discomfort, suggesting that although there are many books, the room is pleasant not cramped.

'...a parade of jars and bottles...' suggests that there is order even though there are many samples collected and stored in the laboratory. The word suggests that the samples are like soldiers; organised and ordered with a clear sense of control and purpose. This reflects Durrell's admiration for the scientist and his belief in the worth of the work being done in the laboratory.

Even everyday objects such as lamps are described using metaphors which are drawn from nature. The '...powerful lamp on the jointed stem leaning like a lily...' shows precisely how the shade of the lamp is large and is the arm of the lamp is down, like a heavy flower on a thin stem. This is a description which adds a sense of grace and beauty to an everyday item and shows Durrell's obsession with nature.

Worksheet 12.1d (2) Evaluating sample responses: Question 2

Response B

The writer explains that there are lots of books. He writes: 'The walls were lined with tall bookshelves' and 'tall' tells us that they could contain lots of books. This helps us see how much the scientist likes to read.

We find out that there is a telescope in the room pointing at the sky. It is described like a dog howling at the moon. This helps us see the shape of it as dogs lift their noses up to howl.

We read that there are lots of creatures still alive in jars in the room. It says 'whirling and twitching' which means that they are spinning around and moving quickly. This helps me to see the way they are moving but isn't very nice as they could be in pain trapped like that.

The microscopes are described as being very shiny. It says they are 'like magpies' which makes me imagine them all black and white with shiny feathers. This helps me to see what the equipment is like and makes them seem alive.

1. a) Does it matter that the six features are not always used?
   b) Does it matter that they are not always used in the order listed on the scaffold?
   c) Which response do you think is the best and why?

2. Now look at your answers to Question 2(d). Compare your work with that of a partner and see whether you can decide which is better, using the underlining techniques that you used on the samples above.

Worksheet 12.1e — Evaluating sample responses: Question 3

Chapter 12: Practice papers and guidance

Read the sample response to **Question 3** below.
- Annotate in the margin with a number 1, 2 or 3 to show where each of the bullets is covered in this response.
- Highlight any uses of details which have come directly from Text C.
- Underline any places where the answer shows an inference which has been drawn from what was written in Text C.

Gerald: Well, although it's a long time ago now, I remember everything – as clearly as if it was yesterday. You see, the thing is, every minute I spent with Theo was magical, fascinating. I was entranced with everything about my visits. Oh my goodness, the day I first saw a Cyclops; well, I'll never forget those eggs – they were in sacs either side of her – like sacks of onions on our old donkey. It really is a joy that the parents here should give to their children.

Interviewer: So you learned a lot?

Gerald: Oh yes – but not just about insects. His library was full of books – on any subject you can think of: botany, astronomy; I soaked it up like a sponge and it helped me so much later in life – at school, and of course in my later career; and just in everyday life. I noticed so much more than my friends – and I understood why things happened the way they did – in nature. Your children (he looks up at audience) need to understand the world they are living in.

Interviewer: He was a clever man?

Gerald: I thought he was a genius – and maybe he was – but most of all he was unusual because he treated me like an equal. He didn't shy away from telling me things because I was young – he told me loads of theories about vampires and my Mum was really cross because she thought I'd have nightmares – but I liked it. I felt like a fellow explorer and it gave me the confidence to ask questions; a really useful skill I think. I respected his knowledge, more than my Grandkids respect me; they just Google everything! But he had stories to go with the facts – and you can't get that first-hand enthusiasm anywhere except from the life experiences of an enthusiast.

Interviewer: I heard that he had lots of slides of samples that he would show you under the microscope?

Gerald: Yes hundreds – he collected samples of everything. He really taught me the joy of observation, of taking your time to really see.

Worksheet 12.1f — Paper 1: self-review

Task Now that you have marked your own response to Practice Paper 1, you should be able to identify your strengths and weaknesses and set targets for improvement. Complete the table below in order to record your findings and conclusions.

Question	Mark	At my target level?	Could be improved	Specific weakness(es)
1(a)				
1(b)				
1(c)				
1(d)				
1(e)				
1(f) Reading				
1(f) Writing				
2(a)				
2(b)				
2(c)				
2(d)				
3 Reading				
3 Writing				

Targets (try to set one for each question type)
1 Explicit meaning
2 Implicit meaning
3 Summary
4 Writer's effects
5 Extended response

Worksheet 12.2a — Practice Paper 2 questions

Question 1

Imagine that your school is considering introducing similar checks on the food that children bring to school.

Write a letter to your school in which you give your views about whether or not teachers should check the food that students eat at school.

In your letter, you should:

- evaluate the views given about the checking of lunches
- give your own views, based on what you have read, about whether the checking of food would benefit students.

Base your letter on the blog, but be careful to use your own words. Address both of the bullet points.

Begin your letter: 'Dear School Governors…'

You should write about 250 to 350 words.

Up to 15 marks are available for the content of your answer, and up to 25 marks for the quality of your writing.

Questions 2–5

Write about 350 to 450 words on **one** of the following questions.

Up to 16 marks are available for the content and structure of your answer, and up to 24 marks for the style and accuracy of your writing.

EITHER

Descriptive writing

2   Describe a scene when a group of people meet to celebrate a happy occasion.

OR

Descriptive writing

3   Describe a quiet garden or park.

OR

Narrative writing

4   Write a story that includes the words, 'she stood in shock as the scene unfolded before her…'

OR

5   Write a story that involves a character who is determined to win.

Worksheet 12.2b — Sample responses: Question 1

Read the paragraphs below, each of which could be part of a letter written in response to this task.

1. Which of them do you think are the most effective and why?
2. What could you add to each of them to improve them?

A   I cannot believe that you and the school board are considering the ridiculous idea that all food brought into the school should be checked by staff. What is this, some kind of prison? Are you going to control every aspect of our lives now? You need to concentrate on teaching us academic subjects, not about nutrition.

B   I cannot imagine who dreamt up the horrifying idea of blaming students for the food that they have been given by their parents. This is not a matter that is in the students' control. They should not be humiliated. Students are extremely sensitive and vulnerable in their teens. Anything which draws attention to them is uncomfortable. I know that just having slightly different hair or uniform is enough to put me on edge. I can't imagine how I'd feel if I had to wear a sticker telling everyone I had 'bad' food with me!

C   I don't mean to be rude but are you sure our teachers are best qualified to be checking our food? Do they have qualifications to do this? Mrs Mackay is hardly the healthiest looking individual and she admits herself that her lunch is a coffee and chocolate bar.

D   I wonder what will happen to the students who have their food confiscated? I learned in my Food and Nutrition class that the energy we need to study comes from the sugar in our meals. Things like a jacket potato can keep you going for hours, whilst having no glucose for your brain to burn can lead to vagueness and sometimes you even fall asleep.

E   This is a great idea. Too many students bring ridiculous food such as chips and candy to school. This just causes them to be out of control all afternoon.

F   Finally, the school is realising that they are responsible for our education as people not just scholars. Couldn't be more pleased about this new initiative.

G   What about the students who can't afford to bring food into school at all? Are they going to be named and shamed, or will they be given healthy food to improve their situation? It seems to me the emphasis is wrong if it's all about punishment.

Worksheet 12.2c: Composition planning: descriptive writing

Description planning

Atmosphere you are going to create ....

Time scale of the description ....

	2	3
Location/environment		
Time of year		
Time of day		
Weather		
What can be seen		
Actions of people/animals/objects		
What can be heard		
Smells		
Tastes		
Textures		

Structure

Choose one of these five possible structures:

- clock-face: exploration of a frozen image
- contrast times of day
- contrast across years
- zoom in/out
- other.

Worksheet 12.2d — Composition planning: narrative writing

Narrative planning

Structure

	4	5
Set-up		
Rising Action		
Crisis		
Falling Action		
Resolution		

Characters

	4	5
1		
2		
3		

Setting

4	5

Chapter 12: Practice papers and guidance

Worksheet 12.2e (1) Composition assessment (1)

Read the sample compositions below carefully, then consider the statements in the success criteria table. How strongly do you agree with the statements? Shade in the box that describes the level of success that you have seen.

	Low	Medium	High
Content: what happens/is described	Some of the things which happen/are mentioned don't seem to fit with the rest of the story/scene being described.	Some of the events/aspects of the scene are developed with details.	The story or scene is entertaining or convincing as if it could be published/ you can imagine being there.
Structure: the way events are organised/the way the description is ordered	The story/scene is incomplete or unbalanced so that some aspects are more focused and clear than others.	There is a sense of a story but it may not build or finish convincingly/only parts of the scene are fully described.	Everything happens in a sequence which builds up and finishes effectively/ you get a full picture of the scene.
Vocabulary: the words that are used	The wrong words are quite often used.	Some words have clearly been chosen for effect.	Words are chosen very carefully to create an overall effect.
Sentence structure: variety and effectiveness	Sentences are very similar and not always punctuated properly.	Some sentences are used and shaped for effect. Most are accurately punctuated.	There is a range of sentence shapes which are used to create an effect and they are punctuated accurately.
Spelling: level of accuracy	Words are often misspelled.	Some more complex or unfamiliar words are incorrect but simple ones are accurate.	Most words are spelled correctly.
Grammar: accuracy	There are lots of mistakes such as wrong tenses or agreement.	There are some mistakes but they are slips rather than major faults.	The writing is grammatically accurate and fluent.

© HarperCollins Publishers Ltd 2018

Worksheet 12.2e (2) Composition assessment (1)

Composition A

From above they look orderly and formal, sat in neat rows, separated by a narrow strip of green turf-like a tidy sandwich; all obediently facing forwards, into the empty white timber pergola strung with ivory roses and blue hydrangea flowers. Sharp cut ends of navy ribbons are twisting and bobbing in the light summer breeze, blurring the crisp white paint on the pergola pillars.

The air is filled with music; humming bass strings and slightly sharp violin bowing which drifts in waves across the garden. There is constant chatter, giggles, and the occasional 'pop' as a balloon strays too close to the tall conifers which wall us all in. A baby is wailing and gentle voices shush it as the music halts.

The garland around my head sends out a sweet tickle of honeysuckle into my nostrils. The floating gauze of our skirts billows like sails as the wind catches us hovering on the steps down from the terrace, and plays in their folds, causing shrieks and a frenzy of patting and clutching.

Serene again we start to walk. Short steps on the uneven grass. We glide between the seated audience feeling the sun warm on our shoulders. There are sighs and a few sobs. When we reach the pergola we stop and turn. A sea of faces, some topped with feathers and ribbons looks on. I step aside and the bride moves on, up the uneven stairs and my sister's wedding begins.

Composition B

A few years ago I arrived home from school one day and faced my worst nightmare.

It was an average day. I don't remember whether it was hot or cold, rain or shine. It wasn't that the front door was open or anything obvious like that, but when I walked into the lounge and dropped my school bag down on the floor by the coffee table, I suddenly knew that there was someone or something else in the house.

As I glanced around me I noticed books pulled out of their place on the shelves, one, my copy of 'The Complete Works of Shakespeare' hanging precariously about to fall onto the carpet which was sprinkled with mud and shredded leaf mould.

'Hello?' I called out, expecting my Mum or sister to have come home early and inexplicably had some kind of mud throwing contest whilst looking for some light reading. 'Are you home early?'

No answer – but a dull thud from the dining room suggested that someone had heard me.

I walked nervously across the room and as I turned the corner into the dining room a flash of something small and solid shot across the room, springing from the dresser to the table and then skidding, with a shudder-inducing scratching sound, across the polished wooden table before landing with a thud against the skirting board.

'Eeeeeeeeeeeew!' I shrieked as I leapt backwards, barrelling into the sideboard and dislodging a pile of mail which cascaded to the floor. The 'thing' didn't like that either, and ping ponged off the wall and back into the lounge, scrabbling up the bookshelf and into the hole which The Complete Works used to occupy.

Determined not to be humiliated by what I strongly suspected was a squirrel I ran to the kitchen to arm myself. A few minutes later I returned, oven glove firmly on my hand, and a large plastic bucket hung over my arm.

The next few minutes were a blur of flying books and fur as I tried to gently encourage the interloper into my bucket. Exasperated I paused for breath, taking in the empty shelves and the squirrel perched triumphantly on the top shelf just out of my reach.

Suddenly I heard the clunk of the front door swinging open. 'Hello! I'm home!' Mum called and I heard her heels clip across the hall and stop as she threw open the lounge door. She stepped in, halted rapidly and glanced around. 'Julia, what on earth is going on?' She stood in shock as the scene unfolded before her.

Chapter 12: Practice papers and guidance

Worksheet 12.2f (1) Composition assessment (2)

Read the sample compositions below. Insert the annotations from the grid below, where you think they are an accurate comment. One has been done for you. Then discuss in pairs the questions that follow each one.

Content: what happens/is described	1 Some of the things which happen/are mentioned don't seem to fit with the rest of the story/scene being described.	2 Some of the events/aspects of the scene are developed with details.	3 The story or scene is entertaining or convincing as if it could be published/ you can imagine being there.
Structure: the way events are organised/the way the description is ordered	4 The story/scene is incomplete or unbalanced so that some aspects are more focused and clear than others.	5 There is a sense of a story but it may not build or finish convincingly/only parts of the scene are fully described.	6 Everything happens in a sequence which builds up and finishes effectively/you get a full picture of the scene.
Vocabulary: the words that are used	7 The wrong words are quite often used.	8 Some words have clearly been chosen for effect.	9 Words are chosen very carefully to create an overall effect.
Sentence structure: variety and effectiveness	10 Sentences are very similar and not always punctuated properly.	11 Some sentences are used and shaped for effect. Most are accurately punctuated.	12 There is a range of sentence shapes which are used to create an effect and they are punctuated accurately.
Spelling: level of accuracy	13 Words are often misspelled.	14 Some more complex or unfamiliar words are incorrect but simple ones are accurate.	15 Most words are spelled correctly.
Grammar: accuracy	16 There are lots of mistakes such as wrong tenses or agreement.	17 There are some mistakes but they are slips rather than major faults.	18 The writing is grammatically accurate and fluent.

© HarperCollins Publishers Ltd 2018

Worksheet 12.2f (2): Composition assessment (2)

Composition A

Chippewa Square is an oasis of shade when the Savannah sun is scorching and the humidity makes you feel as if you are swimming with your clothes on.

It's not really a garden or a park exactly but it has trees, grass, flower beds and benches – so I think it's as good as either of those.

The square isn't big; maybe 60 m by about 90m. It's not quiet either – because the traffic drives around it, so it's a bit like a roundabout – but it is a place to stop and cool off.

In the centre there's a statue of the founder of Georgia, James Oglethorpe. It stands high, on a stone plinth with loops around it like icing on a wedding cake and is made of bronze. There's a lion on each corner. It's black nowadays and looks a bit serious especially with its little low railings around – to keep you off.

The central area of the square is surrounded by Live Oaks. They're called that because they don't shed their leaves in Winter – they stay alive! But what makes them look so special is the stuff that hangs from every twig and branch. It's a bit like dirty dusty cobwebs and gives the idea that its Halloween every day.

Siting in the square it's quite dark and there's a smell of damp around you. The trees mean that the sun can't get in to dry out the soil so it always smells a bit musty and rotten.

Overall I like Chippewa Square – but most of all because it's where Forrest Gump sat on a bench and shared his choclates.

Do you think this is a successful description?

How could you improve it?

Now annotate your own composition.

Worksheet 12.2f (3) Composition assessment (2)

Composition B

Michael was so good at Scrabble he can win against anyone. He nows all the two letter words that don't mean anything. He says he learnt them from his wife who used to have a little book with them all in and he had to learn them too or she'd beat him every time. He used to score 45 just putting down two letters and he didn't even make a real word. 'Zo' whats that. Za whats that. So he would play against his kids and their friends and he always wind.

One day my friend Martin wants to win. He didn't like the fact that an old man could win him so he decided to make sure he got the high score that game. He went through the bag and took out the Z and the O and the A before we called Michael down to play. I reckon he put them up his sleeve or something. I know Michael because he's my Uncle and he moved in with us ten years ago when my Aunt passed away. He was always great fun when we were younger, going out to the park and buying us sweets. He showd me how to play Chess. We played for about 10 minutes and Martin was looking fed up. He was losing and so was I with 42 points when Michael had 80 already. Suddenly whenit was his go Martin started coughing really loudly and then he knocked his drink off the table onto the carpet. Michael got up to get a cloth and when he was in the kitchen Martin dropped the Z O and A out on the table. He whispered to me to help me put these on so I get points but there wasn't anywhere to fit them on. My Uncle came back and mopped up the mess and Martin put down the word Barn which only got him 8 points.

Do you think this is a successful description?

How could you improve it?

Now annotate your own composition.

Worksheet 12.2g — Paper 2: self-review

Task Now that you have marked your own response to Practice Paper 2, you should be able to identify your strengths and weaknesses and set targets for improvement. Complete the table below in order to record your findings and conclusions.

Question	Mark	At my target level?	Could be improved	Specific weakness(es)
1 Reading				
1 Writing				
2/3 Content and structure				
2/3 Style and accuracy				

Targets (try to set one for each question type)
1 Directed writing
a) Reading
b) Writing
2 Composition
a) Content and structure
b) Style and accuracy